THE
IMMORTALS

THE
IMMORTALS
HISTORY'S FIGHTING ELITES

NIGEL CAWTHORNE

ZENITH PRESS

Contents

Highlanders charging English forces at the Battle of Culloden, 1746.

Pages 2–3 US Marine Corps War Memorial, near Arlington National Cemetery, USA.

Spartan King Leonidas.

British soldier of the Parachute Regiment, near Basra, Iraq, 2003.

US troops landing on Omaha Beach, D-Day, 6 June, 1944.

Introduction

The immortals are men and women whose names will live on down the ages because of the glory they have won in battles. They belonged to élite units who fought with little regard for their own safety, concerned only with their honour, their comrades and their cause. But this is not the end of their story, for members of today's élite forces will themselves become the immortals of tomorrow.

It may seem ironic that the first élite formation mentioned in this book – the Persian Immortals – though victorious on the battlefield, were trumped in the fame stakes by those they defeated. The small band of Spartans that bravely held them back for three precious days are, even now, acclaimed as the saviours of Western civilization. The latest movie to feature their exploits – '300' – was released in the year 2007, some 2487 years after they perished at Thermopylae. Fame indeed.

Men who aspire to be among the immortals are often the followers of a charismatic leader, such as Caesar who had his 10th Legion. But they did not always have the most laudable of motives. The Waffen SS were dedicated Nazis and fanatical followers of Hitler. Nor are women immune from such devotion to a cause. Many gave their lives in the Special Operations Executive in the Second World War, and today they fight in Poland's GROM. But history has given us only one dedicated formation of women warriors – the Amazons – and even they may be mythical. Despite doubts about the reality of their existence, they belong here because they embody the martial spirit. Their warlike nature is legendary and they are, in the imagination at least, immortal.

The achievements of Alexander the Great and his cohorts have never – and will never – be equalled. In less than 20 years they conquered almost all of the known world. The Roman Praetorian Guard picked and chose their emperors when Rome was the greatest empire the world had ever seen. The Janissaries did the same in the Ottoman empire, while the Ninja still inspire the imagination of youth of this day.

The wars that tore Europe apart from the Middle Ages produced new élite bands of fighting men – the English bowmen of Crécy and Agincourt, the fighting Irishmen of 'the Wild Geese', the Scots with their Highland Charge, the Prussian Guard and Napoleon's Imperial Guard, referred to in their day as 'the Immortals'. The American Civil War also threw up, and cut down, countless brave men. Here we have chosen the Stonewall Brigade and New York's Zouaves – though it now seems unfathomable to us that Americans would choose to fight the first industrial war in the uniforms of French North Africans.

The Plains Indians produced some of the finest light cavalry that were ever seen. In the dying days of the Native-American nations, there were fighting men who truly saw themselves as 'immortals' – rightly, in fact, since their names live on, such as Geronimo.

In the 19th century, British military might bestrode the world. But even the most well trained army, equipped with the latest weapons, found itself no match for a dedicated formation of Zulus, who massacred an entire British regiment in Natal in 1879. This left the Zulu with an unshakeable sense of pride, undimmed even by the indignities of apartheid.

The British Expeditionary Force who set out to challenge the might of the German army in 1914 were dismissed by the Kaiser as 'contemptible'. They embraced the name and, after four years of the most appalling bloodletting, 'The Old Contemptibles' emerged on the winning side, while the Kaiser had to seek refuge in Holland.

When the Second World War broke out, another small bunch of men stood up to the military might of Germany. This time they were fighter pilots, the men of the Royal Air Force's Fighter Command. And they were not just British, or even fliers from what was then known as the British empire. They included airmen who had escaped from occupied Europe as well as a small band of Americans who had swapped their nationality to fight Hitler in the Battle of Britain. 'Upon this battle,' British prime minister Winston Churchill said: 'depends the survival of Christian civilization.' They won that battle, and could rightfully be compared with the Spartans at Thermopylae.

The Second World War flung up a plethora of new élite units, such as the Screaming Eagles, Merrill's Marauders and the Devil's Brigade. The US Marines and the US Rangers wrote new chapters in the book of honour, while the Office of Strategic Services created a new type of secret warfare that would give birth to the CIA.

A number of units that are now in the front line in the war on terror can trace their origins to the Second World War. Britain's Special Air Service and Special Boat Service were both started then. The Green Berets and the US Navy SEALs drew inspiration from them, and came into their own in the Vietnam War. Delta Force, the most secretive and most élite of America's fighting units, also drew its inspiration from the SAS.

Since the massacre of Israeli athletes at the 1972 Munich Olympics, most Western nations have developed a special forces capability, training élite units to take on terrorists. It seems that as long as there are wars and battles to be won, young men – and women – will find the courage to sacrifice themselves for their beliefs, or for others, and make themselves and their comrades immortal.

Nigel Cawthorne
Bloomsbury, 2009

THE

ANCIENT

WORLD

*The Praetorian Guard accompanied several emperors who also
functioned as generals while on campaign. A notable example were
those with Marcus Aurelius while he conducted campaigns on the
Danubian frontier. This scene from the sarcophagus of Marcus
Aurelius shows a battle against the Barbarians.*

The Persian Immortals

The eventual victors at Thermopylae

In the fifth century BC, the Persian empire spread across the Middle East and North Africa. Its thirst for conquest seemed unquenchable. At the head of its all-conquering army was an élite force known as the 'Immortals'. There were 10,000 of them. They were seemingly immortal because when one of their number was killed or became unfit to serve, he was immediately replaced. The men were pampered and richly rewarded for their work. All they had to do was kill and die for their emperor.

In the sixth century BC, Cyrus the Great and the Achaemenian dynasty established a Persian empire that would stretch from the River Indus to the Aegean Sea. His successor, Darius I, sought to extend the empire into Greece, but his fleet was destroyed by a storm in 492 BC and his army defeated by the Athenians at Marathon in 490 BC. In 480 BC, Darius's son Xerxes attempted expansion once more with a huge army led by an élite corps that the contemporary Greek historian Herodotus called the Ten Thousand or the *Athánatoi* – the Immortals. They were 'a body of picked Persians under the leadership of Hydarnes, the son of Hydarnes' and under the leadership of the *hazarapat*, or commander in chief. According to Herodotus: 'This corps was known as the Immortals, because it was kept up to strength. When any one of them left the number incomplete, whether by force of death or sickness, a substitute was appointed, so that they never were more or less than ten thousand men.'

CONCUBINES AND HOUSEHOLD SERVANTS

The Immortals travelled in covered wagons and were provided with special food carried in a separate train. They were also allowed to bring their concubines and their household servants with them. Herodotus said:

'The dress of these troops consisted of the tiara, or soft felt cap, embroidered tunic with sleeves, a coat of mail looking like the scales of a fish, and trousers; for arms they carried light wicker shields, quivers slung below them, short spears, powerful bows with cane arrows, and short swords swinging from belts beside the right thigh.'

Depictions of these men, who also served as the royal guard, appear in carved reliefs and coloured glazed bricks in Achaemenian capitals, such as the Palace of Artaxerxes in Susa.

Warriors depicted in one of the highly decorated capitals of the ancient Achaemenid empire. Rich architectural ornament and magnificent decorative reliefs were favoured by the Archaemenids – at one time the wealthiest dynasty in the world.

THE PERSIAN IMMORTALS

539 BC Cyrus the Great invades Babylonia

525 BC Cambyses invades Egypt

*c.***514** BC Darius I invades the Indus Valley

513 BC Darius I invades Scythia

490 BC Darius I is defeated by the Athenians at the Battle of Marathon, though the Greeks were heavily outnumbered

*c.***484** BC The birth of Herodotus, the Greek historian whose works are the primary source for our knowledge of the Immortals

480 BC The Immortals outflank the Spartans to win the Battle of Thermopylae

The artefacts show men carrying a wooden spear with a silver blade and a pomegranate insignia. They were also swathed in gold jewellery. Herodotus said that: 'every man glittered with the gold which he carried about his person in unlimited quantity.' An élite of 1000 Immortals was distinguished by having a gold pomegranate fixed at one end of their spears, while the rest merely had silver ones.

THE BATTLE OF THERMOPYLAE

At Thermopylae, some 200,000 Persians, including 20,000 Libyan charioteers, faced just 4,000 Greeks plus 300 Spartans and their helots, or serfs, and 1100 Boeotians from the area northwest of Athens. Thermopylae is a narrow pass some 4 miles (6.5 km) long with the sea on one side and high cliffs on the other. It is the perfect defensive position. Large armies are of little advantage, since it is impossible to manoeuvre in the confined space.

On the first day of the battle, the Persians sent in Median and Elamite contingents. They were easily repelled. The Immortals went in as a second wave, but fared little better. The Greeks were equipped with better armour and with longer spears that could hold the Persians at bay. On the second day, the Persians attacked in force again. Again they had problems manoeuvring and many were forced into the sea and drowned.

However, according to Herodotus, a Greek named Ephialtes then informed the Persian emperor Xerxes that there was a path through the mountains which he could use to outflank the Greeks. That night the Immortals, under the command of Hydarnes, set out for the path. On the way, they encountered a detachment of 1000 Phocian Greeks which the Spartan king Leonidas had sent to guard the path. These men assumed that the Persians had come to fight them, and so they retreated to high ground, preparing to face death, but the Immortals simply bypassed them. They then attacked the Greeks from the rear. Leonidas and his men were massacred in the battle that followed.

But Leonidas' sacrifice allowed the other Greeks time to make an orderly retreat. By the time the Persians reached Athens and burnt it, the city had been evacuated. The Persian fleet was then defeated by the Greek navy at the Battle of Salamis. Facing unrest in Babylon, Xerxes withdrew from Greece, leaving an army there under the Persian commander Mardonius. The Immortals seem to have remained with him, though Hydarnes returned to Persia with Xerxes. Mardonius was defeated at Plataea in 479 BC. There is no further mention of the Immortals, so they may have returned to Asia with Xerxes.

'... one thousand carried spears with golden pomegranates at their lower end instead of spikes; and these encircled the other nine thousand, who bore on their spears pomegranates of silver. The spearmen too who pointed their lances towards the ground had golden pomegranates; and the thousand Persians who followed close after Xerxes had golden apples.'

HERODOTUS OF HALICARNASSUS, *HISTORIES, BOOK VII.4,* C.440 BC

HERODOTUS

Herodotus is considered the father of history. His *History of the Greco-Persian Wars* was the first great narrative history produced in the ancient world and is the primary source for our knowledge of the Immortals. He was born in Halicarnassus in Asia Minor – modern Turkey – around 484 BC. At that time, Halicarnassus was under Persian occupation. Although he was only four at the time of the Battle of Thermopylae, he would have known people who lived at the time. Of course, there were no Greek survivors of the battle, but Herodotus travelled widely in the Persian empire and consulted the work of Persian scribes, giving him a detailed knowledge of the battle and the Immortals' part in it. His work also covers the run up to the Greco-Persian Wars and the Battle of Marathon. He wrote that, on his way to Thermopylae: 'Xerxes ... found here a plane tree so beautiful, that he presented it with golden ornaments, and put it under the care of one of his Immortals.' He went on to relate the Greek victories at Salamis, Plataea and Mycale which finally ended the Persian attempt to invade Greece. The last event Herodotus recorded occurred in 430 BC. It is not known when he died.

A statue depicting the eminent Herodotus. His important writings have led him to be considered as the world's first true historian.

OTHER VICTORIES AND SUCCESSORS

The Immortals are also thought to have played an important role in Cyrus the Great's conquest of Babylonia in 539 BC, his son Cambyses' conquest of Egypt in 525 BC, and Darius's invasion of the Indus Valley around 514 BC and Scythia on the shores of the Black Sea in 513 BC. They also appear to have been at the Battle of Marathon. During his conquest of Persia in the fourth century BC, Alexander the Great faced an élite regiment which bore a small metal counterweight on the butt of their spears to balance the heavy blade that was shaped like an apple, instead of a pomegranate. These 'Apple-bearers' may well have been the successors of the Immortals.

When the Persian king Ardahsir I established the Sasanian empire in AD 208–224, he organized his army along the lines of the Achaemenians. The élite units of their Savaran cavalry were known as the Zhayedan, which is Persian for 'Immortal'. Traditionally, there were 10,000 of them. Their arms and heraldry also reflected Achaemenid ancestry. The Byzantine emperor Michael VII (reigned 1071–8) called one of his élite tagmata cavalry units the *Athánatoi*, or the 'Immortals'. Again they numbered 10,000. Napoleon's Imperial Guard were sometimes referred to as the 'Immortals'. The last shah of Iran, Mohammad Reza Pahlavi (reigned 1941–79), also called the élite Javidan units of his Imperial Guard the 'Immortals'. However, there were only 4000 to 5000 of them, including a battalion of Chieftain tanks. The Javadian units were responsible for the internal and external security of the royal palaces. They were disbanded following the Iranian revolution that brought the Ayatollah Khomeini to power in 1979.

The Spartans

'Come home with this shield or upon it'

The Spartans were known for their self-discipline, courage and fighting ability. Indeed, the Spartan state was designed for one purpose only – to breed and train soldiers. Its single-minded dedication to the military prevented the political unification of classical Greece. However, when the country was threatened, as during the Greco-Persian Wars in the fifth century BC, all Greeks were grateful that the Spartans were in the front line to defend their freedom.

Sparta was the capital of the Laconia district of the southern Peloponnese in Greece. From the ninth century BC it was run by a military oligarchy. In peacetime, there was a 30-man senate. In war, two kings were provided by the ruling families, both said to be descended from Heracles – Hercules in the Roman pantheon. The state was militarized; the arts, philosophy and literature were neglected in favour of building an unbeatable army.

In Greece it was common for sick and weakly children to be left in the hills to die of exposure. In Sparta it was institutionalized. All Spartan males trained for warfare. In return they were given land, which was farmed by helots – serfs from the surrounding countryside which the Spartans had occupied. Helots would also accompany the army on campaigns as light infantry or archers, tasks thought unfit for a true warrior. *Perioeci*, or free non-citizens – merchants, craftsmen and others – also served as light infantry and in auxiliary roles. Only the Spartiate, or native Spartans, could join the élite heavy infantry, the hoplites.

HARDSHIP AND TRAINING

All Greek city-states had hoplites, but the Spartans were better trained, better disciplined and more highly motivated. Boys were taken from their families at the age of seven for military training. They wore a thin tunic in winter and summer, and were given little food. This encouraged them to scavenge, though they would be punished if they were caught. They would also participate in games and mock fights to encourage *esprit de corps*.

At the age of 12, the regimen was tightened. Discipline became stricter and physical exercises tougher. Recruits were taught survival skills and how to endure pain. At 18, some youths were retained as trainers, while the most promising were given specialist training. Once his training was complete, a soldier would be given his citizenship. Those who failed to make the grade were assigned a lesser civil rank.

At the age of 20, trainees were eligible for military service. They joined a *syssitia*, or mess, usually comprising some 15 men of all ages. Up to the age of 30, a man would spend

most of his time with his unit in the barracks, eating all his meals with his fellow soldiers, even if he got married. The marriage ritual itself was rough and brutal. At the end of it, the man would drag off his new wife as if taking her by force. Men in barracks could only visit their wives at night, and other Greeks joked that Spartans had children before they saw their wife's face. Only at 30 did a Spartan become a *homoioi*, or equal, and he was then allowed to live in his own home with his family.

Military service continued up to the age of 60, though in emergencies older men fought. Training was lifelong. The Greek writer Plutarch wrote that the Spartans: 'were the only men in the world for whom war brought a respite from training for war.'

A stone relief memorial in Greece dedicated to the 300 Spartan heroes who faced the might of the Persian army at Thermopylae. Spartans wore their hair long, as can be seen clearly here.

THE SPARTAN WAY OF LIFE

This intense training meant that Spartans had little fear of death. Recruits were taught to abandon individuality for the sake of Sparta. Spartan mothers reputedly told their sons to 'come home with this shield or upon it' as the heavy shield was the first thing a hoplite would abandon if forced to flee. The Sparta shield was marked with the letter *lamba* – for Lacedaemon, the ancient name for Sparta. Spartans soldiers were presented with a bronze cuirass, covering their chest and back, and a bronze helmet. They also wore greaves to protect their legs. However, after the fifth century BC, they abandoned most body armour. Spartans wore distinctive crimson tunics and cloaks, though the cloaks were shed during fighting. For arms they carried a long spear or javelin and a short double-edged sword called a *xiphos*. Like other Greeks, they fought in a phalanx, a close formation of 600 men or more, usually eight ranks deep. When fighting alongside allies, the Spartans would usually take the right flank. Once they had crushed those in front of them, they would wheel to the left and roll up the rest of the enemy formation.

The Spartans prized discipline, self-denial and simplicity. They did not indulge in luxuries and leisure, believing themselves to be the inheritors of the true Greek tradition. The indulgences of civilization brought weakness and disorder, they thought. Instead they valued strength, courage and the moral values which they believed came from self-discipline. It was a creed admired, if not emulated, by the rest of the ancient world. The Spartan philosophy applied to women as well as men. Infant girls were also exposed to die if judged to be weakly. Unlike in other Greek states, women were educated by the state alongside males. As with the males, this was a physical education rather than an academic one. They were trained in gymnastics. With their husbands seldom around, Spartan women also enjoyed freedoms denied to other women in the ancient world.

SPARTAN ARMY SUCCESSES AND DECLINE

Between the eighth and fifth century BC, Sparta subdued neighbouring Messenia, enslaving those who did not flee. Sparta then fell out with Athens, forcing the Athenians to make a pact with the Persian emperor Darius I. But when Darius tried to invade in 490 BC, the Spartans promised Athens their help, but only after the end of their annual religious ceremony. When the Spartans arrived after a march of 150 miles (241 km) in three days, the Battle of Marathon was over. All that was left for them to do was offer their congratulations to the Athenians before marching away.

Three hundred Spartans under their king Leonidas made their heroic sacrifice at Thermopylae in 480 BC, delaying the Persian invasion of Greece. Athenian naval power beat the Persians at sea at the Battle of Salamis. The Spartans then joined an alliance that defeated the Persians at Plataea and Mycale in 479 BC. In 431 BC, there followed the Peloponnesian War which ended with the defeat of Athens by Sparta in 404 BC. But the Spartan hegemony did not last long. In the Corinthian War of 395–387 BC, they faced a coalition of Athens, Corinth, Thebes and Argos. Although the Spartans won a series of battles on land, they lost many of their ships in a naval defeat at Cnidus to a combined Athenian and Persian fleet. Then in 371 BC, the Spartans lost their first land battle fought at full strength against Epaminondas of Thebes at the Battle of Leuctra, a village in Boeotia, territory of Thespiae. They never recovered. Spartan citizenship had to be inherited by blood, and they found

'SO MUCH THE BETTER, WE SHALL FIGHT THEM IN THE SHADE.'

The hero of the Battle of Thermopylae was King Leonidas of Sparta. His name means 'he who has the spirit of the lion', and a statue of Leonidas stands near the site of the battle. When the Persians sought to invade Greece in 480 BC, Leonidas led a small force of 300 Spartans and their helots to join the small Greek garrison defending the narrow pass at Thermopylae. When it was clear they were vastly outnumbered, Leonidas offered to dismiss anyone who wanted to go. The Spartans stayed to a man. They held the Persians back for three days. When an envoy from the Persian emperor Xerxes taunted him, saying: 'Our archers are so numerous that the flight of their arrows darkens the sun', the Spartan Dieneces replied: 'So much the better, we shall fight them in the shade.' When the Persian Immortals found their way through the mountains and attacked the Spartans from behind, Leonidas and his men were massacred. However, this allowed the other Greeks time to make an orderly retreat, and later to defeat the Persians at sea and on land. The Spartan sacrifice at Thermopylae made a deep impression on the Greeks. It gave rise to the legend that the Spartans never surrender, while Spartans could rightfully claim to be the 'defenders of Hellenism'. Although, Leonidas would certainly have craved the glory of such a heroic death, there may have been another reason for his suicidal stand. Before the war, an oracle had foretold that either Sparta would perish or one of her kings would die – Sparta traditionally had two kings at any one time. By his death, Leonidas saved his city.

This sculpture of King Leonidas in Thermopylae, Greece, exemplifies the hallmarks of the Spartan philosophy – he is lightly armored, helmeted and bears a long spear and ornate round shield. The word 'spartan' suggesting hardship and deprivation, derives from this warrior-like way of life.

themselves outnumbered by helots. Neither Philip II of Macedonia nor his son Alexander the Great bothered with Sparta when they took over Greece. However, it is said that Philip II sent a message to Sparta saying: 'If I enter Laconia, I will level Sparta to the ground.' The Spartans reputedly responded with the one-word reply: 'If.'

Spartans did not join the Greek army under Alexander that conquered Persia. However, Sparta took on the Achaean League, a new confederation of Greek states, but was defeated in 222 BC. It was then forced into the Achaean League, which was defeated near Corinth by the Romans in AD 146, led by the Roman General Lucius Mummius. After a final Spartan victory against the Visigoths, Sparta was destroyed in AD 396.

The Amazons

An ancient tribe of fighting women?

The literature and art of ancient Greece is full of tales and depictions of the Amazons – a tribe of warrior women once thought to have invaded Attica. Though they are often dismissed as myth, there is evidence that warlike women did inhabit the area around the Black Sea. This is the area from where classical writers asserted that the Amazons came, at a time before history was recorded.

THE AMAZONS

*c.*800 BC Homer mentions the Amazons in the *Iliad*

*c.*750 BC Arctinus tells how Achilles killed an Amazon named Penthesileia

*c.*500 BC Poet Pindar says there are horse-riding female archers in Anatolia or Thrace

*c.*450 BC Herodotus writes of a war between the Amazons and Greeks in his *Histories*

*c.*400 BC Hippocrates writes of warrior women who removed their right breast

*c.*1 BC Strabo and Plutarch relate tales of Amazons

The ancient Greeks believed that there had once been a tribe of warlike women who lived somewhere to the northeast. The Greek poet Homer, who flourished in the ninth or eighth century BC, mentioned them in the *Iliad*, his epic account of the Trojan Wars. The Trojan king Priam fought against them, and they were later massacred by the Greek hero Bellerophon, though Homer asserts that the Amazon women were in every way equal to men when it came to fighting. The *Iliad* says that there was a tomb at Troy of a woman named Myrine. She was later identified as an Amazon.

The *Aethiopis* of Arctinus of Miletus, written around the seventh century BC, mentions an Amazon named Penthesileia, 'the daughter of great-souled Ares, the slayer of men', coming to the Trojans' aid. Ares was the Greek god of war, the equivalent of Mars in the Roman pantheon. Arctinus says that 'after showing great prowess', she was killed by Achilles and buried by the Trojans. Achilles then slew the Greek soldier Thersites for abusing and reviling him for his supposed love for Penthesileia. Arctinus also mentions that she was 'of the Thracian race' – the easternmost part of Greece, across the Dardanelles from Troy.

'KILLERS OF MEN'

Amazons appear in the visual record from the eighth century BC onwards. At first they were depicted fighting on foot with short swords like men, but wore dresses like Greek women. By the sixth century BC they were shown on horseback, carrying a bow or javelin and a half-round or crescent-shaped shield. They wore trousers, jackets and leopard skins like the 'barbarians' from Thrace or Scythia – the area to the north of the Black Sea.

The fifth-century Greek poet Pindar also mentioned horse-riding female archers who lived somewhere between Lycia in southwestern Anatolia, now Turkey, and the Danube in

A detail from an amphora (a vessel used for holding liquids) depicting Heracles, on the left, fighting against the Amazons in about 530–520 BC.

THE WARRIOR WOMEN OF EURASIA

Some 50 ancient burial mounds near the town of Pokrovka, Russia, near the Kazakhstan border, have yielded skeletons of women buried with weapons, suggesting the Greek stories concerning the Amazons may have had some basis in fact. The Sauromatian nomads buried their dead in that region from around 600 BC. This is the very area – to the north of the Sea of Azov – where Herodotus said the descendants of the Amazons and the Scythians lived. In general, females buried there have a wider variety and larger quantity of artefacts buried with them than males, and seven female graves have been found to contain iron swords or daggers, bronze arrowheads and whetstones to sharpen these weapons. Some scholars have argued that weapons found in female burials served a purely ritual purpose, but this is not borne out by the bones. The bowed leg bones of one teenage girl show that she spent much of her short life on horseback, and a bent arrowhead found inside the body of another woman suggests that she had been killed in battle. The Pokrovka women were not Amazons, who were thought to have lived far to the west, but their existence does show that there were nomadic tribes of warrior women in that part of the world during the Early Iron Age.

northern Thrace. The playwright Aeschylus also took up the story, saying they came from Lake Maeotis – the Sea of Azov – in Scythia, but that they had moved to Themiscyra on the River Thermodon – what is now the Terme river in northern Turkey. Aeschylus also described them as being 'man-hating' and 'manless'.

Later in the fifth century BC, Herodotus, the first historian, wrote of a time when the Greeks fought the Amazons. He says that they were called *oiorpata* in the Scythian tongue, which means 'killers of men'. He says that the Greeks had won a great victory on the Thermodon and carried away on three ships as many Amazons as they could take alive. But once they were out at sea the Amazons attacked the crew and killed them. He wrote:

> *'But they knew nothing about ships, or how to use rudder or sail or oar; and with the men dead, they were at the mercy of waves and winds, until they came to the cliffs by the Maeotian lake; this place is in the country of the free Scythians. The Amazons landed there, and set out on their journey to the inhabited country, and seizing the first troop of horses they met, they mounted them and raided the Scythian lands.'*

Herodotus said they later intermarried with the Scythians, producing the Sauromatae people. According to custom, no woman could marry until she had killed an enemy in battle. Surviving papyrus fragments mention Heracles fighting against the Amazons and, later, one of his famous Twelve Labours was to obtain the girdle of Hippolyte, the queen of the Amazons, after invading her realm. In another tale, the Athenian hero Theseus attacked the Amazons. The Amazons responded by invading Attica, but were defeated. Along the way, Theseus married Antiope, the sister of Hippolyte. In another version, Antiope took revenge after Theseus refused her and married Phaedra instead. The mythic battle between Amazons and Athenians spawned a genre of art – amazonomachy – seen in marble bas-reliefs such as those from the Parthenon or the sculptures of the Mausoleum of Halicarnassus.

Did Amazons have children?

A tribe exclusively made up of women, naturally, had a problem with procreation. The historian Strabo said that the Amazons solved this by going up a nearby mountain that separated them from the Gargarians, for two months a year:

> *'to unite with them, and under cover of darkness, without fixed partners, in order to beget children. After impregnating them, they sent them away. The Amazons keep all female children that were born, but they send the male children away to be reared by the Gargarians.'*

In other accounts, the male children were killed.

Strabo also said that Amazons had their right breast cauterized at a tender age so they could: 'easily use their right arm for all purposes, especially spear-throwing.' They also fired bows and arrows, he said. A bow could more easily be drawn if the right breast was missing. Earlier, Hippocrates also mentioned that the Sauromatian women had no right breast:

> *'... for while they are yet babies their mothers make red-hot a bronze instrument constructed for this very purpose and apply it to the right breast and cauterize it, so that its growth is arrested, and all its strength is diverted to the right shoulder and right arm.'*

The Greek biographer and author Plutarch, writing at the end of the first and beginning of the second century AD, said there were a large number of tombs of Amazons near Scotussa and Cynoscephalae, and statues of Amazons were found all over Greece.

This statue of a powerfully built woman archer is reputed to be an Amazon from ancient times and stands in Villa Torlonia, Rome, Italy.

'Concerning his voyage into the Euxine Sea, Philochorus and some others write that he made it with Hercules, offering him his service in the war against the Amazons, and had Antiope given to him for the reward of his valour; but the greater number, of whom are Pherecydes, Hellanicus and Herodotus, write that he made this voyage many years after Hercules, with a navy under his own command, and took the Amazon prisoner – the more probable story, for we do not read that any other of all those that accompanied him in this action, took any Amazon prisoner.'

PLUTARCH, *THE LIFE OF THESEUS*, C.AD 100

The Sacred Band of Thebes

The invincible Greek band of lovers

There were so many wars in ancient Greece that many learned Greeks put a great deal of thought into what made a fighting unit invincible. According to Homer, the Greek hero Nestor thought it was best if men fought together in families and tribes, since kinsmen would naturally aid each other. But Plato thought it was better if lovers fought alongside each other. This was the idea behind the Sacred Band of Thebes, who dominated the battlefields of Greece for 40 years.

The Sacred Band of Thebes was an élite unit formed by 150 pairs of homosexual lovers. The idea of a military band of lovers has been attributed to the Athenian philosopher Plato, although it was later – some time after 385 BC – that he wrote in his *Symposium*:

> *'And if there were only some way of contriving that a state or an army should be made up of lovers and their loves, they would be the very best governors of their own city, abstaining from all dishonour, and emulating one another in honour; and when fighting at each other's side, although a mere handful, they would overcome the world. For what lover would not choose rather to be seen by all mankind than by his beloved, either when abandoning his post or throwing away his arms? He would be ready to die a thousand deaths rather than endure this. Or who would desert his beloved or fail him in the hour of danger? The veriest coward would become an inspired hero, equal to the bravest, at such a time: Love would inspire him. That courage which, as Homer says, the god breathes into the souls of some heroes. Love of his own nature infuses into the lover. Love will make men dare to die for their beloved – love alone.'*

It was not necessarily homosexual love alone that inspired such devotion and willingness to sacrifice one's own life, Plato maintained. He quoted the example of Alcestis, the daughter of Pelias, who willingly laid down her life on behalf of her husband when no one else – not even his father or mother – would do so. Plato wrote:

> *'The tenderness of her love so far exceeded theirs, that she made them seem to be strangers in blood to their own son, and in name only related to him, and so noble did this action of hers appear to the gods, as well as to men, that among the many who have done virtuously she is one of the very few to whom, in admiration of her noble action, they have granted the privilege of returning alive to earth.'*

Depiction by Dutch painter Isaak Walraven (1686–1765) of the death of Theban commander Epaminondas at the Battle of Mantinea, 362 BC, in which a Spartan army was defeated.

THE SACRED BAND OF THEBES

387 BC Theban general Gorgidas forms the Sacred Band of Thebes

AFTER 385 BC Plato outlines the military advantages of creating a fighting unit out of lovers

379 BC Pelopidas takes command of the Sacred Band and forges them into a single élite unit

375 BC The Sacred Band defeats a numerically superior Spartan force at Tegyrae

371 BC The Sacred Band leads the Theban army that inflicts the first defeat on the Spartan army at full strength

338 BC The Sacred Band stands and is slaughtered by the Macedonian army under Philip II and his son Alexander the Great at Chaeronea

1818 The monument to the fallen of the Sacred Band is found at Chaeronea

1890 The site at Chaeronea is excavated and 254 bodies found

It is generally assumed that Plato was homosexual because, as a teacher, he surrounded himself with young men and boys. However, he had little time for sexual passion, believing that sex belonged to the realms of animals. But he conceded that homosexual practices were generally widespread throughout Greece.

'A BAND CEMENTED BY FRIENDSHIP...'

The Theban general Gorgidas had formed his Sacred Band in 387 BC. Three hundred men were hand-picked from his army. Their exploits were chronicled by Plutarch, who said:

> *A band cemented by friendship grounded upon love, is never to be broken, and invincible; since the lovers, ashamed to be base in sight of their beloved, and the beloved before their lovers, willingly rush into danger for the relief of one another. Nor can that be wondered at; since they have more regard for their absent lovers than for others present; as in the instance of the man, who, when his enemy was going to kill him, earnestly requested him to run him through the breast, that his lover might not blush to see him wounded in the back.*

The couples usually consisted of an older *heniochoi*, or charioteer, and a younger *paraibatai*, or companion. Such pederastic relations were common among the Greeks while, generally, homosexual relations between older men were decried. As the élite city guard, the Sacred Band was housed, provisioned and trained at the city's expense. In battle Gorgidas dispersed members of the Sacred Band among the front ranks of the Theban army so that they would inspire others with their courage.

After the Theban general and statesman Pelopidas retook the citadel of Thebes from the Spartans in 379 BC, he took over command of the Sacred Band with his friend Epaminondas. Pelopidas changed strategy. Unlike Gorgidas, he kept the Sacred Band together as a single unit which served as a personal guard on the battlefield. For the ensuing 40 years from 378 to 338 BC, it was considered invincible.

VICTORIES AND DESTRUCTION

At the Battle of Tegyrae in 375 BC, Pelopidas's Sacred Band faced a Spartan force that outnumbered them by at least three to one. Fearful of these odds, one of Pelopidas's men said despairingly: 'We are fallen into our enemy's hands.' But Pelopidas simply replied: 'And why not they into ours?' Pelopidas brought up his cavalry to charge the Spartan phalanx. Then he formed his infantry into a tight formation. The Spartan line opened to let them through, thinking they were trying to escape, but the Thebans turned and slaughtered the Spartan ranks. Writing of the Sacred Band's triumph at the Battle of Tegyrae, Plutarch remarked: 'The Spartans were never before beaten by a smaller company than their own; nor, indeed, in a set battle, when their number was equal.'

The Sacred Band of Thebes under Pelopidas distinguished itself again at the Battle of Leuctra in 371 BC. The Theban army, under the overall command of Epaminondas, killed the Spartan king Cleombrotus and left nearly 1000 Spartan dead on the battlefield. The Greek writer Pausanias said this battle finally established the independence of Thebes and was the most decisive battle fought between Greek city states. It left Sparta weakened.

THE MONUMENT AT CHAERONEA

According to the second-century Greek geographer and travel writer Pausanias, the Thebans erected a 6-metre (20-ft) marble statue of a lion as a memorial to the Sacred Band at Chaeronea around 300 BC. This was rediscovered by English travellers in 1818. It was pieced together and now stands on a plinth on the site. Later the site was excavated and 254 bodies were found, laid out in seven rows. Though Plutarch implies that all 300 men of the Sacred Band died in the battle, it seems that some 46 of them actually survived.

A marble statue of a lion was erected in memory of members of the Sacred Band who fell at the Battle of Chaeronea in Boeotia, Greece.

Philip II of Macedonia was held hostage in Thebes from 370 to 360 BC, where he could observe the Theban military at close quarters. After being returned to Macedonia, Philip became king and began his campaign against the Greek city states. In 338 BC, he faced the Thebans at Chaeronea, with his son Alexander the Great commanding his left flank. Philip himself showed great personal courage taking on the Sacred Band. He was in danger of being killed or captured when Alexander rode to his rescue. The Sacred Band, for the first time, broke. Though the battle was lost, they fought on. Of their 300-strong force, only 46 were captured. The other 254 died where they stood.

According to Plutarch, when Philip came upon the place the Sacred Band lay dead after the battle, he said: 'Perish any man who suspects that these men either did or suffered anything that was base.'

'It is likely, therefore, that this band was called sacred on this account; as Plato calls a lover a divine friend. It is stated that it was never beaten till the battle at Chaeronea: and when Philip, after the fight, took a view of the slain, and came to the place where the three hundred that fought his phalanx lay dead together, he wondered, and understanding that it was the band of lovers, he shed tears ...'

PLUTARCH, *THE LIFE OF PELOPIDAS*, C.AD 100

Alexander the Great's Companion Cavalry

With his élite horsemen, Alexander never lost a battle

The Macedonians under their king Philip II (r. 359–336 BC) conquered Greece with an army led by a corps of horsemen known as the Companion Cavalry. When Alexander the Great succeeded his father – possibly by arranging his assassination – he used the corps his father had developed to smash the Persian empire, which had dominated the region for some 200 years, and then to go on to conquer most of the known world.

The Macedonians revolutionized war in ancient Greece with the introduction of the *hetairoi* – or Companions. These horsemen were traditionally recruited from the ranks of the nobility of Macedonia, but when Philip II, the father of Alexander the Great, increased their number from 600 to over 3000, men from Thessaly and other parts of the Greek world were also recruited.

The inner core was a royal guard of some 300 to 400 men. There were smaller groups of 200 – known as *ilai*, or wings – who acted as shock troops. They carried a metal-tipped wooden spear or *xyston* some 3.3–4.3 metres (11–14 ft) long and a 1 m (3 ft) kopis, a short slashing sword that was curved inward towards the blade. The rider would be protected by a helmet and a bronze or iron breast-plate or heavy linen corselet reinforced with metal scales. Shields were only used in action when the *hetairoi* were dismounted. Their horses were protected by layers of thick felt draped over their sides, while their head and breast were shielded with metal plates to fend off spears, javelins and other missiles.

THE ROLE OF THE CAVALRY

The Macedonian cavalry played several roles. Light cavalry were used as *prodromoi*, or scouts. On reconnaissance missions they carried javelins, while in battle they carried a cavalry version of the *sarissa*, a 4–6.4 metre (13–21 ft) pike introduced by the Macedonians. Cavalrymen were also used to protect the flanks of the infantry in battle. The Companion Cavalry usually fought on the right flank, next to the *hypaspist* or shield-bearing infantry guard, while the infantry phalanx would be in the centre.

During Alexander's campaign against Persia, he had eight squadrons of Companions each comprising 225 horsemen. He led them personally in battle. They would attack in a wedge formation, aiming to punch through the enemy's line of infantry. Then they would turn and attack from behind, forcing the enemy onto the Macedonian phalanx.

At the Battle of Granicus in 334 BC – Alexander's first victory in Asia – he led his Companion Cavalry in a decisive charge against the centre of the Persian line. Easily identified by his splendid armour and the large white plumes on his helmet, Alexander was attacked by two Persian commanders, Rhoesaces and his brother Spithridates. Alexander's lance broke on Rhoesaces' body armour, but he had the presence of mind to jab the Persian in the face with the shaft of his shattered lance. Meanwhile, Spithridates struck Alexander on

The Alexander mosaic, found at Pompeii and dating from about 100 BC, is one of several famous depictions of the Battle of Issus, when the young Alexander the Great achieved victory over the Persian army of King Darius.

'Many a night did he spend without sleeping. Many a blood-stained day did he pass amid combats unceasing against irresistible forces and innumerable tribes, against impassable rivers and mountain fastnesses whose summit no arrow could reach, furthered by wise counsels, steadfast purpose, manly courage, and a prudent heart.'

PLUTARCH, *ON THE FORTUNE OR THE VIRTUE OF ALEXANDER*, C.AD 100

the head with a battleaxe, chopping off one of his plumes and slicing through the helmet to the scalp. Spithridates was about to deliver the fatal blow when Alexander's Companion Cleitus ran him through with a spear, while Alexander finished off Rhoesaces with a sword. With the death of Spithridates, the Persian line broke, the Macedonian phalanx poured through and the Persian infantry fled.

The following year, Alexander faced the Persian emperor Darius III himself at Issus. This time he moved his Companion Cavalry to the right, stretching the Persian line until a gap opened. Alexander then wheeled his Companions left through it in an attempt to reach Darius and kill him, finishing off the Persian empire with a single blow. Although the Persians were winning the battle, Darius fled, fearing for his life.

At the Battle of Gaugamela in 331 BC, Alexander used the same tactic, moving his Companion Cavalry to the right. The Persian left wing, fearing it would be outflanked, did the same. Although the Macedonians were vastly outnumbered, the tactic worked a second time. As the line stretched, a gap opened. The Companions wheeled through it, followed by the phalanx and a welter of lightly armoured troops. The Persians deserted. Darius fled – to be killed by his own men the following year – and the Persian empire fell to Alexander.

A stone bust of Alexander the Great (356–323 BC), at one time the most powerful ruler in the ancient world.

TROUBLE WITH THE COMPANIONS

Instead of returning to Greece, Alexander headed on eastwards. His men became homesick and discontented. Fearing that they were plotting to kill him, Alexander had Philotas, the commander of the Companion Cavalry, tortured and executed. No longer trusting the command of the Companion Cavalry to one man, Alexander split the command between Cleitus and his former school friend and – probably – one-time lover, Hephaestion.

During a brawl at a drinking party in 328 BC, Alexander broke free from the Companions who tried to restrain him and ran Cleitus through with a spear, killing him on the spot. When Alexander saw what he had done he was overcome with grief. He pulled the

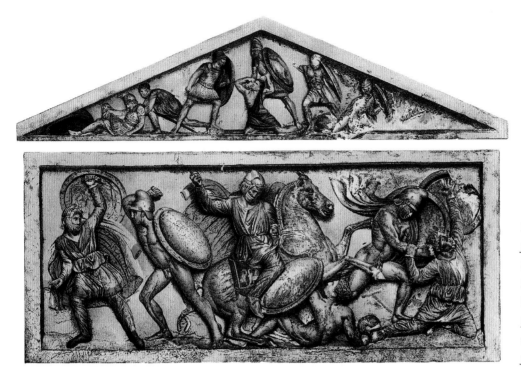

Reproduction of the marble frieze on the Alexander Sarcophagus showing Macedonian soldiers in battle. The sarcophagus was probably that of a Persian noble, and depicts scenes from Alexander's life.

spear from Cleitus's body and tried to impale himself. Restrained, he locked himself in his quarters and tried to starve himself to death. He eventually consoled himself with the thought that Heracles, who he claimed as an ancestor, had killed his wife and children in a fit of rage and undertook his Twelve Labours in expiation.

Alexander grew angry with the Companions when they refused to prostrate themselves in front of him in the Persian style. Nevertheless, the Companions gave him another victory at the Battle of Hydaspes in 326 BC when they faced the battle elephants of the rajah Porus. Although India was now at its feet, the Macedonian army refused to go on. Alexander eventually called the Companions together and gave the order to turn back.

A NEW COMPANION CAVALRY

The Companion Cavalry then boarded ships to sail down the River Indus, while the rest of the army marched along the banks. As they travelled down the Makran coast towards Persia they passed through the Gedrosian Desert, where 700 of the Companions died of heat and thirst. Arriving at Susa, Alexander held mass weddings, marrying the surviving Companions to the daughters of the Persian and Mede aristocracy. He then dismissed the veterans and announced that he was forming a new élite Companion Cavalry comprising only Persians. A mutiny was narrowly avoided, and the remaining Greeks and Macedonians set off home. When Hephaestion died in 324 BC, no one was appointed to take over his position as head of the Companion Cavalry. Alexander himself died the following year.

When Alexander died, his newly conquered empire split apart into warring states run by his generals. Seleucus and his successors who took over Babylonia had their own Companion Cavalry. They were more lightly equipped, though they had arm and leg protection and partial horse armour. The Companions of the Ptolemys, who were to rule Egypt until the death of Queen Cleopatra, carried a large round aspis cavalry shield, not dissimilar to those carried by the Spartan infantry.

The Roman Praetorian Guard

The palace bodyguard who used assassination to choose their emperor

The Praetorian Guard regularly proved themselves on the battlefield against Rome's enemies, but they were no less a force at home within the empire. They assassinated emperors they did not favour and replaced them with those they did – or simply sold the throne to the highest bidder. They also took up arms against rival candidates and were a powerful political and military force in the Roman empire for over 300 years.

A detail from Death of Caligula *(1871) by Lawrence Alma-Tadema (1836–1912). A Praetorian guard reveals the body of the emperor he is supposed to protect.*

The Praetorian Guard was formed by Augustus, the first emperor of Rome, to protect him from assassins following the murder of Julius Caesar. Its name derives from the *praetorium* – the headquarters or tent of the commander or *praetor* of a Roman army in the field. The practice of forming a Praetorian Cohort – or *cohors praetoria* – was begun by the Roman general Scipio Africanus the Younger when he took a corps of 500 friends as a bodyguard while he re-established discipline among the legions in Spain and besieged the hill town of Numantia in 133 BC.

Having a Praetorian Cohort of handpicked Roman citizens to act as a bodyguard became commonplace. Julius Caesar, Mark Anthony and Octavian – later Augustus – all had one. During the Gallic War, Julius Caesar ordered that his favoured Tenth Legion be mounted, so they could act as a bodyguard in the field. On horseback, they distinguished themselves as a fighting force.

After his victory at the Battle of Actium in 31 BC, Octavian made his Praetorians into a standing corps and divided them into nine cohorts of 500 men, each commanded by a tribune of equestrian rank, like a regular legion. When Octavian became the emperor Augustus, he kept three cohorts on duty in Rome, though they had no barracks there. The others were stationed in surrounding towns. In 2 BC, Augustus appointed two Praetorian prefects to be in overall command.

Members of the Praetorian Guard of the emperor Augustus, depicted in a marble bas-relief, dated the 2nd century AD and probably from the Forum of Trajan, Rome.

THE SYMBOL OF THE SCORPION

As well as acting as the emperor's bodyguard, the Praetorians served as a police force in Rome, though they still fought on the battlefield when the need arose. Then they were equipped with the same weapons as the normal legions, though the Praetorians' equipment was distinguished by a scorpion symbol. In the city, they dispensed with their shield and armour, wearing a plain tunic and carrying just a sword. They received double the pay of other soldiers and had a rank equivalent to a centurion in other legions. Their term of service was originally fixed by Augustus as 12 years, which was later increased to 16. When a soldier had served his time, he received a pay-off of 20,000 sesterces.

When Tiberius succeeded Augustus as emperor, Lucius Aelius Sejanus rose to power. He joined his father Seius Strabo as a Praetorian prefect, then became sole prefect. An ambitious man, Sejanus is thought to have murdered Tiberius's son, Drurus, but was refused permission to marry Drurus's widow, Livilla. In AD 23, he managed to persuade Tiberius to let him move the Praetorian Guard to a fortified camp – the Castra Praetoria – on the outskirts of Rome. This gave him immense power which he used to kill off his enemies.

31

In 27, Sejanus persuaded Tiberius to retire to the Mediterranean island of Capri. Two years later he succeeded in having Augustus's grand-daughter Agrippina exiled, along with her sons – who were in direct line of succession. In 31, Sejanus was made consul and served alongside Tiberius as co-ruler. However, when Tiberius was warned that this might not be the pinnacle of Sejanus's ambitions, he paid the Praetorian Guard ten gold pieces each to have Sejanus arrested and executed. His body was dragged through the streets, to the delight of those who had suffered at his hand.

THE ASSASSINATION OF CALIGULA

With the rise and fall of Sejanus, the Praetorians had already shown that they were the most powerful body in the state. But soon they went further. In 41, Cassius Chaerea and Cornelius Sabinus, two tribunes of the Praetorian Guard, killed the emperor Caligula at the Palatine Games. The Praetorian Guard then made Caligula's uncle Claudius emperor. He rewarded them with a gift of 150 gold coins a head to buy their loyalty. Claudius sentenced Cassius Chaerea to death for daring to slay an emperor. It is said that Cassius Chaerea asked to be executed with the same sword that he had used to kill Caligula. Cornelius Sabinus took his own life soon afterwards.

In 68, the Praetorian Guard abandoned the unpopular Emperor Nero, who fled Rome before committing suicide. However, when Servius Sulpicius Galba succeeded him, he refused to pay the Praetorian Guard a reward, so they killed Galba in the Forum and installed Marcus Salvius Otho as emperor. He gave them the right to choose their own prefects in an attempt to ensure their loyalty. However, the legions in Germany had already declared for Aulus Vitellius. Instead of remaining in Rome with the Praetorian Guard, Otho headed north to take on Vitellius, but he was defeated and committed suicide.

By the time Vitellius reached Rome in July 69, the legions in the east had declared for Vespasian. Vitellius considered abdication, but the Praetorian Guard forbade it. He therefore disbanded them, forming a new guard of 16 cohorts. However, the men he had dismissed simply switched their allegiance to Vespasian. When Vespasian entered Rome, Vitellius was savagely murdered by his own men. Vespasian also tried to tame the Praetorian Guard. He cut the number of cohorts and installed his son Titus as Praetorian prefect. Titus himself was the son-in-law of a former prefect.

AUCTIONING THE THRONE

Under the emperor Commodus, the Praetorian prefect Sextus Tigidius Perennis used his position to take over the running of the Roman empire. He was executed in 185, while Commodus was murdered in 192. Commodus's successor, the emperor Pertinax, was killed by the Praetorian Guard after he had ruled for just 87

A statue of a Praetorian Guard from an arch of Trajan. These arches were built in a number of places in the Roman Empire by the Emperor Trajan to commemorate military achievements.

THE FALL OF LUCIUS AELIUS SEJANUS

With Tiberius out of the way on Capri, Sejanus went ahead and married Livilla. However, a letter from Livilla's mother, Antonia, warned Tiberius of Sejanus's imperial ambitions. He sent for his great-nephew the exiled Gaius Caesar Germanicus – the future Emperor Caligula – who was the son of Agrippina the Elder and the popular general Germanicus Caesar. Having secured his heir, Tiberius sent a series of messages to Sejanus promising future advancement while systematically opposing everything he was doing. It soon became apparent to Romans that Sejanus no longer had any real power, and the crowd of people around his door asking for favours quickly thinned.

Then Tiberius sent Naevius Sertorius Macro, the new prefect of the Praetorian Guard, to Rome to tell Sejanus that he was going to be given the powers of a tribune. Sejanus made his way to the senate where the announcement was to be made. Meanwhile, Macro ordered any of the Praetorian Guard who might still be loyal to their former prefect Sejanus to return to barracks. Then he had the senate building surrounded by the city's Night Watch. Meanwhile, what the first-century Roman poet Juvenal called a 'long and wordy letter from Capri' was being read out in the senate. It began by praising Sejanus, who still thought he was going to be made tribune. But, little by little, the letter began to undermine him. The other senators began to back away from Sejanus, who sat slumped in his seat unable to believe his ears. When the reading of the letter was finished, the consul Regulus asked whether there was any reason why Sejanus should not be imprisoned. When the answer 'no' was given, Sejanus was led away by the Night Watch to be executed.

There was rejoicing when his body was dragged through the streets, then thrown in the River Tiber. His children were also put to death, though his daughter had to be raped first – it was against the law in Rome to execute a virgin. Livilla was spared, even though Sejanus's first wife confirmed that Drusus had been poisoned by the ambitious couple. This act of mercy was done out of consideration for Livilla's mother Antonia, who had warned Tiberius of Sejanus's plot. Antonia was not so forgiving, however, and starved her daughter to death.

days. The Praetorian Guard then announced the throne would be sold to the highest bidder. Didius Julianus paid 25,000 sesterces, but after 66 days, Roman general Septimius Severus marched into Rome and took over. Seeing the Praetorian Guard as unreliable and seditious, he disbanded them and banished them from the city.

But an emperor needed a bodyguard, and Severus was forced to reinstate the Praetorian Guard, though it was organized along new lines. There were to be four times as many of them. Previously only Italians were allowed to serve. Now he recruited the best troops from all over the empire. In 235, the emperor Severus Alexander was murdered and the Praetorian Guard proclaimed Maximinus Thrax emperor. Praetorian cohorts accompanied Aurelian when he went to Palmyra in Syria in 271 to reclaim the eastern provinces of the Roman empire. But the status of the Praetorian Guard suffered when the emperor Diocletian moved to Nicomedia in Asia Minor and established two new corps there. By the end of Diocletian's reign in 305, the Castra Praetoria housed only a small garrison.

Diocletian retired, dividing his empire among four successors. In the resulting power struggle, the Praetorian Guard picked the wrong side. They were defeated at the Milvian Bridge in 312 by Constantine the Great, who dispersed the survivors to the four corners of the empire and demolished Castra Praetoria. Instead he instituted a *scholae palatine*, or palace guard, who were much more strictly regulated than their predecessors.

The Sacred Band of Carthage

'... distinguished for valour and reputation as well as for wealth ...'

During their war against the Carthaginians in Sicily in the fourth century BC, the Greeks faced a major Carthaginian force that bore comparison to their own Sacred Band of Thebes. Though the Greek historians recorded no victories for the Carthaginian Sacred Band, they were the beginnings of a citizen army that, under the command of Hannibal, would eventually threaten Rome.

THE SACRED BAND OF CARTHAGE

341 BC The Sacred Band of Carthage fights Timoleon of Corinth at the Battle of Crimissus on Sicily

311 BC Carthaginian citizen army defeats Greek tyrant Agathocles at the Battle of Himeras

310 BC The Sacred Band takes on Agathocles outside Tunis

264–241 BC First Punic War

240 BC The Mercenary or Truceless War

218–201 BC Second Punic War takes Hannibal to the gates of Rome

149–146 BC Third Punic War sees the destruction of Carthage, its army and whatever remained of the Sacred Band

The Sacred Band of Carthage is the name used by Greek historians to refer to an élite infantry unit of Carthaginian citizens who served in the army of Carthage from the fourth century BC. It was notable because the bulk of the Carthaginian army was made up of mercenaries and infantry levied from Carthage's colonies. Outside the Sacred Band, Carthaginian citizens usually only served as officers or cavalry. Members of the Sacred Band of Carthage came from wealthy Carthaginian families. Plutarch notes: '...no others were superior to these in birth or wealth or reputation.' They were also distinguished by: 'the splendour of their armour and the slowness and good order of their march.' They were a heavy infantry unit of around 2000 to 3000 men. Trained to be great warriors from a young age, they were spearmen who fought in a phalanx, Greek-style. They were dressed in white, a colour the Carthaginians associated with death, and were the only military unit allowed within the walls of the city. It is also assumed that the members were homosexual lovers. But this may have been inferred from the obvious comparison to the Sacred Band of Thebes.

THE BATTLE OF CRIMISSUS

The Sacred Band of Carthage first appeared around 341 BC, when the Carthaginians were fighting the Greeks for control of Sicily. At the Battle of Crimissus they faced an army under the Greek general Timoleon of Corinth. The Sacred Band was caught by Timoleon's cavalry crossing a river in a rainstorm. Plutarch said: 'These withstood his first onset sturdily, and owing to the iron breast-plates and bronze helmets with which their persons were protected, and the great shields which they held in front of them, repelled the spear thrusts.' But their

Some of the Sacred Band of Carthage wore expensive and richly decorated armour, like this golden breast-plate with bas-reliefs, dating from the Second Punic War; it was perhaps even a trophy.

A 19th-century coloured engraving of Hannibal at the time the Carthaginians made their legendary crossing of the Alps in the Second Punic War. The engraving was based on a drawing by German artist Alfred Rethel (1816–59).

copious tunics filled with water and, hampered by their heavy armour, they had trouble fighting in the mud. Once a man fell over, he was an easy target for the lightly clad Greeks. The Greek historian Diodorus of Sicily noted:

> 'In the end, even the Carthaginians who composed the Sacred Battalion, twenty-five hundred in number and drawn from the ranks of those citizens who were distinguished for valour and reputation as well as for wealth, were all cut down after a gallant struggle. In the other elements of their army, more than ten thousand soldiers were killed and no less than fifteen thousand were taken captive. Most of the chariots were destroyed in the battle but two hundred were taken. The baggage train, with the draught animals and most of the wagons, fell into the hands of the Greeks. Most of the armour was lost in the river, but a thousand breast-plates and more than ten thousand shields were brought to the tent of Timoleon … nor is it recorded that so many native Carthaginians ever perished in a single battle before.'

Those who had fallen were clearly wealthy men. 'For those who stripped the bodies made very little account of bronze and iron; so abundant was silver, so abundant gold.' And among the spoils were: 'a thousand breast-plates of superior workmanship and beauty.'

THE GENERALSHIP OF HANNO

Agathocles, the Greek tyrant of Syracuse, rose to power in Sicily, but was defeated by the Carthaginians at the Battle of Himera in 311 BC. Determined to take his revenge, the following year he took an army of 66,000 men to North Africa. Outside Tunis he would meet the Sacred Band, under a general named Hanno. Agathocles opposed them on the battlefield with 1000 hoplites. Agathocles's men were poorly equipped and afraid, but Agathocles had a plan. He released owls, which flew into the Carthaginian ranks and perched on their shields and helmets. The owl was deemed sacred to Athena and the word passed among the soldiers that the goddess was predicting their victory. And the auguries were not wrong as Hanno, who was commanding the Sacred Band on the right, was accompanied on the left by the general Bomilcar, a political enemy. According to Diodorus of Sicily:

> 'The fight began with a charge of the Carthaginian war-chariots. The Greeks stood their ground; some of the drivers were shot, some were let pass right through the ranks, but the more part were forced to wheel round and take shelter among the foot-soldiers. Then the horsemen charged; but the Greeks never wavered, so that these too had to flee with heavy loss. The onset of the infantry proved more dangerous, and a fierce fight began along the whole line. Hanno and the Sacred Band wrought a great slaughter among the Greeks, until the light troops came up to the rescue.'

Hanno's motives were also suspected:

> 'A gallant battle developed, and Hanno, who had fighting under him the Sacred Band of selected men and was intent upon gaining the victory by himself, pressed heavily upon the Greeks and slew many of them. Even when all kinds of missiles were hurled against

him, he would not yield but pushed on though suffering many wounds until he died from exhaustion.'

Bomilcar took advantage of this turn of events.

'The Carthaginians fought on under a rain of arrows till at last Hanno fell with many wounds. The Greeks now felt that the victory was theirs, and began to press hard on the enemy. Bomilcar meanwhile saw the discomfiture of the right wing, and withdrew his own troops, sending word to the rest to retire to the camp in good order. Such a command naturally meant the ruin of the army, and Bomilcar was strongly suspected of treasonable designs in wishing to bring about the overthrow of the Sacred Band; for not only would the weakening of Carthage make it easier to upset the government, but with the Sacred Band many of the staunchest oligarchs would perish. The right wing, thinking from the withdrawal of Bomilcar that the battle was already lost, was swept away in headlong rout.'

DIODORUS OF SICILY

The primary source for the Sacred Band of Carthage is the *Bibliotheca Historica*, the 'historical library' – more commonly known as the 'universal history' – of Diodorus Siculus, who lived in Agyrium (now Agira), Sicily, in the first century BC. It consisted of 40 books, 15 of which still survive. It is divided into three sections. The first covers the mythic history of Greece and the Middle East up to the destruction of Troy. The second ends with the death of Alexander the Great, and the third ends with the beginning of Julius Caesar's Gallic War. The last event mentioned is in 21 BC. The author was a wealthy man – he mentions no literary patron. He travelled extensively in Egypt, visited Rome and quotes many earlier sources. Plutarch, who also mentions the Sacred Band of Carthage, quotes largely from Diodorus.

Nearly the whole army returned, a disordered rabble, to the gates of Carthage.

'... those who were leading the Sacred Band after the death of its general Hanno, at first resisted stoutly and, stepping over the bodies of their own men as they fell, withstood every danger, but when they perceived the greater part of the army had turned to flight and that the enemy was surrounding them in the rear, they were forced to withdraw.'

THE LEGACY OF THE SACRED BAND OF CARTHAGE

After the Battle of Tunis, there is no further mention of the Sacred Band of Carthage in the historical record. This may be because it was the Greeks who had given them that name and the Greeks and the Carthaginians did not fight again after the defeat of Agathocles in 307 BC. However, Carthaginian citizen armies did take to the field again during the Punic Wars against Rome and in the Mercenary or Truceless War of 240 BC when their mercenary army rebelled, and élite bands of citizens were used as royal guards for members of the Carthaginian government as well as for important figures such as Hannibal.

'The Carthaginians recognized that their generals in Sicily were conducting the war in a spiritless manner and decided to send out new ones, together with heavy reinforcements. Straightway they made a levy for the campaign from among their noblest citizens and made suitable drafts among the Libyans.'

DIODORUS OF SICILY, LIBRARY OF HISTORY, BOOK XVI.73.3, FL 60–30 BC

THE
MEDIEVAL
WORLD

The Ninja

Japan's legendary 'invisible ones'

Ninja is the dark side of the samurai tradition. While the samurai faced their enemy openly in honourable conflict, the ninja operated by stealth to spy, assassinate or knife an opponent in the back. Nevertheless, the samurai often employed the ninja's special skills to achieve objectives that would have proved too costly using conventional forces of arms.

A 17th-century portrait of a man making the secret ninja sign with his finger. The Ninja remained a closed and secret society well into the 20th century.

This 19th-century woodcut depicts a samurai initiated in ninjutsu, *the martial art embracing 'invisibility'. Such initiates were known as ninja.*

Although the ninja appeared in medieval Japan, their origin is Chinese and they can trace their roots back to the military classic *The Art of War* written by Sun Tzu – or Sonshi as he is known in Japan – in the fourth century BC, which emphasizes the importance of stealth and subterfuge.

The Art of War was introduced to Japan by Kibi Makibi (AD 693–775) who visited China twice as an ambassador and brought back classic texts. These included the *Shoku Nihongi*, compiled around 747, which contains quotations from *The Art of War*. However, the *Kojiki* or the *Record of Ancient Events* – Japan's first book presented to court around 714 – tells the tale of Prince Yamato, who dresses as a woman with a sword concealed under his skirt to kill rebellious chieftains. And according to legend, the hero Raiko (the historical Minamoto Yorimitsu, 944–1021) and four companions disguised themselves as monks in order to get the ogre of Oeyama drunk before assassinating him.

THE BEGINNINGS OF *NINJUTSU*

Around 900, following the collapse of the T'ang dynasty, exiled Chinese generals arrived in Japan, bringing with them their martial arts. Then, in 1024, Chinese mystics came to live in the forests and caves of the Kii Peninsula, where their ways were taken up by the warrior-priests who lived in the wilderness. The fusion of mysticism and martial arts resulted in *ninjutsu*, which was gradually formalized into a systematic code of combat and espionage.

Defeated in battle – and consequently losing his samurai status – Daisuke Nishina of the village of Togakure escaped to the pine forests of the Kii Peninsula when he met Kain Doshi, a warrior-monk who had fled from the military upheavals in China. Daisuke put aside his samurai code and adopted the Chinese and Tibetan ways he learnt from Kain. Over the next three generations, Daisuke's family developed and refined these ideas into the *Togakure-ryu* – or school – of *ninjutsu*, and came to be called ninja.

Other *ryu* then sprang up in the mountains of Honshu island, each with their own speciality. The *Koto-ryu*, for example, specialized in bone-breaking techniques known as *koppojutsu*, which later evolved into *jujutsu* and *karate*. The *Fudo-ryu* concentrated on

夜叉五良
中村芝翫

市川圀丸筆

THE NINJA

throwing *shuriken*, or steel blades, ranging from small knives to the notorious ninja stars. The *Kukishin-ryu* used conventional weapons in unconventional ways. The *Kusunoki-ryu* developed a huge network of spies. The *Gyokko-ryu* developed *koshijutsu* – attacking the nerve centres by pinching or finger jabs, while the *Togakure-ryu* employed the *shuko* – a spiked band worn around the hand which could deflect a sword or allow the wearer to climb a wall or a tree like a cat. They also used the *tetsubishi*, small spike weapons that were scattered on the ground to injure the unwary.

THE SECRET ORGANIZATION

There were three ranks of ninja. The *jonin* was the commander or 'wise man', whose identity was kept secret. His orders were passed to *chunin* or middle men, and then on to *genin* or field agents. When they were not out on operations, the *genin* lived in remote mountainous areas where they posed as farmers, but spent their time training. Different groups of *genin* often had no idea they were working for the same *jonin*.

The ninja were a hereditary organization. Their children were trained from birth. Even their children's games were designed to develop balance and agility. They then went on to learn unarmed combat and, later, fighting with the sword and traditional Japanese stave. In their early teens they would be taught the specialty of their *ryu*. While developing their strength and stamina, they would be instructed in methods of concealment, information gathering, subterfuge, gaining surreptitious entry to buildings, climbing walls, preparing medicines and drugs, map making and tying up victims. Psychological strength was developed, along with methods of using opponents' weaknesses against them.

In the 12th century the Gempei War broke out between two samurai families. However, ninja methods were used. At the Battle of Yokota ga hara in 1182, the Genji of Shinano divided up his force of 2000 men into seven bands and gave them enemy banners. When the enemy saw them coming, they cheered. But as the Genji's men approached, the seven bands joined together, threw away the banners, unfurled their own and attacked. And at the time of the Battle of Ichi-no-tani in 1184, ninja entered enemy castles by stealth – in one instance on a suicide mission. In 1441, the Akamatsu family used ninja methods to assassinate the shogun Ashikaga Yoshinori during a banquet, but the shogun was avenged and the Akamatsu banished. To restore their fortunes, the Akamatsu again adopted ninja methods to assassinate the emperor and steal the crown jewels.

THE NINJA OF IGA AND KOGA

In 1487, the writer Sugiyama records 'ninja … said to be from the regions of Iga and Koga' going 'freely into enemy castles in secret. They observed hidden things and were taken as being allies'. Over 50 years later, ninja took Kasagi castle in a surprise attack. In 1561, ninja from Iga entered the fort at Futo: 'in secret, started fires in the castle, and at this signal the keep and the second bailey were conquered.' In 1562, ninja from Koga took the castle built on top of a cliff at Kaminojo, which would have been costly to take by a conventional assault. Wearing enemy uniforms, they scaled the cliff and entered the castle under the cover of darkness. They set fire to the fort and slaughtered the defenders. The victor even sent a letter of thanks to the head of a prominent family in Koga. The sons of the owner of the castle were allowed to return, but began causing trouble again. The ninja returned to kill them.

THE *KUSUNOKI-RYU*

During the Nambubokucho Wars that raged between the emperor and the shogun from 1319 to 1338, the samurai strategist Kusunoki Masashige (1294–1336) who backed the emperor began the *Kusunoki-ryu*. Using guerrilla tactics, he captured the fortress of Chihaya near Nara in Japan in 1332 and restored imperial rule. As head of the imperial forces, he defeated the forces of the new shogun Ashikaga Takajuki in 1335.

However, the following year the emperor Go-Daigo ordered him to take on the forces of Ashikaga Takajuki again in a conventional pitched battle. Kusunoki Masashige was defeated and committed suicide rather than face capture.

This statue of Kusunoki Masashige stands outside the Imperial Palace in Tokyo, Japan.

Throughout the wars of the 16th century, ninja worked as mercenaries and spies for both sides. Ninja were also employed to thwart the efforts of opposing ninja. As well as burning castles and gathering intelligence, they would steal, murder, spread misinformation and devise plots to disrupt the enemy.

THE DECLINE OF THE NINJA

In 1573, General Nobunaga Oda and his army, newly armed with muskets, overthrew the last of the Ashikaga shoguns. A supporter of Christianity that was beginning to take hold in Japan, Nobunaga was determined to suppress the ninja, who had a religious element to their martial code. He sent his son Katsuyori to attack the ninja stronghold in Iga, but at the Battle of Tensho Iga no Ran in 1579, Nobunaga's samurai troops were defeated by the ninja under Sandayu Momochi. Nobunaga retaliated, leading a massive army that outnumbered the ninja ten to one into Iga, where they slaughtered men, women and children.

The surviving ninja retreated into the mountains to regroup. In 1582, Nobunaga was murdered by his ally Ieyasu Tokugawa, but the Tokugawa shogunate brought peace and stability – leaving the ninja unemployed. They joined the military and the police force, or took to a life of crime. When Commodore Perry's 'black ships' arrived in 1853 to force Japan to open its ports, a ninja named Yasusuke Sawamura was ordered to board Perry's flagship to search for information. He returned with two letters from a Dutch sailor praising the virtues of British women in the kitchen and French women in the bedroom.

'The Iga shu entered Kasagi castle in secret and set fire to a few of the priests' quarters. They also set fire to outbuildings in various places inside the San no maru.'

THE TAMON-IN NIKKI DIARY OF ABBOT EISHUN, *26TH DAY OF 11TH MONTH OF THE 10TH YEAR OF TEMBUN* (1541)

The Ottoman's Janissaries

The sultan's feared bodyguard

Traditionally, Christian slaves converted to Islam, the Janissaries owed their only allegiance to the sultan, who led them into battle. They gained such a fearsome reputation that, when other European nations decided to keep standing armies of their own, they modelled them on the Janissaries. However, the Janissaries became so powerful politically that they could remove any sultan they opposed, so they were forcibly disbanded.

A woodcut from 1576 depicting an Ottoman Janissary. These élite soldiers were well equipped and well paid, and they enjoyed a high living standard and respected social status.

The Janissaries – or 'new soldiers' – were members of a powerful force of the Ottoman empire from the late 14th century until they were disbanded in 1826. Usually, recruits were Christian slaves between the ages of seven and ten, taken from their villages in the Balkans. They were deprived of any further contact with their family and then converted to Islam, since non-Muslims were not allowed to bear arms. As the personal property of the sultan, these soldiers had no other allegiance. Their loyalty was reinforced with strict training and regular pay, at a time when other soldiers were only paid during wartime. The Janissaries also shared in the spoils of war.

Janissary units were begun either by the Ottoman bey Orhan I, who ruled from 1326 to 1359, or by his son the first sultan, Murad I, who reigned from 1360 to 1389. Traditionally, after a successful campaign, one-fifth of the army's bounty was due to the sultan who often took it in kind. Consequently he had access to large numbers of prisoners of war, who were kept as slaves. Christian captives were given uniforms and trained as the sultan's soldiers, who could then be used to replace tribal warriors, whose allegiance could not be depended upon. The Janissaries were at the forefront of the expansion of the Ottoman empire over the next 100 years.

THE DEVSIRME SYSTEM

Later, new recruits were supplied by the devsirme system, whereby provinces occupied by the Ottoman had to give up one boy from every 40 houses. They were usually collected by Janissaries who, themselves, had been forcibly taken from their homes. Greek or Albanian recruits were preferred. Training took between three and seven years. During that time, they would learn Turkish and Ottoman lifestyles, speaking Turkish and reading Arabic.

Recruits were strictly disciplined and expected to remain celibate even after they became fully fledged Janissaries at the age of 24 or 25. They were only allowed to marry when they retired. As the Ottoman empire expanded, Bulgarians, Armenians, Bosnians, Serbs, Poles,

Ukrainians and southern Russians were also recruited. While other Muslims wore beards, converts from these countries were only permitted to wear moustaches, since a beard was considered the emblem of a free man.

The number of the sultan's Janissaries varied from as few as 100 to, it is estimated, over 50,000. Initially they were trained as expert archers, but they adopted firearms as soon as they became available in the mid-15th century. As the technology developed, they were also equipped with hand-grenades and light artillery. In battle, they also used sabres and battleaxes but, in peacetime, they only carried cutlasses or clubs unless on frontier duty.

The Battle of Kahlenberg (by the 17th-century Flemish artist Franz Geffels) at the Second Siege of Vienna, when Turkish forces tried to take the city. However, despite the presence of the Janissaries, the attack ended in failure.

45

THE OTTOMAN'S JANISSARIES

c.1365 First Janissary units formed from Christian prisoners of war

1453 Janissaries fight at the capture of Constantinople

1529 Janissaries act as engineers during the Siege of Vienna

1566 Permission to marry granted to the formerly celibate Janissaries

1622 Janissaries murder Sultan Osman II

1648 Janissaries depose and murder Sultan Ibrahim I

1683 The devsirme forcible recruiting system abandoned

1807 Revolt of the Janissaries deposes Sultan Selim III

1826 Mahmud II disbands the Janissaries by force

The corps was divided into three divisions – the sultan's bodyguard, frontier guards and a small group of musketeers. At full strength, there would be 165 to 196 battalions. As the first standing army in the region since the Rome legions, they were much studied and emulated by the European powers who, traditionally, only raised armies in times of war.

As an élite fighting unit, the Janissaries had a *cebeci*, or logistical, corps to carry their weapons and ammunition. Other backup groups – the Azabs – made roads, pitched tents and baked bread. The Janissaries even had their own medical corps and field hospitals staffed by Muslim and Jewish doctors. These innovations made the Ottoman army the most formidable force in Europe for a long period.

POLITICS AND POWER

In action, the Janissaries were led by the sultan himself and took part in all the major Ottoman campaigns, including the capture of Constantinople in 1453, the defeat of the Egyptian Mamelukes and the wars against Austria and Hungary. In the siege of Vienna in 1529, they demonstrated their considerable skills as engineers, acting as their own sappers undermining the city walls.

Like the Praetorian Guard before them, the Janissaries became a political force. Until the 16th century, around two-thirds of the grand viziers of the Ottoman empire had been Janissaries, as were many other officials of the empire, forcing out the traditional Turkish nobility. When the Janissaries were allowed to recruit outside the devsirme system in the late 16th century, Muslim Turks enrolled, looking for a lucrative career. Even Janissaries' sons were allowed to join up. Becoming a Janissary became so popular that the devsirme system was abandoned completely in 1683.

Janissaries were given permission to marry in 1566. They left their barracks and began involving themselves in business, where their intimidating methods made them unpopular with civilian traders. Although outside interests undermined their effectiveness as a fighting force, the Janissaries still had power over the sultan, regularly staging palace coups.

When the teenage Osman II came to the throne he tried to discipline the Janissaries by closing down their coffee shops and cutting their pay. Then in 1622 he announced that he was going to make a *hajj* to Mecca. Suspecting that his real intention was to recruit a new army in Syria and Egypt, the Janissaries strangled him. They also deposed and murdered Sultan Ibrahim I in 1648.

'They found the Turks coming right up under the walls and seeking battle, particularly the Janissaries, who are soldiers of the Turkish sultan; none of them are afraid of death, but they came on like wild beasts, and when one or two of them were killed, at once more Turks came and took away the dead ones, carrying them on their shoulders as one would a pig, without caring how near they came to the city walls.'

NICOLO BARBARO, *DIARY OF THE SIEGE OF CONSTANTINOPLE*, 1453

Janissary Music

The Janissaries pioneered the military marching band. Traditionally, they used a wide variety of drums, triangles, cymbals and bells, adding varieties of oboe and trumpet. It began to become fashionable throughout Europe in 1720, when it was adopted by August II of Poland. Other armies soon followed suit. Gluck, Mozart, Haydn and Beethoven all incorporated the Janissary style into their compositions. The music fell into disfavour following the bloody end of the Janissary corps that had supplied most of the musicians. In the middle and late 19th century, the genre went into decline along with the Ottoman empire. With the collapse of the Ottoman empire, the director of Istanbul's military museum tried to revive the tradition, and by 1953 – celebrating the 500th anniversary of the Fall of Constantinople – the tradition had been fully restored as a band of the Turkish armed forces. A Janissary band that is resident at the military museum in Istanbul gives regular performances.

The band of the Janissaries was called the mehterhane. *They accompanied the soldiers into battle and used music to communicate instructions – such as retreat or attack – during the fighting. (Ottoman miniature, early 18th century.)*

A PROGRAMME OF WESTERNIZATION

Following the French Revolution, Sultan Selim III began a programme of Westernization. This was halted in 1807 by a revolt of the Janissaries who deposed him. But the need for reform was pressing. Although their numbers had swollen to some 135,000, the Janissaries still failed to prevent Greece gaining its independence in the 1820s. This demonstrated that they were not the great military force they once had been.

It was not until 1826 that Selim's successor, Mahmud II, tried once more to introduce reforms, reorganizing the army along European lines. The Janissaries rebelled in what became know as the 'Auspicious Incident'. It is suspected that this revolt was the result of deliberate provocation by the sultan, who then declared war on the rebels. When they would not surrender, he turned cannon on their barracks. Over 4000 died. Those taken prisoner were either executed or banished to the furthest outposts of the empire. The age of the Janissaries was over and the corps was disbanded. The Ottoman empire would then gradually crumble, coming to an end in 1922.

Ivan the Terrible's Streltsy

The tsar's musketeers

Ivan the Terrible formed an élite band of musketeers to defend Russia from the Tartars and expand its empire east and west. The units stationed in Moscow became the tsar's bodyguard. Lack of pay and harsh treatment forced some units to rebel. Others involved themselves in politics, and their opposition to Peter the Great finally led to their downfall.

The Streltsy were formed between 1540 and 1550 by Ivan the Terrible, the grand prince of Moscow who became tsar of all the Russias in 1547. They were armed with the harquebus, a muzzle-loading weapon fired from the shoulder that was invented in Spain in the mid-15th century. Initially, free trades people and peasants were recruited into the Streltsy. Later, military service in this unit became lifelong and hereditary.

The Streltsy first saw combat at the Siege of Kazan in 1552, which resulted in a massacre of the population and the total destruction of the city. With the fall of Astrakhan in 1556, the Volga became a Russian river and the Tartars were no longer a threat. The Streltsy saw action again when Ivan the Terrible invaded Livonia in 1558. This led to a full-scale war with Poland, Sweden and Lithuania. In the 17th century, they fought against the Polish and Swedes again, and also fought in the Crimea.

Engraving (dated 1813) showing how the Streltsy would have looked in about 1550, shortly after the unit was formed by Ivan the Terrible.

ORGANIZATION, TRAINING AND EQUIPMENT

The Streltsy were then divided into a contingent stationed in Moscow, and municipal units stationed in other Russian cities. The Moscow Streltsy guarded the Kremlin and, when not involved in military operations, acted as a police force and fire brigade. The Municipal Streltsy were charged with garrison and border duties. They came under the authority of the *Streletsky prikaz*, or Streltsy Department, but also carried out the orders of the local authorities, except in time of war.

Both the Moscow and local Municipal Streltsy received the same training and equipment – sabres, sometimes pikes, harquebuses and long poleaxes – which were sometimes used to steady the gun while firing. Later, muskets were introduced. They also wore the same uniforms – usually red, blue or green coats, with yellow boots.

Although they often faced highly mobile horseborne troops such as the Tartars, the Streltsy were used in static formations or deployed from fortifications. They employed a portable wooden defence known as a *gulyai gorod*, or 'walking fort'. The Streltsy were trained to fire in rotating volleys. As the first line of men fired and then stepped back to reload, the second line stepped forward to fire.

By the end of the 16th century, there were 20,000 to 25,000 Streltsy. In 1681, this number reached 55,000, including 22,500 in Moscow alone. Then the Streltsy were split into *prikazy*, or regiments, under the command of a nobleman appointed by the government. The regiments were subdivided into *sotni*, or hundreds, and *desyatki*, or tens. By that time, they had both mounted and infantry units.

Members of the Streltsy in action, from a painting by Viktor Vasnetsov (1848–1926). Note the portable wooden defence, the muskets and the long poleaxe – typical Streltsy equipment.

DISCONTENT AMONG THE RANKS

The Streltsy lived in their own neighbourhoods or districts in settlements. The Streltsy settlement in Moscow was close to where the main campus of Moscow State University now stands. They received money and bread from the State Treasury. However, the government in Moscow rarely had much cash, so the Streltsy were often not paid the four roubles a year they had been entitled to since the 1550s. To supplement their income, they were allowed to farm or go into trade, but this reduced their effectiveness as a combat unit, as men wanted to stay at home during the planting and harvesting seasons. Outside interests also interfered with training and, in the second half of the 17th century, the Streltsy could not compete with other army regiments that had been reorganized along Western European lines.

The government then took to paying them in land instead of money. Discontent spread. Regular Streltsy units were no longer prepared to undergo the hardships of military service for no money, or put up with the abuse of their officers or the local authorities. The poorest

49

units joined the rural anti-serfdom uprisings of the 17th and early 18th centuries, as well as urban uprisings such as the Moscow Uprising of 1682, the Streltsy Uprising of 1698 and the Astrakhan Uprising of 1705–06.

THE STRUGGLE FOR POWER

However, the top Streltsy men enjoyed a high social status. They tried to quell these revolts and keep the rank and file on the government's side. Then a Praetorian element of the Moscow Streltsy began to get involved in politics. In 1676, Tsar Alexis had died and was succeeded by his son Fyodor III, who died childless in 1682. The Miloslavsky family, relatives of Fyodor's mother Mariya, wanted to put his younger brother Ivan on the throne. But 15-year-old Ivan was a sickly and feeble-minded child. Meanwhile, the Naryshkina family, relatives of Alexis's second wife Natalya, backed her son, Fyodor's nine-year-old half-brother, Peter. Determined to maintain Miloslavsky power, Ivan's sister, 25-year-old Sophia, encouraged the Streltsy to revolt. They killed many of Peter's supporters and demanded that Ivan become tsar. In the event, both Peter I and Ivan V were crowned, with Sophia as regent. Sophia then progressively excluded Peter from public affairs, and the young tsar grew fearful that he might be murdered by the Streltsy.

In 1689, Peter, then 17, came of age and the Naryshkina family insisted that Sophia stand down as regent. Instead she proclaimed herself tsarina. This time the Streltsy deserted her, and Sophia was banished to a convent. Although Ivan was allowed to retain his title until his death in 1696, Peter the Great took power. He then tried to limit the Streltsy's military and political power. The corps was run down, and eight Moscow regiments were transferred to Belgorod, Sevsk and Kiev. Despite this, while Peter the Great was away on his 'Great Embassy' to western Europe in 1698, the Streltsy revolted again in a last-ditch attempt to put Sophia on the throne. The revolt was put down by Patrick Gordon, a Scottish general who had entered imperial service under Tsar Alexis in 1661. When Peter returned to Russia he crushed the Streltsy with savage reprisals, including public executions and torture.

However, with the Russian defeat at Narva in 1700, Peter needed the Streltsy again. Their regiments took part in the Great Northern War of 1700–21 and in Peter's Prut Campaign of 1711 against the Ottomans. Gradually, the Moscow Streltsy became incorporated into the regular army. At the same time, Peter began to disband the Municipal Streltsy, though units were kept in some cities until the late 18th century. Meanwhile, the Imperial Guard's Izmailovsky and Preobrazhensky regiments – formed by Peter himself – replaced the Streltsy as the tsar's bodyguards.

IVAN THE TERRIBLE'S STRELTSY

1540–50 Ivan the Terrible forms the Streltsy

1552 The Streltsy see action at the Siege of Kazan

1558–83 The Streltsy participate in the Livonian War

1681 The Streltsy are re-formed into regiments

1682 The Streltsy participate in the Moscow Uprising to prevent Peter the Great becoming tsar

1689 The Streltsy desert the regent Sophia, allowing Peter the Great to take the throne

1698 The Streltsy Uprising: the Streltsy revolt and try to put Sophia on the throne; they are defeated and executed or exiled

1700–21 A rump of the Streltsy take part in the Great Northern War

1711 The Streltsy join Peter the Great on his Prut Campaign

1720s The Streltsy are finally disbanded

'Peter organized the execution of the Streltsy like a theatrical production. The blood of the beheaded Streltsy poured into the unearthed coffin of the boyar Miloslavsky, whom Peter regarded as the ideological inspiration for the Streltsy movement. The coffin itself was brought to the place of execution on a sleigh harnessed to a team of pigs.'

RUSSINA JOURNALIST GRIGORY PASKO, 2007, QUOTING EARLIER HISTORIANS

THE STRELTSY UPRISING

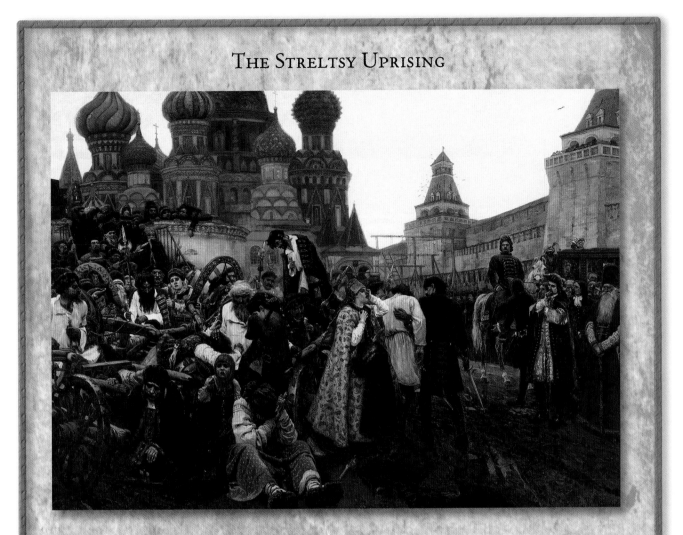

The Moscow Streltsy had participated in Peter the Great's Azov campaigns of 1695–6, and four regiments were left in Azov as a garrison. However, in 1697, they were sent to the western city of Velikiye Luki instead of being returned to Moscow. They were left without provisions and, lacking horses, had to carry their own equipment. In March 1698, 175 Streltsy left their regiments and went to Moscow to complain. There they secretly established contact with Sophia, who was incarcerated at the Novodevichy Convent. When the delegation were returned to their regiments empty-handed, discontent spread. On 6 June, the Streltsy removed their commanding officers and approximately 4000 men rode to Moscow with the intention of putting Sophia on the throne. Peter the Great was out of the country, but ordered four regiments and a cavalry

Painting by Vasily I. Surikov (1848–1916), showing the morning of the execution of the Moscow Streltsy rebels by Tsar Peter the Great in September 1698.

unit under the command of Patrick Gordon and the boyar Aleksey Shein to attack the Streltsy. On 18 June, the Streltsy were defeated 25 miles (40 km) west of Moscow. Fifty-seven Streltsy were executed; the rest were sent into exile. When Peter the Great returned in August, he ordered a full investigation. Another 1182 Streltsy were then executed or sent into exile – 601 of them were whipped or branded with hot irons first. The executions continued until 1707. Other Moscow regiments that had not participated in the uprising were later disbanded, and former Streltsy members and their families were banished from Moscow.

The Bowmen of England

From Crécy and Poitiers to Agincourt

In the 14th century, the English longbow was introduced to the battlefields of Europe. It ended the medieval social order of battle fought between mounted knights, since they could now be cut down by peasants armed only with bows. The weapon made England the dominant power in Western Europe for 100 years.

The English longbow seems to have been developed in Wales. It was as tall as a man and fired arrows half that length. A trained archer could fire six aimed shots a minute with an effective range of 183 metres (600 ft) – though it was possible to fire an arrow twice as far.

The effectiveness of the English longbow was first demonstrated against the Scots at the Battle of Dupplin Moor in 1332 and Halidon Hill in 1333. Flemish crossbows proved they were no match at the Battle of Cadzand in 1337. And the French got their first taste of them at Sluys in 1340.

Nevertheless, they seemed unprepared when the English King Edward III and his son, Prince Edward, landed at Cherbourg in July 1346. They were heading for Rouen when they heard that Philip VI of France was massing an army near Paris. With the bridges across the Seine cut, Edward moved his army north to retreat into Flanders. But his way was blocked by the River Somme. Now with a massive French army on his tail, he eventually made a crossing near Blanchetaque. Then he turned to face the French outside the village of Crécy.

THE BATTLE OF CRÉCY

Vastly outnumbered, Edward deployed his army for a defensive battle. On the left he had 3000 archers, 1000 dismounted knights and some Welsh foot soldiers. On the right, near Crécy itself, there were another 3000 archers, 1000 men-at-arms and 1000 Welsh infantry. Behind them on a ridge were a reserve of 2000 archers and 700 dismounted knights. Eleven thousand in all, they faced an army of 60,000 French, including 12,000 mounted men-at-arms and the flower of Continental nobility. The French foot soldiers had been marching for 18 hours when they spotted the English at around six in the evening. Philip wanted to make camp, but the knights were eager to join battle. They cried out 'Kill!' giving the impression that battle had already begun. Unable to restrain his men, Philip decided to attack.

The French were to be led into battle by 6,000 crossbowmen from Genoa. They were followed by a line of knights under the command of the Count of Flanders and Count Charles II of Alençon, the king's brother. As they approached the English, the Genoans loosed off their first volley, which fell short. As they began to reload, they were hit by a storm of English arrows. Some 60,000 missiles rained down in the next 60 seconds.

THE BOWMEN OF ENGLAND

1332 English longbows cut down the Scots at the Battle of Dupplin Moor

1333 English bowmen triumphant again at Halidon Hill

1337 Longbows outperform Flemish crossbows at the Battle of Cadzand

1340 The French face English longbows at Sluys

1346 Longbows give the English victory over superior French forces at Crécy

1356 English bowmen cut down mounted knights at Poitiers

1415 English bowmen cut down dismounted knights at Agincourt

1453 Bowmen overwhelmed by French firearms at Formigny

Pounded by boulders from English catapults, the Genoans turned and ran. The fleeing crossbowmen blocked the knights' advance and Philip ordered his knights to kill them. The English were then treated to the sight of the French slaughtering their own mercenaries, while being pummelled by English arrows. When the French knights finally turned on the enemy, few were left and they made little impact on the English lines. By nightfall, the French had made 15 charges, to no avail. Over 1500 French men-at-arms lay dead, along with countless foot soldiers. Among the dead were the counts of Alençon and Flanders.

THE BATTLE OF POITIERS

Ten years later, the Black Prince was leading some 7000 men on a raid from Bordeaux into central France. They were pursued by a French force of over 35,000 men led by Philip's successor, John II. The English turned to fight in the thickets and marshes south of Poitiers. Forgetting the lessons of Crécy, the French sent in their heavily armed knights, who quickly became bogged down in the mud, making them easy targets for the English bowmen. King John and his son Philip were captured, along with 17 lords, 13 counts and 5 viscounts. The

At the Battle of Crécy the English army, with longbow archers, won a decisive victory against a numerically superior French army. Prince Edward, the Black Prince (1330–76), is shown middle right commanding English forces. (Illustration from Chronicles *by French writer Jean Froissart (c.1337–c.1405).)*

French suffered 2500 dead and wounded, and 2000 captured. The Black Prince reported casualties of just 40 dead.

At Crécy and Poitiers, English longbowmen showed that they could defeat mounted knights. At Agincourt in 1415, they inflicted an even more telling defeat on French dismounted knights. By then, Henry V was king of England and he laid claim to the French throne. Landing 11,000 men in Normandy in August, he captured Harfleur the following month. By then, he had lost nearly half his troops, largely due to disease. They headed for Calais, hoping to sail back to England, but they were stopped by a huge French force near the village of Agincourt – now Azincourt – in the Pas-de-Calais.

THE BATTLE OF AGINCOURT

Henry had some 5000 archers and 900 men-at-arms; the French fielded between 20,000 and 30,000 men. Chivalrously, the French chose a battlefield flanked by two woods 900 metres (about 2950 ft) apart. This would hamper the larger French force manoeuvring and prevent them outflanking the English. The battle lines formed up in sight of each other, around 900 metres (about 2950 ft) apart. They were separated by a ploughed field, muddy after days of rain. Henry only had enough men-at-arms to form a single line. The archers were formed up on the wings, raked forward so that they could provide flanking fire. They were protected by thickets of 2.4-metre- (8-ft-) long pointed stakes hammered into the ground and angled forward to impale charging French horsemen.

The French men-at-arms formed three lines. The two front lines were dismounted and carried lances cut down for fighting on foot. The rear line remained mounted. As every French nobleman wanted to be in the front rank and have his banner prominently displayed, the archers and crossbowmen were positioned out to the flanks along with the artillery and the cavalry – 800 on the right and 1600 on the left.

The English were trapped, so the French delayed the attack for five hours. Henry waited, too, knowing that an attack would be costly. He also knew that he had to fight that day. The English had no food and they would only get weaker, so he gave the order to advance to within 275 metres (900 ft) of the French position, where the archers hammered their stakes in again. At that distance a flight of arrows is not very effective, but the first volley produced a thunderous noise when it hit French armour. This was enough to pique the cavalry into charging. The dismounted knights followed across the muddy field.

'Every man being the King's subject, ... (except spiritual men ... justices and barons) ... shall ... use and exercise shooting in longbows ... and also that the fathers, governors and rulers of such as be of tender age, do teach and bring them up in the knowledge of the same shooting; and that every man having a man-child ... of the age of seven years and above, till he shall come to the age of seventeen years, a bow and two shafts to induce and learn them and bring them up in shooting ...'

THE UNLAWFUL GAMES ACT OF 1541

THE ENGLISH LONGBOW

The English – or Welsh – longbow was up to 2 metres (6.5 ft) long and was made from yew, though ash and other woods were also used. The draw of around 76 centimetres (30 in) required between two and three times the effort taken to draw a modern bow. Longbows were accurate only to 7 metres (23 ft). However, flights of arrows were effective against an approaching army at much greater distances. While aiming at a target slowed the archer's firing rate to six a minute, skilled archers could loose off flights of up to 20 arrows a minute – several clouds of arrows would be in the air before the first hit its mark. Typically an archer would be provided with 60 to 72 arrows, permitting between three and six minutes of continuous fire. They would be stuck in the ground in front of the archer for ease of loading.

This engraving shows 15th-century archers using the longbow. The weapon was deadly when sending volleys of arrows into enemy ranks from a distance.

In the 40 seconds it took the French horsemen to reach the English lines, the archers loosed off another six flights of arrows, each more deadly as the French advanced. With the woods preventing a flanking attack, the French horsemen had to make a frontal assault, with the riders behind pushing those in front onto the English stakes. Shying away from the hail of arrows, the cavalry turned onto the dismounted men-at-arms who were making slow progress over the muddy ground. The English archers were able to fire into their flanks. Their arrows were equipped with 'Bodkin points', specially designed to penetrate armour.

THE COMPRESSED FRENCH LINE

As the French advanced on the English, the field narrowed by 140 metres (460 ft), compressing the French line. Arrows from English archers on the flanks compressed it further. By the time the men-at-arms arrived at the English line, they did not have enough room to wield their weapons. Sheer weight of numbers pushed the English back. But the French men-at-arms then slipped in the mud or fell over others. In full armour, it was difficult to get back up again.

With the battle joined, the French artillery, archers and crossbowmen had no clear line of fire, while English archers could pour arrows into the crush of French knights. More piled in and many were crushed to death. At Henry's signal, the archers dropped their bows to finish off the French knights with swords and axes. With the first two French lines either killed or taken prisoner, the third line of mounted men refused to attack. By early afternoon, the prisoners taken outnumbered the English army, but the battle was not yet over. Fearing the prisoners were a threat to his rear, Henry ordered that they be killed. The English men-at-arms refused, so Henry picked out 200 of his archers – tough, professional soldiers – and threatened to hang them if they did not obey his order. Within minutes 2000 French men-at-arms lay dead, along with some 10,000 killed in the fighting. Ten members of the nobility were dead and another five survived captivity. The English lost fewer than 450 men.

After Agincourt, the English bowmen remained supreme until the Battle of Formigny in 1453, when they were overwhelmed by fire from French handguns and cannon.

The Military Orders of the Holy Land

The Knights Hospitaller and the Knights Templar

During the crusades, religious orders of knights were founded to look after the needs of pilgrims visiting the Holy Land. While they continued to fight to maintain crusader strongholds, they considered themselves a special force because of their religious and humanitarian calling as well as their military prowess.

In the 11th century, a hospital was founded in Jerusalem by Italian merchants from Amalfi to care for sick and injured pilgrims who had fallen on hard times. When Christian forces took Jerusalem during the First Crusade in 1099, the Blessed Gerard, the superior of the hospital, extended his work in Jerusalem and set up hostels on the route from Europe to the Holy Land. To look after them, the Order of the Knights of St John of Jerusalem was founded on 15 February 1113 by a papal bull issued by Pope Paschal II.

Gerard's successor Raymond de Puy acquired money and lands, and the order began providing armed escorts to the pilgrims. These grew into a large force, and the Hospitallers, along with the Templars, founded in 1119, became the most formidable military order in the Holy Land. Wearing a white cross on their black surcoat, they distinguished themselves in battle against the Muslim forces trying to recapture the city.

By the middle of the 12th century, the order was divided into those who cared for the sick and those who administered to the religious brothers. Exempt from tithes, the Hospitallers built seven large forts in the Holy Land and had 140 estates in the area. In 1185, they were granted the protection of the Holy Roman Emperor Frederick Barbarossa. However, they could not stem the tide of Islam and, in 1187, Jerusalem fell.

THE HOSPITALLERS MOVE TO CYPRUS, RHODES AND MALTA

When Acre was captured by the Muslims in 1291, the Hospitallers withdrew to Cyprus. In 1309, after two years of campaigning, they took Rhodes, which they ruled until 1523 as the Order of the Knights of Rhodes. They also had holdings in Aragon, Auvergne, Castile, England, France, Germany, Italy and Provence.

The Knights of Rhodes fought the Barbary pirates and thwarted invasions by the sultan of Egypt in 1444 and the Ottoman sultan Mehmed II in 1480. In 1522, Süleyman the Magnificent laid siege to Rhodes. Four hundred ships landed 200,000 men to take on just

7000 Hospitallers. After six months, the Hospitallers capitulated and, on 1 January 1523, sailed from Rhodes. For seven years, they wandered from place to place. Then in 1530, the Holy Roman Emperor Charles V gave them the Maltese archipelago – in return for the annual fee of a falcon to be presented to his representative, the viceroy of Sicily – and thereafter they became the Knights of Malta.

In 1565, Süleyman sent an invasion force of 40,000 men to take the island that was held by just 700 knights and 8000 men. With no aid forthcoming from their allies, the Hospitallers under grand master Jean Parisot de la Valette were besieged in their castles. Over half their number died, but they held out against all odds. By the time a small relief force from Sicily arrived, the Turks were exhausted and the siege was lifted. In 1571, the Knights of Malta sent ships to join the Christian fleet that finished off the Turkish navy at the Battle of Lepanto.

The new capital of Malta was named Valetta after Jean Parisot de la Valette, and the Hospitallers built a large hospital there. They continued to run Malta as a sovereign state, but gave up warfare and devoted themselves to medical work until Napoleon landed in 1798. In

A siege led by Godfrey de Bouillon in 1099, during the First Crusade. It shows Saracens firing arrows at Christian forces as they attempt to scale the walls under cover of their own longbowmen. (Illustration from the 14th-century illuminated manuscript The Story of Godfrey de Bouillon.*)*

Knights Templar were equipped with armour and weapons, but they also wore a tunic emblazoned with a large cross to denote their allegiance to Christianity.

1834, they established themselves in Rome as the Knights Hospitaller of St John of Jerusalem. Since 1961, they have been the Sovereign Military and Hospitaller Order of St John of Jerusalem, of Rhodes and of Malta. Although the order no longer exercises territorial rule, it still issues passports.

THE POOR KNIGHTS OF CHRIST

The Knights Templar (originally called the Poor Knights of Christ and the Temple of Solomon) were founded by eight or nine French knights who, in 1119, vowed to protect the pilgrims visiting the kingdom of Jerusalem. The king of Jerusalem, Baldwin II, gave them quarters in the captured Al Aqsa Mosque on Temple Mount, and also gave them their name. The Knights Templar took vows of chastity and poverty, reflected in their emblem of two knights riding on one horse. Their courageous service in the Holy Land quickly won them new recruits.

St Bernard of Clairvaux wrote their rules of life and won them the endorsement of the Catholic Church at the Council of Troyes in 1128. Pope Innocent took them under direct papal authority in 1139. They became a key element in the defence of the Holy Land, garrisoning every major town there. Some 80 Templars joined the army of Baldwin IV that defeated Saladin at the Battle of Montgisard in 1177.

Noblemen who fought with the Templars deposited their assets with the order since, individually, they were sworn to a vow of poverty. Pilgrims also deposited money with the order before setting out on their journey to the Holy Land. In return they were given a letter of credit which allowed them to retrieve money in the Holy Land. This was the beginning of European banking, and it made the order wealthy.

At the height of their powers the Templars consisted of around 20,000 knights; they had their own naval fleet and they owned the island of Cyprus. They became bitter rivals of

MILITARY ORDERS OF THE HOLY LAND

1099 Crusaders capture Jerusalem

1113 The Order of the Knights of St John of Jerusalem founded

1119 The Poor Knights of Christ and the Temple of Solomon (Templars) founded in Jerusalem

1139 The Templars taken under direct papal authority

1177 The Templars defeat Saladin at the Battle of Montgisard

1185 The Hospitallers granted the protection of the Holy Roman Emperor Frederick Barbarossa

1187 The fall of Jerusalem

1291 The fall of Acre

1303 The Templar garrison at Ruad taken by the Mamelukes

1307 The Templars arrested by Philip IV of France

1309 The Hospitallers take Rhodes

1312 The Templars suppressed; their wealth transferred to the Hospitallers

1314 The Templars' grand master burnt at the stake in Paris

1523 The Hospitallers ejected from Rhodes by the Ottomans

1530 Charles V grants the Hospitallers possession of Malta

1565 The Ottomans besiege Malta

1571 The Turkish fleet defeated at the Battle of Lepanto

1798 Napoleon lands on Malta

1834 The Hospitallers are established in Rome as the Knights Hospitaller of St John of Jerusalem

'[A Templar Knight] is truly a fearless knight, and secure on every side, for his soul is protected by the armour of faith, just as his body is protected by the armour of steel. He is thus doubly armed, and need fear neither demons nor men.'

BERNARD DE CLAIRVAUX, *DE LAUDE NOVAE MILITAE* – '*IN PRAISE OF THE NEW KNIGHTHOOD*', C.1135

THE SIEGE OF MALTA

On 18 May 1565, a Turkish fleet of 138 galleys approached the island of Malta. About 38,000 men disembarked at Marsaxlokk, and 11 days later another 3000 men from a further 38 ships joined them. They faced just 700 knights and 8000 Maltese volunteers or mercenaries. But the Hospitallers were ready for them. Their grand master, Jean Parisot de la Valette, ordered all the crops to be harvested, even though they were not ripe – to deprive the invaders of food – and poisoned the wells.

The Turks attacked Fort St Elmo, bombarding it with three dozen guns. It is said that over 60,000 cannon-balls were fired during the attack. Within a week the fort was reduced to rubble. But the garrison repulsed numerous assaults until, on 23 June, the Turks took what was left of the fort. But taking St Elmo cost the Turks 4000 men, including half the Janissaries.

The Turks then took possession of most of the island, destroying the cities and slaying nearly half of all the knights. Queen Elizabeth I of England said: 'If the Turks should prevail against the Isle of Malta, it is uncertain what further peril might follow to the rest of Christendom.' Six hundred Sicilians managed to slip through the blockade, and Turkish deserters warned about a plan to attack the Hospitallers' position at Senglea from the south, giving them time to build a line of defensive stakes. They successfully repulsed the attack that followed. Fort St Michael held out, and a fusillade from Fort St Angelo stopped an amphibious attack, sinking all but one of the vessels and drowning over 800 Turks. Senglea resisted a bombardment of some 65 siege guns. When the walls were breached, the Turkish attack was broken off after a chance attack on one of their field hospitals led them to believe that Christian reinforcements had arrived.

Attempts were then made by the Turks to take Fort St Michael using siege engines, but they were toppled by Maltese engineers. By now, the Turks were becoming disheartened. On 8 September, a relief force of 8000 Spanish and Italian soldiers arrived from Syracuse. Dispirited, the Turks sailed home with only a quarter of their army intact. During the siege, Malta had lost 219 knights and 9000 inhabitants.

the Hospitallers but, like them, were ejected from the Holy Land in 1291. They withdrew to Limassol in Cyprus, though they established a garrison on Ruad Island off Tortosa (now Tartus in Syria) in 1300. This was besieged by the Egyptian Mamelukes, and the remaining Templars found themselves cast into a jail in Cairo.

With the order's military purpose gone, Pope Clement suggested that they merge with the Hospitallers. Neither order was agreeable to this arrangement. Meanwhile, rumours began to circulate about their secret rites of initiation. These were said to involve blasphemies and irreligious practices. Although these accusations were probably false, King Philip IV of France had every Templar in France arrested on 13 October 1307 and seized their property to help fund his war against the English.

In 1312, the Templars were suppressed and their remaining property in Europe was confiscated by the state or given to the Hospitallers. Templars were imprisoned or executed and, on 18 March 1314, the order's last grand master, Jacques de Molay, was burned at the stake on the Île de la Cité in Paris.

The Mongol Hordes of Genghis Khan

The merciless horsemen of the steppes

Founding an empire that stretched from Korea in the east to Poland in the west, and from Vietnam in the south to the Arctic Ocean in the north, Genghis Khan was victorious not by force of numbers and barbarity alone, but also by his meticulously organized military campaigns.

At the age of 33, Genghis Khan became undisputed leader of the Mongol hordes. Like Attila the Hun 700 years before, he organized his men in ten squadrons, or *ordus* (hence 'hordes'), comprising ten units of ten horsemen. Their leaders were family and trusted clan members, and discipline was rigid. His fast, mobile units comprised mounted bowmen, light cavalry and heavy cavalry who wore leather armour and wielded lances and sabres.

When the Chin Dynasty had appealed to him for help, Genghis reasoned that they must be weak. So he attacked China, breaching the Great Wall in 1208 and taking Beijing in 1215. By then the Mongols controlled the Middle Kingdom – China north of the Yellow River – and forced those outside their rule to deliver 500 young men and women, plus 3000 head of livestock, as the price of peace. Then he turned west.

THE SIEGE OF OTAR AND OTHER CITIES

In 1218, a Mongol army of 20,000 swept through the Qara-Khitai empire in what is now Kazakhstan. The Korean peninsula also fell that year. In 1219, Genghis Khan assembled between 150,000 and 200,000 horsemen on the border of Khwarezm, which covered what is now northeast Iran, Afghanistan, Turkmeniya, Uzbekistan and Tadzikistan. Shah Mohammed's army easily outnumbered Genghis Khan's, but they were spread thinly. Instead of mounting a cavalry attack, the Mongols besieged the walled city of Otar. During their campaign in China, they had captured much siege machinery – along with Chinese soldiers who could use it. The Chinese had also perfected gunpowder and knew how to make bombs and mortars. They had rockets and bombards – primitive cannon firing metal balls.

The Mongols also had siege engines of their own. These dated back 1000 years. They were massive crossbows mounted on trestles that fired huge arrows over 180 metres (590 ft), and catapults that could fling huge boulders. Under covering fire, sappers tunnelled under the walls of Otar. Towers with extendable ladders were trundled up, while the gates were pummelled by huge battering rams. The city held out for a month until the defenders ran out

The conquest of Baghdad in 1258 was a pivotal battle, in which the Mongol hordes destroyed the centre of Islamic power. It was a victory for Hulagu Khan, a grandson of Genghis Khan. (Illustration from an illuminated version of Jami' at-tawarikh, a record of the Mongol dynasty written by Rashid ad-Din in the late 13th century.)

THE MONGOL HORDES OF GENGHIS KHAN

1194 Mongol Temüjin named Genghis Khan, which means 'Universal Ruler'

1202 Mongols defeat the Tartars

1206 Genghis Khan emerges victorious in civil war

1208 Mongols attack China

1215 Mongols capture Beijing

1218 Hordes sweep through western China

1220 Mongols sack Samarkand

1222 Mongols invade Russia

1226 Mongols put down rebellion at the Battle of the Yellow River

1227 Genghis Khan dies on the banks of Lake Baikal

1237 Mongolian 'Golden Horde' attacks Russia again

of arrows. For resisting the Mongols, the governor of the city had molten silver poured into his ears and eye sockets.

A second Mongolian column butchered the inhabitants of Sighnaq. A third attacked Banakat. The city's craftsmen were assigned to combat units or sent back to Mongolia. The women were distributed among the clans. The rest were taken to be used as a human shield in the next battle. Khojend was taken by damming the river that protected its fortress. The Mongols entered the city of Nur disguised as caravanners. Once they were inside the city walls, the people were driven out, the city looted and the booty sent back to Mongolia.

Next to fall was Bukhara, a city sacred to Muslims. The defenders were slaughtered. Genghis Khan rode into the great mosque, believing it to be the shah's palace. Sacred Koranic books were thrown in the dirt. Devout Muslims killed themselves rather than submit to the barbaric invaders. Men killed their own wives, as the Mongols made a practice of making men watch while they raped their womenfolk. The city was then burnt to the ground. For dozens of years afterwards Bukhara was inhabited only by thousands of putrefying corpses.

Genghis Khan was born Temüjin in Mongolia in 1162. Legend has it that he was born with a blood clot grasped in his fist – a sign that he was destined to be a great leader.

THE SACK OF SAMARKAND

The Mongols then turned on Samarkand. The city had recently been fortified. Genghis Khan was impressed when he arrived in the spring of 1220, so he had thousands of prisoners dress as Mongols and marched them towards the city walls. When the city's garrison attacked, the unarmed prisoners absorbed the assault. The Mongols then counter-attacked. Thirty thousand were massacred and the city was sacked.

At the capital of Khwarezm, Urgench, the garrison had stockpiled weapons, food and water, ready for a long siege. Under fire, Mongol prisoners began filling in the moat. It took 12 days. Sappers then advanced under the cover of siege engines and started chipping away at the brickwork. Once the walls were breached, the defenders fought ferociously. Both sides used burning naphtha to set fire to houses where their foes took shelter. After seven days of fighting, the Mongols lost patience and torched the rest of the city.

Then Genghis Khan turned north to Termez. It fell after seven days and everyone was disembowelled after a woman had swallowed some pearls rather than hand them over. The ancient city of Balkh, capital of Bactria, surrendered on the understanding that its citizens would go unmolested. Thousands were put to the sword anyway. When the Mongols passed that way again in 1222, they massacred the survivors and tore down the walls.

MERCILESS HORDES

The Mongols spared some cities, but if there was the slightest sign of opposition, they were merciless. As well as massacring the inhabitants, they would destroy the irrigation system that had taken centuries to construct. Many cities that the Mongols ravaged were destroyed forever. When Nessa resisted, its inhabitants were used by Mongol archers for target practice. Seventy thousand died. In February 1221, the Mongols arrived at Merv. After the city surrendered, the population was divided up among the army units. Each man, it was said, had to kill between 300 and 400 people. One source says that Tolui left 700,000 corpses there. Another said he stopped counting after 1,300,000.

THE BATTLE OF KALKA

At the Battle of Kalka, 20,000 Mongols were attacked by 80,000 knights under Prince Mstislav. After a short engagement, they withdrew, apparently in disorder. The Russians pursued them at high speed, stretching out their army in the process. Then, when the Mongols outnumbered the advance guard, they turned and fought. When the rest of the Russian army arrived, they would come upon a scene of appalling butchery.

The Russian knights wore steel armour and had shields, axes, swords and lances. They were heavy and slow compared with the Mongol horsemen and easy prey for Mongolian archers. Prince Mstislav was captured and executed by being wrapped up in a carpet and suffocated. The Mongols held him in great respect; they would not shed his blood. The rest of the Russian army were intimidated by Mstislav's defeat and withdrew.

At Neyshabur, severed heads were stacked in three pyramids – one for men's heads, one for women's heads, and one for children's. Not even the cats and dogs were left alive. At Herat, one source says there were 1.3 million dead, another quoted 2.4 million.

After Shah Mohammed died, his successor Prince Jalal a-Din scored one victory against the Mongols, when a force of 60,000 held up in a fortress at Ghazi saw off a smaller force. The victors drove nails into the ears of their prisoners. When Genghis Khan heard of this, he rode for two days to reach Ghazi. His men did not even stop to eat or drink, but rather – in the Mongol way – cut a nick in the back of their horse's neck and nourished themselves with its blood. When they reached Ghazi, the garrison was massacred. The prince fled, but was cornered on the banks of the Indus. While his remaining men were being hacked to death, the prince made a break for it, jumping off a cliff on horseback into the river. Genghis Khan was full of admiration – first for how the prince had saved his own life at the expense of his men's, then for the leap into the river. He was an example to all Mongols, the khan said, and was allowed to escape.

HEADING INTO RUSSIA

After a brief incursion into India, the Mongols headed northwards into Georgia, defeating the Georgian cavalry who were supposed to be the mightiest in the region. Then they moved on into Russia. The Mongols went on to plunder the warehouses of Sudak in the Crimea. They looted the kingdom of the Bulgars, then they turned for home, cutting a swathe through Kazakhstan. Genghis Khan himself returned to Mongolia where he died in 1227. He left orders that, if anyone gazed on his coffin, the next coffin would be theirs.

In 1237, ten years after the death of Genghis Khan, the Mongolian 'Golden Horde' attacked Russia again, using similar barbarous tactics. In 1347, during the Siege of Caffa on the Crimea, they invented biological warfare, catapulting the corpses of plague victims over the walls to infect those within. The Mongols continued to attack the Russians for centuries.

THE

18TH & 19TH

CENTURIES

*This 18th-century hand-coloured copperplate engraving shows the
Highlanders charging against the English lines at the Battle of
Culloden, 16 April 1746. The defeat of the Highlanders marked the last
Highland Charge in history.*

The Wild Geese

Louis XIV's fighting Irishmen

Britain's 'Glorious Revolution' of 1688 replaced the Catholic King James II with the Protestant William of Orange. Irish supporters of James went to France with their exiled king. For the next 100 years, until the French Revolution, these 'Wild Geese' and their descendants served France as the Irish Brigade.

In the late 1600s the Irish supported King James II, the Catholic king of Great Britain, who had been deposed in 1688 in favour of his nephew and son-in-law, the statholder of the United Provinces of the Netherlands, the Protestant William of Orange. (Statholders were provincial leaders in the Netherlands, first appointed in the 15th century.) James had fled England, and the fight for the throne moved to Ireland where the Jacobite Irish had been promised the support of the Catholic king of France, Louis XIV. But before any help could arrive, James was defeated at the Battle of the Boyne on 12 July 1690 and fled to France.

The Irish forces under Patrick Sarsfield continued the Jacobite war for another year, but after losing their stronghold at Limerick on 3 October 1691, they were forced to surrender. The victorious William gave Sarsfield the choice of returning to his lands in Ulster and swearing allegiance to parliament and the new king, or taking his army and leaving Ireland forever. Unwilling to submit, Sarsfield and some 14,000 men and their dependants left the country to join James in France. This exodus from Ireland was known as the 'Flight of the Wild Geese'.

A scene from the Battle of Fontenoy, during the War of the Austrian Succession. The Irish Brigade distinguished itself in the skirmish, causing the British to withdraw with 50 percent losses. (Painting by French artist Pierre L'Enfant (1704–87).)

THE IRISH BRIGADE

The expatriates were incorporated into the Irish Brigade of the French army and fought against William of Orange in the Nine Years' War that pitted France against England, Holland, Spain, Sweden and the Holy Roman Empire. It ended in 1698 by the Treaty of Ryswick, which recognized William as king of England and disbanded the Irish Brigade. However, with the outbreak of the War of the Spanish Succession in 1700, Louis called upon his fighting Irishmen again. Four battalions of Irish foot soldiers and two squadrons of Irish dragoons fought at the Battle of Chiari in September 1701 and at the Battle of Cremona in February 1702.

'Cuimnidh ar Luimneach agus ar Feall na Sasanach!'
(*'Remember Limerick and the Saxon Faith'*)

THE BATTLE CRY OF THE WILD GEESE

THE WILD GEESE

1688 The Glorious Revolution replaces the Catholic James II with the Protestant William of Orange on the British throne

1690 James and the Irish Jacobites defeated at the Battle of the Boyne

1691 The defeated Irish Jacobites leave for France

1698 The French Irish Brigade is disbanded under the Treaty of Ryswick

1700 The outbreak of the War of the Spanish Succession prompts the recall of the Irish Brigade

1701 The Wild Geese fight at the Battle of Chiari

1702 The Wild Geese distinguish themselves against the Austrians at the Battle of Cremona

1745 The British try to stop the French recruiting in Ireland after the Jacobite Uprising; the Wild Geese help defeat the British at the Battle of Fontenoy

1791 The Irish Brigade disbanded

The French continued recruiting in Ireland. Many Irish Catholics were eager to join, since they hoped to return a Catholic Stuart to the throne of Britain. Although Britain was rarely at peace with France, the British allowed this as it was better to have disgruntled Irishmen of military age in the French army than at home in Ireland plotting insurrection. However, the British authorities tried to stop the French recruiting in Ireland after France backed the Jacobite Uprising of 1745 in Scotland.

THE BATTLE OF FONTENOY

Two months before Bonnie Prince Charlie had set foot in Scotland for the Uprising, the Irish Brigade had distinguished itself in the Battle of Fontenoy. Its attack against the British right flank forced the British to withdraw with 50 percent losses. 'Cursed be the laws which deprived me of such subjects,' said King George II. Fontenoy was a famous victory for the French during the War of the Austrian Succession (1740–48) and a defeat for the English commander, George II's son the duke of Cumberland, who went on to brutally suppress the Jacobite Uprising.

With the failure of the 1745 Uprising, all hope of a Stuart returning to the British throne was gone. But a trickle of young Irishmen still fled their homeland to join the Irish Brigade. Their numbers were also bolstered by deserters from the British army and prisoners of war. The majority of the recruits came from the counties of Clare, Limerick, Cork, Kerry and Galway. They were taken to France by the French ships that arrived on the west coast smuggling in brandy and wine. Captains would list the departing Irishmen on their manifests simply as 'Wild Geese'.

During the Seven Years' War (1756–63), the French had six regiments of Irish foot soldiers plus one cavalry unit. During the passage of time, these units became increasingly more diluted in terms of their Irish composition. By the end of the 18th century, even the officers of the units came from families who had been in France for several generations and were in reality French.

'The Wild Geese come in their thousands with the October moon. They blacken the sky and they cry the coming of Autumn. About the estuary of the Shannon, and all up the river into Limerick, they must have whizzed and moaned, that winter of 1691, when Ginkel offered the terms that ended the Jacobite War, and started bitter quarrels among the tired and tattered Irish. The flying Irish, down the Shannon or down the Lee with Sarsfield, looked up at the skies, and took the name, The Wild Geese. It was the end of a period. It was all but the end of a race.'

SEÁN O'FAILÁIN (1900–91), IRISH SHORT STORY WRITER

THE BATTLE OF CREMONA

An allied army under Prince Eugene of Savoy attacked the French at Chiari on 1 September 1701, driving them from the field. The French fell back on the town of Cremona, where on 1 February 1702 they were caught in a night attack. The French garrison, under Marshal François de Neufville, duc de Villeroi, was taken completely by surprise. A small unit under Eugene of Savoy himself launched a commando-style attack which succeeded in capturing the duc de Villeroi and other high-ranking French officers. A thousand French soldiers were killed in the attack, many of them in their sleep. But the assault was not a complete success. A large allied force under Charles Thomas de Lorraine-Vaudemont was to have taken the Po gate, but this was held by the Irish Brigade.

Just 25 men under Captain Stuart held off the Austrians until reinforcements under Major Daniel O'Mahony reached them. As the Austrian losses mounted, Prince Eugene sent one of his own Wild Geese, Francis MacDonnell, to bribe them. 'Countrymen,' he said, 'Prince Eugene sends me to say to you that if you will change [sides], you shall have higher pay in the Imperial army than you have had in the French service … If you reject [this offer], I do not see how you can escape certain destruction.

We are masters of the city, with the exception of your post. It is on this account, his Highness only awaits my return to attack you with the greatest part of his force, and to cut you to pieces, should you not accept his offers.' O'Mahony replied: 'Prince Eugene seems to fear us more than he esteems us, since he causes such propositions to be made to us. We wish to gain the esteem of the prince by doing our duty, not by cowardice or treachery, unworthy of men of honour.' O'Mahony then made MacDonnell his prisoner.

When Prince Eugene realized that MacDonnell was not coming back, he asked the captured duc de Villeroi to order the Irish to surrender or he would be forced to put them all to the sword. De Villeroi said he had 'no longer any orders to give in the town'. The Austrians then attacked in force and were slaughtered. The Irish held out until 3 p.m. when they were finally ordered back. On the way, they blew up the bridge, stranding the main Austrian force on the wrong side of the river. Prince Eugene then found the other gates to the city were also held by Irishmen. Eventually Prince Eugene began to see that the city was becoming a trap, rather than a prize, and left without taking the citadel. It was said that Cremona was 'taken by a miracle, and lost by a greater one'.

THE END OF THE IRISH BRIGADE

With the outbreak of the French Revolution in 1789, the Irish Brigade ceased to exist. It was subsequently disbanded on 21 July 1791. Many of those involved in the Brigade considered that their oath had been sworn to Louis XVI, who was deposed during the Revolution, and so they left the service. The rest were absorbed into the infantry of the line. However, after the failure of the Irish Rebellion of 1798, the French military leader Napoleon Bonaparte raised a small Irish unit from the exiled veterans.

Other Wild Geese fought in the armies of Austria, Poland, Russia, Spain and Sweden. They also fought in South America and with the French army of General Rochambeau, who helped defeat the British at Yorktown.

The Prussian Guard

Frederick the Great's fearless cuirassiers

Frederick the Great made Prussia a great military power. In most of his campaigns he was outnumbered both in men – in one instance by 20 to one – and by the nations allied against him, but through bold and offensive action, he nearly always won. At the head of his army since its inception in the 18th century were the soldiers of the Prussian Guard, who continued to play key roles in the German army until 1945.

The Prussian Guard was the personal bodyguard of the king of Prussia and, following the unification of the German empire in 1871, also of the German kaiser. The Prussian Guard was founded in 1740 by Frederick the Great, with Prussian nobleman Friedrich von Blumenthal as its first commander. He died suddenly in 1745 and his brother Hans assumed command in 1747.

By then the Prussian Guard had already tasted victory at the Battle of Hohenfriedberg in the War of the Austrian Succession. Fought on 3 June 1745, the Prussians under Frederick the Great faced the Austrians under Charles of Lorraine with their Saxon allies. Early that morning, the Prussians attacked the Saxons encamped at Striegau in the disputed province of Silesia, and defeated them before the Austrians could come to their aid.

Then they turned upon the Austrians and, after a desperate fight, succeeded in routing them. The Austrians and Saxons lost 9000 soldiers either killed or wounded, 7000 soldiers taken prisoner, including four of their generals, and 66 guns. The Prussians lost 5000 men. After the battle, Hans von Blumenthal and several other officers of the Prussian Guard were awarded the '*Pour le Mérite*' medal, popularly know as the Blue Max, for deeds of gallantry in the regiment's first action.

THE BATTLE OF LOBOSTIZ

The Prussians faced the Austrians again during the Seven Years' War. On 1 October 1756, they met at the Battle of Lobostiz in Bohemia. The battle began with an artillery duel. As the Prussian cavalry advanced, the Austrian horse attacked from the left. Colonel Hans von Blumenthal led a counter-charge in an attempt to outflank them, but this brought the Prussians within musket range of defensive positions in the village of Sullowitz.

Von Blumenthal had his horse shot from under him and suffered a crippling sabre blow in the neck. Nevertheless, Prussian cavalry charged the Austrian position twice more, but in vain. Believing the battle to be lost, Frederick wanted to leave the battlefield, saying: 'These

are no longer the same Austrians.' But the duke of Brunswick-Bevern, commanding the Prussian left wing, chased the Austrians from the field with an infantry charge. The battle was won, but the wounded von Blumenthal had to retire from the regiment.

A scene from the Seven Years' War. On 5 December 1757 the Prussians, led by Frederick the Great, stormed Leuthen graveyard and defeated the Austrian army. (Watercolour painting by German artist Carl Röchling (1855–1920).)

TRAINING FOR THE CAVALRY

For a time the regiment was used as a training ground for officers as part of a programme to expand the cavalry. This increased their reputation as an élite throughout the army. Early officers included the rake and memoirist Friedrich von Trenck. He joined in 1740, but after an affair with Princess Amelia of Prussia in 1745 he was imprisoned but escaped and joined the Russian military. In 1754, he was again arrested and held in the fortress of Magdeburg until 1763. After a career in writing, he was guillotined in Paris during the French Revolution.

Describing his time in the Prussian Guard, von Trenck wrote of the arduous life of sleep deprivation and physical stress endured by officers, as well as the huge cost of belonging to the élite corps. They had to buy their own uniforms and the costly cuirasses, or breast-plates, were silver plated. Nevertheless, the highest bravery was expected from them and they never failed to live up to these high expectations. At the Battle of Torgau on 3 November 1760 – the bloodiest battle of the Seven Years' War – the Prussian Guard led the charge against a larger Austrian force. As they emerged from a wood in the cold and rain, they were cut down by the Austrian artillery. But they had shown the way. The infantry continued the attack over their dead bodies and Prussia won the day, though they had lost 20,000 men against the Austrians' losses of 16,000.

THE GROWING CORPS

While the rest of the Imperial German Army was formed by regiments recruited locally, the Prussian Guard was recruited nationally. As Prussia expanded under Frederick the Great, the Prussian Guard eventually reached a full corps strength. By the Seven Weeks' War of 1866, it had its own artillery. Under Major General Kraft, Prince zu Hohenlohe-Ingelfingen, the Prussian Guard's Artillery Brigade saw action in the Franco-Prussian War of 1870–71 at Gravelotte and Sedan, and it went on to bombard the fortifications of the city of Paris.

With the German empire now secure, the kaiser surrounded himself with Prussian Guards as his bodyguard and personal advisors. Prussian Guard officer Walther von Brauchitsch rose to become a member of the general staff in the First World War. Although the Prussian Guard was disbanded after Germany's defeat in 1918 and the exile of the kaiser, former members of the Prussian Guard retained influential positions in the military establishment. Walther von Brauchitsch became head of the Germany army in 1938. Like other Prussian aristocrats, he disliked the Nazis, but was dazzled by Hitler personally. Promoted to Field Marshal in 1940, von Brauchitsch commanded the German forces in Russia in the winter of 1941. But Hitler blamed him for the defeat before Moscow and, after suffering a heart attack, von Brauchitsch resigned on 19 December. He survived the war, but died in 1948 before he could be tried as a war criminal.

> *'Were he still alive today, we should now not be here in Prussia.'*
>
> NAPOLEON BONAPARTE ON FREDERICK THE GREAT, 1807

THE UNIFORM OF THE PRUSSIAN GUARD

The regiment of the Prussian Guard wore a white cuirassier uniform. Their court uniform included a red tunic for officers and a white metal eagle, poised as if to fly, on a bronze helmet. The regiment's full dress, worn on ceremonial occasions until 1914, also included a sleeveless *supraweste* over the tunic with the star of the Order of the Black Eagle – Prussia's highest order of chivalry – on the front and back. They also wore black iron cuirasses edged with red, presented by the Russian tsar in 1814. These replaced the normal white metal breast-plates worn on certain special occasions. Traditionally, Prussian Guards also grew a luxuriant moustache.

The Battle of Gravelotte

The Prussian Guard's infantry brigades attack the French army at the Battle of Gravelotte. The battle was a victory for the Germans, but both sides lost many troops.

The Prussian Guard played a crucial role in the Battle of Gravelotte, the biggest battle of the Franco-Prussian War. The battle began at 8 a.m. on 18 August 1870. At first, it appeared to favour the French with their superior Chassepot rifle. However, the Prussian artillery fielded the new Krupp breech-loading gun. Nevertheless, by 4 p.m., the German attack was in danger of stalling. Then at 4.50 p.m., the 3rd Prussian Guard Infantry Brigade with the 2nd Army opened an attack against the French positions at St Privat. At 5.15 p.m., the 4th Prussian Guard Infantry Brigade joined the advance, followed by the 1st Prussian Guard Infantry Brigade . The Prussian Guard were pinned down by lethal French fire, but at 6.15 p.m. the 2nd Prussian Guard Infantry Brigade, the last of the 1st Guard Infantry Division, was committed to the attack on St Privat.

The Prussian 1st Army, to the north, had been defeated, so all its artillery was brought to bear to support the action at St Privat. At 7 p.m., the survivors of the 1st Guard Infantry Division launched a fresh attack against the ruins of the town. By 8 p.m., the Prussians of the 1st Guard Infantry Division had captured St Privat, decimating the French and forcing them to withdraw.

The following morning, the French Army of the Rhine retreated to Metz where they were besieged and forced to surrender two months later. The Germans had lost 20,163 killed, wounded or missing. The French had lost 7855 killed and wounded, along with 4420 prisoners of war, half of whom were wounded. The Prussian Guard Infantry Division had lost 8000 of the 18,000 men it had put in the field.

The Highland Charge

Claymore-wielding warriors

The sight of a bunch of screaming Highlanders, clad in plaid kilts, brandishing their claymores and dashing through the heather, was designed to terrify any formation of conventional troops lined up to face them. Their opponents often turned and ran. For over a century it proved a battle-winning technique, but eventually new weapons and tactics cut down the clansmen and put an end to this fearsome sight.

The Highland Charge was a battlefield tactic used by the fighting clans of the Scottish Highlands in the 17th and 18th centuries designed to instil fear in the enemy – particularly the English. It was devised as a response to the development of firearms. Traditionally, Highlanders had fought in tight formations, led by a heavily armed warrior élite that carried mighty battleaxes, or two-handed broadswords known as claymores. But once the use of musket and cannon became widespread, these formations were vulnerable and a new style of attack had to be devised.

David Morier's (c.1705–70) painting 'Culloden' depicts the ill-fated Highland Charge of 1746. It shows Highlanders still wearing the plaids they usually set aside before battle, when they would fire a volley and then run full tilt at the enemy with sword and targe, wearing only shirts.

The man credited with developing the Highland Charge was Alasdair MacColla. A member of the clan MacDonald, he fought with the Royalist forces and their Irish confederates when the English Civil War spilled over into Scotland and Ireland in what has become known at the Wars of the Three Kingdoms. In the Charge, the aim was to cover the ground between the Highlanders and their adversaries as quickly as possible and punch a way through the enemy line.

HAND-TO-HAND FIGHTING

The heavy battleaxes and broadswords were dropped in favour of the lighter, one-handed sword with a basket hilt that protected the hand. Highlanders would carry a dirk – a poniard or dagger – in the other hand and have a light shield, or targe, strapped to their body for protection. Lightly equipped, the Highlanders closed with their enemy at great speed. As the Charge developed, the clansmen sometimes carried muskets themselves, firing them at close range. The speed of the charge was designed to reduce the time that they were in range of the enemy muskets, and so reach the enemy line before suffering too many casualties. The Highlanders knew that they had an advantage over conventional soldiers in hand-to-hand fighting, even when the enemy were better armed and better trained, so closing on them fast was a vital tactic.

'Lord, what am I, that I should be spared when so many brave men lie dead upon this spot?'

ATTRIBUTED TO THE DUKE OF CUMBERLAND, 1746

The Highland Charge also had an enormous psychological impact. In the face of huge waves of screaming Highlanders, regular troops often fired one ill-aimed volley and then turned and ran. The lightly armed Highlanders would soon catch up with them, and the enemy would have to fight the clansmen not as a disciplined unit, but as a mass of panicking and retreating individuals. The result would be a bloodbath or a rout.

THE HIGHLAND CHARGE

1644–50 The Wars of the Three Kingdoms

1644 The Battle of Tippermuir

1745–6 The Second Jacobite Rising

1746 The Battles of Falkirk and Culloden

THE BATTLE OF TIPPERMUIR

At the Battle of Tippermuir in 1644, a Royalist Scots and Irish army of 3000 men under James Graham, first marquess of Montrose, faced 7000 Scottish Covenanters, allies of the English Parliamentarians, under Lord Elcho outside Perth, Scotland. After initial harassment of the Royalist lines, the Covenanters advanced with the battle-cry of: 'Jesus and no quarter.' The Royalists were not only outnumbered, but also ill-equipped. Montrose told those who had no sword to pick up a stone, rush up to the first Covenanter he saw, beat out his brains and take his weapons. The Royalists then roared down the slopes and overwhelmed the enemy. The Covenanters manning the cannon turned and fled as their position was overrun by Highlanders, who then went on to rout the musketeers who stood behind the guns.

The Irish attacked the centre, waiting until their matchlocks were a pike's length away before blasting a volley into a dense mass of pikemen. They then reversed their muskets and charged in, beating the Covenanters with the butts. Behind them came more clansmen. Again some were armed only with stones, but the savagery of their attack was too much for the newly raised Covenanters. Soon the road back to Perth was jammed with men desperate to escape the carnage. The Covenanters lost 2000 dead and 1000 taken prisoner. The Royalists claimed they lost only one man.

THE BATTLES OF FALKIRK AND CULLODEN

During the Second Jacobite Rising, the Highland Charge won Charles Edward Stuart – also known as the Young Pretender or Bonnie Prince Charles – a great victory over the Hanoverian forces of the British at the Battle of Falkirk on 17 January 1746. A storm had rendered the British muskets ineffective, so they sent in their dragoons. The Jacobites waited until they were in pistol range, then fired, cutting them down. Other clansmen crouched down, stabbed the oncoming horses in the belly, then dispatched the riders as they fell.

With the horses routed, the Highland musketeers fired one volley, flung down their muskets and charged the British infantry with their claymores. The infantry returned one fruitless volley, then turned and ran, leaving the field to the Jacobites who had, once again, routed a numerically superior force. The Hanoverians suffered some 350 casualties, with another 300 captured. The Jacobites lost around 50 dead and 70 wounded.

The battle was won, but the war was not. The Jacobites failed to take advantage of their victory at Falkirk. They retreated into the Highlands, while the Hanoverians regrouped around Edinburgh. The two sides would face each other on 16 April at Culloden. This time, the British forces were led by the duke of Cumberland, the third son of George II. Fighting on the Continent during the War of the Austrian Succession, he had learnt a new tactic.

'They have not had such a thrashing since the days of Old Noll [Oliver Cromwell] … what a pity it is that so much resolution and bravery as our troops had that day could not be united in the confederate arms and fall upon the grand enemies of the liberties of Europe …'

MAJOR RICHARD WEBB, ENGLISH SOLDIER, AFTER THE BATTLE OF CULLODEN, 1746

THE CLAYMORE

Clansmen traditionally carried a heavy two-handed broadsword known as a *claidheamh mòr* or claymore – meaning 'great sword' in Scottish Gaelic. These were double-edged weapons with a crossed hand-guard turned down to protect the hilt. This traditional claymore was based on the medieval broadsword, though slightly smaller. But for the Highland Charge, a lighter, single-handed sword was needed. These typically weighed between 0.9 and 1.4 kilograms (2–3 pounds), compared with the 2.5 kilograms (5.5 pounds) of the two-handed model. The blade was 76–89 centimetres (30–35 in) long – compared with 107 centimetres(42 in) – and typically single-edged. A basket hilt, often lined with velvet, protected the hand. Frequently, though inaccurately, this single-edged sword is called a claymore, and the older, double-edged sword is referred to as a *claidheamh da laimh* – 'two-handed sword' – to distinguish it from its successor.

A Scottish Highlander armed with a later-style, one-handed sword. The original version was a two-handed weapon.

Cumberland put his infantry in three ranks. The front rank were ordered not to fire until the Highlanders were only 11 metres (36 ft) away. While the front rank reloaded, the second rank fired their guns. By the time the third rank had fired their guns, the first rank were ready to fire again. This system had first been used by the Swedish king Gustavus II 100 years before, but Cumberland's infantry now used muskets known as firelocks, which were faster to reload than the old matchlocks.

At Culloden, for once, the English did not run away when the Highlanders charged. Their disciplined volleys brought down many of the Highlanders before they reached the English lines. The new guns were also fitted with bayonets, so even if some of the Highlanders managed to reach the English front lines, Cumberland's men were able to defend themselves against their claymores. Cumberland had also taught his infantry not to bayonet the man directly in front of him, but to attack the exposed side of the man to the right. Unable to get close enough to use their broadswords, some Highlanders even resorted to throwing stones. This was the ignominious end of the last Highland Charge in history. A thousand clansmen lay dead, while the Hanoverians lost just 50 men.

Bonnie Prince Charlie returned to France, and there were no further attempts to put a Stuart back on the British throne. But this was not the end of the fighting Highlanders. They became a valuable part of the British army.

Napoleon's Imperial Guard

The emperor's national guard that other French soldiers referred to as 'the Immortals'

Hand-picked war veterans, the Imperial Guard were Napoleon's personal bodyguard who surrounded him day and night. On the battlefield, they were the most feared troops in Europe. They followed him in ascent to power and were only once ordered to retreat – at Waterloo. Even then, they sacrificed themselves to protect the rest of the French army.

The corps that became the Imperial Guard was originally formed as the *Gardes de la Prévôté de l'Hôtel* in 1789 to guard royal residences. Following the French Revolution, it became instead the unit that guarded the various national assemblies, conventions and legislatures. In November 1795, the Directory took over from the *Garde du Directoire* to protect its members.

On 9 November 1799 – or 18 Brumaire, Year VIII on the French Revolutionary Calendar – Napoleon overthrew the Directory and set up a three-man consulate. The *Garde du Directoire* and the *Garde du Corps Législatif* were then combined to form the *Garde des Consuls*. They saw action defeating the Austrians and winning 79 *Armes d'Honneur* at the Battle of Marengo in June 1800.

FEATURES OF THE IMPERIAL GUARD

In 1804, Napoleon crowned himself emperor, so the *Garde des Consuls* became the Imperial Guard. From just 3000 men in 1800, it had swelled to nearly 10,000 strong. The number had climbed to over 112,000 by the time of the Battle of Waterloo.

A recruit would have needed to have served in the army for ten years, fought in at least two campaigns and to be of good character. He also had to be over 1.8 metres (6 ft) tall to be a grenadier and 1.7 metres (5.5 ft) tall to join the cavalry. The Imperial Guard were better paid, better equipped and better provisioned than all other soldiers in Napoleon's *Grande Armée*, and Napoleon personally approved each detail of the design of their uniforms.

In 1804, the Guard consisted of one regiment of grenadiers – two battalions of eight companies each – and a similar formation of *chasseurs à pied*. Two companies of artillery with 16 guns were then incorporated into the Guard. When a second regiment of foot grenadiers was formed, along with another regiment of *chasseurs*, the service requirement was dropped to eight years. The men of these units comprised the Old Guard, though some of their number went on to serve as officers in units of the Guard formed later. The Middle

French emperor Napoleon Bonaparte inspects his Imperial Guard following their victory over the Prussian-Saxon army at Jena in 1806. (Oil painting by French artist Horace Vernet (1789–1863).)

THE BATTLE OF WATERLOO

The Imperial Guard were in the thick of the action throughout the years of the Napoleonic Wars. They distinguished themselves at Austerlitz and Jena, but their finest moment came at the moment of their downfall at Waterloo. When the Prussian troops under General von Blücher arrived late in the day, Napoleon could have withdrawn in good order and saved his army. Instead, he sent in his Imperial Guard to hold the Prussians on the left. At 7 p.m. he withdrew several battalions, in the belief that one more charge up the centre by the veterans of the Imperial Guard would break the British forces who were holding the ridge.

To the beat of the drum, the Imperial Guard, magnificently attired in their tall bearskin caps decorated with long red feathers, marched up the ridge. The duke of Wellington ordered his own guardsmen to lie down so that shot from the French artillery flew harmlessly over their heads. When the Imperial Guard reached the top of the ridge they were met with a fusillade of musket fire and grapeshot. With the Imperial Guard just 18 metres (about 60 ft) away, Wellington is reputed to have given the order: 'Up Guards and at 'em.'

They leapt to their feet, let off a volley of fire at close range, then charged with fixed bayonets, pushing the Imperial Guard back. Seeing this, the cry went up among the French: '*La Garde recule*' – 'The Guard is retreating.' This was the first retreat in their history. With the retreat, French morale collapsed completely.

The Middle Guard broke completely, but the Old Guard and some Young Guard battalions formed a square in the middle of the battlefield to screen Napoleon's retreat. They were annihilated by British and Prussian artillery fire and cavalry charges.

Guard were those who served during the campaigns of 1805 and 1809. The Young Guard were the best of the annual intake of conscripts after the draft was introduced in 1798.

EXPANDING THE *GARDE IMPÉRIALE*

The *Génie de la Garde Impériale* was created in 1804 from the engineers of the Consular Guard. They saw more action than many combat units. By 1810, there were 140 sappers, all members of the Old Guard. In 1813, this was increased to two companies. Later there was one battalion of four companies totalling 400 sappers. The first two companies were considered Old Guard, while the third and fourth companies were Young Guard.

In 1806, the artillery was expanded with a regiment – six companies – of horse artillery. Then in 1808, the horse artillery was cut back to 32 guns, but three companies of foot artillery and three companies of conscript cannon were formed. Later more were added.

'La Garde meurt, mais ne se rend pas!'
(*'The Guard dies, but does not surrender!'*)

ATTRIBUTED TO GENERAL PIERRE CAMBRONNE AT WATERLOO, 1815

At the Battle of Waterloo Napoleon's Old Guard finally meet defeat at the hands of English and Prussian forces.

In 1810, a third regiment of grenadiers was formed from the disbanded Dutch army. A fourth was raised in 1815 for the Hundred Days campaign that ended at Waterloo. A third and fourth *chasseur à-pied* regiment also existed briefly during the Hundred Days campaign. Two regiments of conscripted grenadiers were also formed in 1809 and served with the Young Guard.

TIRAILLEURS AND FLANQUEURS

Two regiments of fusilier-grenadiers were raised in 1810, but they were disbanded when Napoleon fell from power in 1814. In 1809, two regiments of *tirailleurs* (skirmisher) grenadiers were formed from conscripts who could read and write. Other regiments of *tirailleurs chasseurs* were also formed as part of the Young Guard. There were six regiments in the 1812 Russian campaign. This increased to 16 regiments in 1813–14. Regiments of *flanqueurs grenadiers* and *flanqueurs chasseurs* were also formed in preparation for the invasion of Russia.

Created from the *tirailleurs chasseurs* in 1810, the *Régiments de Voltigeurs* (literally acrobats) *de la Garde Impériale* became one of the largest corps in the Guard, eventually absorbing the *Régiments de Conscrits-Chasseurs* to make 16 regiments by 1814. The 14th Regiment was created from the Spanish volunteers who had retreated with the French army when it had been forced out of the Peninsula by the duke of Wellington in 1813.

The Horse Grenadiers – the *Régiment de Grenadiers-à-Cheval de la Garde Impériale* – were the senior cavalry regiment of the Guard, having originally been part of the Consular Guard. Although classed as heavy cavalry, the regiment did not wear a cuirass, but was known for its distinctive bearskin head-dress and black horses. A regiment of *chasseurs à cheval* was also created from the Consular Guard. They usually provided personal escort to Napoleon and he often wore their uniform. A second regiment was created briefly from the *Regiment d'Éclaireurs Lanciers* in 1815.

There were other regiments of *éclaireurs* (scouts) of the Guard. They were badly depleted after bloody skirmishes with Cossacks in Russia and were reorganized in 1813. One regiment joined the *Regiment de Dragons de la Garde Impériale*. Formed in 1806, this had three squadrons headed by 60 officers, each selected by Napoleon. The regiment was named the Empress' Dragoons. Added to that were regiments of lancers from Poland, Holland and Lithuania, a squadron of Mamelukes from Egypt, and an élite unit of gendarmes attached to the General Staff and Guard of Honour, created in 1813 from the Young Guard who dressed as hussars.

NAPOLEON'S IMPERIAL GUARD

1789 The *Gardes de la Prévôté de l'Hôtel* become the *Garde de l'Assemblée Nationale*

1795 The *Garde de l'Assemblée Nationale* become the *Garde du Corps Législatif*; the *Garde du Directoire* formed

1799 The *Garde du Directoire* and the *Garde du Corps Législatif* combined to form the *Garde des Consuls*

1800 The *Garde des Consuls*, under Napoleon's command, taste victory at the Battle of Marengo

1804 Napoleon crowned emperor; the *Garde des Consuls* becomes the Imperial Guard

1805 The French Imperial Guard defeat the Russian Imperial Guard at the Battle of Austerlitz

1806 The Old Guard spearhead victory at the Battle of Jena and head the victory parade through Berlin

1812 Imperial Guard suffer heavy losses during the withdrawal from Russia

1813 New recruits levied into the Young Guard

1814 Imperial Guard reach maximum strength; Napoleon deposed

1815 Napoleon returns from exile in Elba; re-forms Imperial Guard in Hundred Days campaign; defeated at Waterloo

The Ever-Victorious Army

China's imperial force under Frederick Townsend Ward and General 'Chinese' Gordon

The Ever-Victorious Army was a powerful force of Chinese soldiers trained and led by an American and European officer corps. It was the first Chinese army drilled in modern Western strategy and tactics. Under the Qing Dynasty, it put down the Taiping Rebellion and became a model for later Chinese armies.

This illustration, one of a series of 'Fancy Portraits' from the satirical magazine Punch, *shows Charles George Gordon depicted as an illuminated Chinese lantern held aloft by Chinese figures.*

A contemporary Chinese painting of Taiping rebels storming a town during the Taiping Rebellion.

The Ever-Victorious Army had its origins in a force of mercenaries led by American soldier of fortune Frederick Townsend Ward in Shanghai in 1860. At the time, the city was being threatened by the forces of the Taiping Rebellion under the leadership of Hung Hsiu-ch'üan, who claimed to be Jesus Christ's younger brother and who sought to oust the Manchus from the imperial throne.

Ward had distinguished himself on the *Confucius*, an armed riverboat employed by the Shanghai Pirate Suppression Bureau. Then, wealthy banker Yang Fang gave him the money to set up a force of foreign nationals to defend Shanghai against encroaching Taiping forces. The 100-strong Shanghai Foreign Arms Corps was equipped with the latest weapons, including Colt revolvers. It joined imperial forces to retake captured towns but, without artillery, failed to take the fortified city of Sung-Chiang.

Back in Shanghai, Ward recruited more Westerners and eight Filipinos, and acquired some artillery. They took Sung-Chiang, but out of 250 men, 62 were killed and 100 were wounded, including Ward. The Shanghai Foreign Arms Corps then suffered 50 percent casualties trying to take Ch'ing-p'u and Ward was wounded again, shot through the jaw. Ward was in Shanghai when the city beat off a Taiping besieging force. He then began recruiting a new Shanghai Foreign Arms Corps on terms so attractive that sailors on British warships deserted to join. In May 1861, Ward led another assault on Ch'ing-p'u. Again it failed, with heavy casualties, putting an end to the Shanghai Foreign Arms Corps.

RECRUITING A CHINESE ARMY

Now a Chinese citizen, Ward joined forces with the local imperial commander Li Heng-sung to form a Chinese contingent, to be trained and commanded by the remnants of Ward's foreign mercenaries, and equipped by the British. Dressed in Western-style uniforms and Indian sepoy turbans, the Chinese recruits were taught to respond to Western bugle calls and verbal commands. Crucially, they were also trained to hold their fire until the enemy was within range.

'This life is only one of a series of lives which our incarnated part has lived. I have little doubt of our having pre-existed; ... So, therefore, I believe in our active employment in a future life, and I like the thought.'

CHARLES GEORGE GORDON, LETTER, 1877

In January 1862, a 120,000-strong Taiping force marched on Shanghai. With 1000 trained and disciplined men, Ward repeatedly routed the enemy in both offensive and defensive actions, though he was wounded five times. In March 1862, his men were officially named the Ever-Victorious Army and Ward was made a mandarin. The Ever-Victorious Army continued to live up to its name, taking to the rivers and canals in steamers to increase mobility. By the time Ward died, after being shot in the abdomen in the Battle of Cixi in September 1862, his army was 5000 strong, organized in four battalions and had its own artillery corps.

GORDON'S EVER-VICTORIOUS ARMY

Command of the Ever-Victorious Army passed to the British officer Charles George Gordon, known as 'Chinese' Gordon, who had already taken Beijing and burnt down the emperor's summer palace during the Second Opium War of 1856–60. In May 1862, he was in Shanghai strengthening its defences. Gordon led his men into battle armed only with a walking stick. Alongside the imperial forces, the Ever-Victorious Army acted as a force-multiplier to put down the Taiping Rebellion. Nanking fell in 1864 and Hung Hsiu-ch'üan committed suicide.

By then, there were six regiments numbering between 250 and 650 men. Each comprised six companies of 80 men, with two Western officers and seven Chinese non-commissioned officers. There was one Chinese interpreter per regiment. Commands were given exclusively in English, which had to be learned by rote. Gordon replaced Ward's original bodyguard of Filipinos with a company of Europeans and Africans and 100 handpicked Chinese soldiers. By 1863, his army had six batteries of heavy and light artillery, each with five foreign officers, 19 Chinese non-commissioned officers and 120–150 Chinese gunners.

Infantry wore dark green in winter dress with red facings and shoulder straps in regimental colours. The bodyguard wore blue uniforms with scarlet facings and green shoulder straps carrying their unit identification in Chinese characters. Artillerymen wore light blue uniforms with red facings and trouser stripes. In summer, all branches wore white uniforms with scarlet facings. And all units wore green turbans.

Ward's flotilla of 12 armed paddle-steamers, supported by around 40 Chinese gunboats, dwindled under Gordon's command to only six steamers. They were fitted with either 9-pounder or 12-pounder bow-guns, though the 27-metre (90-ft) *Hyson* carried a 32-pounder gun as well as a 12-pounder howitzer.

When Gordon refused to allow his men to loot captured cities, the army mutinied. Gordon responded by shooting dead one of its ringleaders, then threatening to shoot one

Frederick Townsend Ward and Charles George Gordon

Born in Salem, Massachusetts, in 1831, Ward became second mate on a clipper by the age of 16. The following year he landed in Hong Kong. In 1849, he enrolled at the American Literary, Scientific and Military Academy in Vermont to study military tactics, strategy and drill before returning to sea. He joined the invasion of Mexico as a filibuster in 1853. After visiting China again, he served in the French army during the Crimean War, where he honed his military skills. Thus he was well versed in the latest European weapons and tactics when he arrived in Shanghai in 1860 to set up the Ever-Victorious Army.

Gordon is murdered at the hands of the Muslim insurgents in Khartoum just days before a relief force arrives.

'Chinese' Gordon was born in Woolwich, London, in 1833. At 19, he was commissioned in the Royal Engineers, fighting in the Crimea from 1853 to 1856, where he was mentioned in despatches and decorated for bravery. In 1859, he was promoted to captain and sent to China where he fought in the Second Opium War. After leading the Ever-Victorious Army to victory in the Taiping Rebellion,

he returned to England and renovated forts at Gravesend and Tilbury. Promoted to full colonel in 1871, he was sent to Sudan in 1873 as governor, and set about suppressing the slave trade. In 1880, he went to India as secretary to the viceroy and served in China, Mauritius and South Africa, where he championed home rule for Botswana, South Africa and Ireland. King Leopold of Belgium offered him the governorship of the Congo. In 1884, the Muslim fundamentalist leader Muhammad Ahmad al-Mahdi revolted against Anglo-Egyptian rule in Sudan. Gordon was sent to lead an orderly withdrawal of the British and Egyptian forces. He arrived in the Sudanese capital Khartoum in February 1884, where he soon found himself besieged by the Mahdi. The British government delayed sending relief until October. It arrived two days after the city fell. By then, Gordon and the city's population were dead. Gordon became a national hero and is now known as Gordon of Khartoum.

mutineer every hour until the mutiny was over. It was over within the first hour. However, Gordon's harsh discipline led to desertions. By June 1863, the force had dwindled to 1700 men and Gordon took to recruiting from Taiping prisoners who had been persuaded to change sides. Gordon resigned when the Manchus had the leaders of the rebellion executed. He refused to continue in command even when he was promoted to the rank of mandarin in the Chinese army and was offered 100,000 gold pieces. The Ever-Victorious Army was disbanded in May 1864. Its 104 foreign officers and 2288 Chinese soldiers were paid off, and its artillery and some of its infantry were transferred to the Chinese imperial forces.

Stonewall Brigade

The Confederates' finest fighting unit

Trained and initially led by General Thomas J. 'Stonewall' Jackson, the unit that shared his *nom de guerre* set a standard for marching, fighting and sacrifice rarely equalled. Despite crippling losses, the brigade fought throughout the Civil War, from the First Battle of Manassas to the Appomattox Campaign. Although the war was lost, the brigade lived on.

With the outbreak of the Civil War on 12 April 1861, there was a rush to volunteer. At Harpers Ferry, on 27 April, the 2nd, 4th, 5th, 27th and 33rd Virginia Infantry Regiments, plus the Rockbridge Artillery Battery, were organized into a brigade under General Thomas J. Jackson. All of its soldiers were from the Shenandoah Valley and the surrounds. They were largely farmers, blacksmiths, building workers or machinists. Many were Irish and Scotch-Irish. Few were slaveholders and the units were close-knit, with male family members all joining up together.

Jackson himself was born in Clarksburg and brought up in Jackson's Mill, in what is now West Virginia. After attending West Point, he became a professor at the Virginia Military Institute, where he was known as 'Deacon Jackson' and compared to Oliver Cromwell.

THE BATTLES OF MANASSAS

At Harpers Ferry, Jackson brought the discipline of West Point to the raw recruits and built them into an effective fighting force, known initially as Virginia's 1st Brigade. But on 21 July 1861, at the First Battle of Manassas – known as the First Battle of Bull Run in the North – General Barnard E. Bee of South Carolina compared Jackson and the brigade to a 'stone wall' for their fortitude in the face of the enemy. Bee's remark rallied his troops. It was seen as the turning point of the battle, and the Union Army was repulsed. Jackson was promoted, though the brigade that now shared his nickname remained under him.

Jackson's second-in-command, Richard B. Garnett, took over. The Stonewall Brigade then joined the left wing of the Army of Northern Virginia operating in the Shenandoah Valley. At the Battle of Kernstown on 23 March 1862, after two hours spent fighting, out of ammunition and almost surrounded, Garnett ordered a withdrawal. He wrote later:

A photograph of Thomas 'Stonewall' Jackson, taken some time between 1861 and 1863.

'Had I not done so we would have run imminent risk of being routed by superior numbers, which would have resulted probably in the loss of part of our artillery and also endangered our transportation.'

Nevertheless, Garnett was relieved of his command, arrested and court-martialled. But the trial was suspended with the beginning of General Robert E. Lee's Maryland Campaign. Garnett went on to serve creditably and was killed during Pickett's Charge at the Battle of Gettysburg.

Brigadier General Charles S. Winder took over. Marching the brigade over 400 miles (645 km) in four weeks and winning six engagements, he won their respect as a commander. The brigade's speed in the Valley Campaign – notably covering 57 miles (92 km) in 51 hours – earned it a new nickname: 'Jackson's foot cavalry.'

At Gaines's Mill on 27 June 1862, the brigade helped break the Union right and gave Lee one of his hardest-fought victories. Then at Cedar Mountain on 9 August 1862, it suffered heavy casualties and Winder was killed. But Jackson arrived in person to rally his 'Old Brigade' and win the battle.

'Stonewall' Jackson is mortally wounded during the Battle of Chancellorsville in Virginia, on 2 May 1863. (Lithograph by Kurz & Allison, 1889.)

'The men of the brigade will be, some day, proud to say to their children "I was one of the Stonewall Brigade".'

GENERAL THOMAS J. 'STONEWALL' JACKSON AFTER THE BATTLE OF CHANCELLORSVILLE, 1863

STONEWALL BRIGADE

APRIL 1861 1st Virginia Brigade formed at Harpers Ferry under General Thomas J. Jackson

JULY 1861 The brigade earns the *nom de guerre* 'Stonewall' at the First Battle of Manassas

MARCH 1862 The brigade forced to withdraw at the Battle of Kernstown

JUNE 1862 Wins a hard-fought victory at Gaines's Mill

AUGUST 1862 Victories at Cedar Mountain and the Second Battle of Manassas, despite heavy losses

SEPTEMBER 1862 The brigade defends Lee's left at the Battle of Sharpsburg

DECEMBER 1862 Victory at the Battle of Fredericksburg

MAY 1863 Jackson killed at Battle of Chancellorsville; the 1st Virginia Brigade officially designated the Stonewall Brigade

JUNE 1863 Capture of six Union regiments at Stephenson's Depot

JULY 1863 Fight at Battle of Gettysburg

MAY 1864 The brigade fights at the Battle of the Wilderness and Spotsylvania Court House; reduced to the strength of a regiment

JULY 1864 Victory at the Battle of Monocacy

APRIL 1865 The Confederate forces surrender at Appomattox Court House

On 30 August 1862, at the Second Battle of Manassas, the Stonewall Brigade repulsed the Union's Iron Brigade and rallied for a counter-attack, despite its losses. Its acting commander, Colonel William Baylor, was killed and the brigade reduced to regimental strength. Under the temporary command of Lieutenant Colonel Andrew J. Grigsby, the Stonewall Brigade defended Lee's left on 17 September 1862 at the Battle of Sharpsburg, known as the Battle of Antietam in the North. The fighting around West Woods was so fierce that Grigsby took over command of Jackson's 'Stonewall Division' when its senior officers were incapacitated.

However, Grigsby was not given permanent command of the brigade and resigned. One of Jackson's staff officers, Colonel Elisha F. Paxton, formerly commander of the 27th Virginia, took over. This was not a popular choice with the men, who preferred the notoriously profane Grigsby. However, after the Confederate victory at the Battle of Fredericksburg, 11–15 December 1862, Paxton was accepted. The brigade had lost more than 1200 men in 1862.

'REMEMBER STONEWALL JACKSON!'

On 2 May 1863, at Battle of Chancellorsville, the brigade took part in Jackson's flanking movement. That evening, they attacked along the Orange Plank Road behind Major General 'Jeb' Stuart's cavalry. Paxton was killed and more than 600 men out of the brigade's 2000 were killed or wounded. The same night Jackson was hit by friendly fire and mortally wounded. Stuart exhorted the brigade to: 'Remember Stonewall Jackson!' They rallied and resumed the attack. On his deathbed, Jackson said: 'The name "Stonewall" ought to be attached wholly to the men of the Brigade, and not to me; for it was their steadfast heroism which earned it at First Manassas.' On 30 May 1863, the Confederate War Department officially designated the unit the Stonewall Brigade.

Brigadier General James A. Walker of the 4th Virginia now took over. Again the veterans were unenthusiastic about their new commander. However, at the Second Battle of Winchester, they foiled the Union's attempt to turn Lee's left flank and, in a spirited counter-attack at Stephenson's Depot on 15 June 1863, they captured six Union regiments.

At Gettysburg on 1 July 1863, the brigade arrived late in the afternoon at the end of the first day's fighting. Over the next two days it took part in hard-fought frontal assaults against the Union entrenchments on Culp's Hill. Then at the Battle of the Wilderness of 5–7 May 1864, the brigade saw another two bloody days of fighting along the Orange Courthouse Turnpike. A week later, at Spotsylvania Court House, they were on the left of the critical salient remembered as the 'Bloody Angle'. Some 6080 men were captured, including Walker, who was seriously wounded, and the brigade was reduced to just 200 men.

Survivors were consolidated into one small regiment. It joined the remnants of the Stonewall Division under Lieutenant General Jubal A. Early. They saw success at the Battle

The Old Stonewall Brigade

After the end of the Civil War, the *Southern Illustrated News* wrote the following:

'The Old Stonewall Brigade! What a host of thoughts, memories, and emotions do these words excite! How like a call to the charge sounds the simple mention of the famous band! These veterans have fought and bled and conquered on so many battlefields, that memory grows weary almost of recalling their glories.

Gathering around Jackson in the old days of Patterson in the Valley, when Stuart had but a handful of cavalry to watch the whole border, and [Brigadier General Turner] Ashby, our dead hero, was a simple captain – they held in check an enemy twenty times their number, and were moulded by the hand of their great leader into that stern phalanx which no bayonet could break, and no odds intimidate. They were boys and old men, the humblest of the sons of toil, and the flower of the land – but united, trained, and looking with supreme confidence to their commander. And then commenced their long career of glory – their wonderful marches over thousands of miles – their incessant combats against odds that seemed overpowering – their contempt of snow and rain, and cold and hunger, and want of rest.

The soul of their leader seemed to have entered into every breast – and "Stonewall's Band" became the terror of the enemy. To meet that enemy, was to conquer him, it might almost be said, so obstinately did the eagles of victory continue to perch upon the old battle-flag. The laws of the human body seemed to have been reversed for these men. They marched, and fought, and triumphed, like war machines, which felt no need of rest, or food, or sleep.'

of Monocacy on 9 July 1864, routing the Union defenders and opening the road to Washington. But Early did not have the manpower to take the capital and he was defeated by General Philip Sheridan's Army of the Shenandoah. What remained of the Stonewall Brigade rejoined Lee at the Siege of Petersburg and fought in the Army of Northern Virginia's rearguard action to Appomattox. By the time the surrender was signed at the court house there, the brigade had fought in 39 engagements. Only 210 of the 6000 who served in the Stonewall Brigade were left – none above the rank of captain.

However, the Stonewall Brigade did not disappear completely. The 5th Virginia, one of the original five regiments, became the 1st Brigade 'The Stonewall Brigade' of the 29th Infantry Division (Light), Virginia Army National Guard. Later it became the 116th Infantry Regiment, then the 116th Infantry Brigade Combat Team. Its shoulder sleeve insignia shows 'Stonewall' Jackson on his horse – it is nicknamed 'Stony on a Pony' – and its colours carry battle streamers for the Stonewall Brigade's actions in the Civil War.

This monument to 'Stonewall' Jackson can be seen at the site of the Manassas Battlefield, Virginia.

New York's Zouaves

The Civil War units inspired by the fighting men of French North Africa

With their exotic African uniforms, the Zouaves who fought in the American Civil War may have looked out of place, but they were a highly disciplined fighting force who demonstrated their courage under fire. Their reputation grew to a point where their baggy pants, tight buttonless jackets, broad sashes and fezzes were awarded to other units who showed conspicuous gallantry.

The original Zouaves were members of the Zouaoua tribe from Algeria mixed with some French settlers who served with the French army during France's North Africa campaign of the 1830s. General George B. McClellan, while still a captain, had been an observer of the Crimean War of 1853–6. He saw the élite 'Zoo-Zoos' in action and called them the 'beau-ideal of a soldier'. Their uniform – baggy trousers, short jacket and fez – became famous throughout Europe. Queen Victoria even had one of her colonial regiments, the West India Regiment, kitted out in it. By 1860, the Zouave craze of outlandish attire coupled with superb military capabilities hit the United States.

The Battle of Fredericksburg raged on 11–15 December 1862. The 5th New York Volunteer Infantry – 'Duryée's Zouaves' – served with distinction, though the Union experienced a heavy defeat and suffered over 12,000 casualties. (Oil painting by German artist Carl Röchling (1855–1920).)

In 1861, following the outbreak of the Civil War, the famous US colonel Elmer E. Ellsworth turned to the firemen of New York to form the backbone of his new regiment. 'I want the New York firemen for there are no more effective men in the country and none with whom I can do so much,' he said. Within 48 hours of his call to arms, the muster rolls of the 11th New York Volunteer Infantry were full.

THE ZOUAVES' FIRST ACTION

The New York Fire Zouaves then took the train to Washington, and camped on the banks of the Potomac. On the morning of 24 May, one day after the public ratification of Virginia's secession, Ellsworth's regiment were ferried to Alexandria, becoming the first Union regiment on enemy soil. Leading a detachment to take the local telegraph office, Ellsworth saw a Confederate flag on the Marshall House Hotel. He scaled the roof and cut it down. But then he was killed by a gun blast from the hotel's proprietor, James T. Jackson, and became the first prominent Union casualty of the Civil War. Jackson himself was shot and bayoneted. Ellsworth's body was returned to Washington. A funeral service was held in the White House. His body was laid in state in New York City Hall and Albany. Thousands of mourners turned up. Some joined New York regiments that called themselves the 'Ellsworth Avengers'.

Command of the Fire Zouaves passed to Lieutenant Colonel Noah L. Farnham, who led them at the First Battle of Bull Run (21 July 1861). With a battalion of marines, they were to escort two Union artillery batteries into position when they came under Confederate fire.

A 19th-century engraving depicting the fatal shooting of Elmer Ellsworth, Colonel of the New York Fire Zouaves.

The artillery men were cut down and the escort broke, but some Zouaves stood their ground and returned fire. Colonel Farnham was injured, later dying of his wounds, and the regiment broke when run down by the First Virginia Cavalry. They were disbanded a few months later.

NEW YORK'S ZOUAVES

1830s French form Zouave regiments in North Africa

1853–6 Zouaves perform heroically in the Crimean War

1859 US Zouave Cadets formed in Illinois

1860 Zouave craze started by tour of Ellsworth's Cadets

1861 Zouave units formed in New York

1862 Duyrée's Zouaves take heavy losses in the Civil War at the Second Battle of Bull Run

1863 New York's Fire Zouaves parade down Broadway

1864 General Meade selects the 114th Pennsylvania Zouaves as his headquarter's guard in honour of their 'discipline and soldierly bearing'

1865 Last casualty of the Civil War is a Zouave

BATTLE HONOURS

Meanwhile, the 5th New York Volunteer Infantry had proved themselves at Big Bethel on 10 June 1861 under Colonel Abram Duryée, a drillmaster who had been impressed by Ellsworth's Zouave Cadets. 'Duryée's Zouaves' continued their attack even after their officers had been wounded and the rest of the Union forces had given up. The fight cost the 5th New York six dead and 13 wounded. At Gaines's Mill on 27 June, they charged the superior forces of the 1st South Carolina Rifles three times. Two Zouave standard-bearers stood 30 paces in front of the regiment's line, inspiring the 1st to go in with the bayonet. The unit won respect for their precision manoeuvres and steady bearing under fire. 'I doubt whether it had an equal,' said General George Sykes, 'and certainly no superior among all the regiments of the Army of the Potomac.' Many observers considered the 5th New York to be the best-drilled volunteer unit in the Union army.

At the Second Battle of Bull Run (28–30 August 1862), they were with the 10th New York 'National Zouaves' when they were hit from three sides by James Longstreet's corps. Within seven minutes, 120 men of the 5th were killed or mortally wounded, 179 were injured and 27 were captured. Out of a total of 550 men, 326 were listed as casualties. In the entire war, no other Union infantry regiment lost so many men in such a short time.

The 5th went on to serve at the battles of Antietam, Shepherdstown, Fredericksburg and Chancellorsville. After that, their three years of service were up. Returning to New York, Duyrée's Zouaves paraded down Broadway. The *New York Times* reported: 'The men were brown and rugged; their colours were weather-stained and bullet-torn; their uniforms were tattered and stained with Virginia mud and the smoke of hard-fought conflicts. They looked magnificent.'

Of 1508 men on their rolls, they lost 211 dead. However, nine of their soldiers attained the rank of general – five the full rank, and four by brevet. Duyrée's Zouaves remained an inspiration. After the Second Battle of Bull Run, officers of the 5th raised the 165th New York. Men from the 5th who had not served out their three years were transferred to the 146th, while Colonel Cleveland Winslow raised the 5th New York Veteran Volunteers in an effort to preserve the name of Duyrée's Zouaves.

In 1863 and 1864 three Union regiments – 146th New York, 140th New York and 155th Pennsylvania – were issued with Zouave uniforms in recognition of their drill proficiency and battlefield performance. However, problems with resupply meant that Zouave uniforms were gradually replaced by the standard issue. But the Zouave tradition remained strong and the last Union casualty of the war was reported to be a Zouave of the 155th Pennsylvania.

'Les Zouaves sont les premiers soldats du monde.'
(*'The Zouaves are the premier soldiers of the world.'*)

MARSHAL DE SAINT-ARNAUD, AFTER THE BATTLE OF ALMA, CRIMEA, 1854

COLONEL ELMER E. ELLSWORTH

Born in Malta, New York, on 11 April 1837, Elmer E. Ellsworth showed what his mother called a 'military propensity' from an early age. In the schoolyard he put the other boys, armed with sticks, through their drill. After failing to get into West Point, he worked as a grocery clerk before moving to New York City where he would watch the drilling of the 'Dandy 7th' – the 7th Regiment, New York State Militia, also nicknamed the 'Old Greybacks' for their grey uniforms. Later, as a struggling law student in Chicago, he met Charles A. DeVilliers, a former French army surgeon who had served with the Zouaves in the Crimea.

Colonel Elmer E. Ellsworth was the first conspicuous casualty of the American Civil War.

Ellsworth then took command of Illinois's volunteer National Guard Cadets, who were on the verge of disbanding, and turned them into the US Zouave Cadets. In September 1859, they won the state drill competition in Springfield. The following year, he took his Zouaves on a tour of 19 East Coast cities, giving a drill display that lasted over four hours and included over 500 manoeuvres. Even the Old Greybacks admitted that no other unit could match the Zouaves. One Chicago newspaper said:

'A Zouave is a fellow who can climb a greased pole feet first, carrying a barrel of pork in his teeth – that is a Zouave … A fellow who can take a five-shooting revolver in each hand and knock the spots out of the ten of diamonds at 80 paces, turning somersaults all the time and firing every shot in the air – that is a Zouave.'

By the time he returned to Chicago, Ellsworth was said to be: 'the most talked-of man in the country.' However, maintaining the unit proved too expensive. The Zouaves were disbanded and Ellsworth entered the law office of Abraham Lincoln, then the Republican presidential nominee. He went on the stump for Lincoln and became, in the words of Lincoln's future personal secretary John Hay: 'one of the most popular speakers known to the schoolhouses and barns of central Illinois.' Lincoln himself said that Ellsworth had: 'a power to command.' When Lincoln won the election, Ellsworth accompanied him on his journey to Washington with the aim of starting a National Militia Bureau with himself as head.

With the outbreak of the Civil War, Ellsworth headed to New York where he recruited the 11th New York Volunteer Infantry, also known as the 1st New York Fire Zouaves, becoming their colonel on 7 May 1861.

After the war, other militia units adopted the Zouave uniform. New York boasted three post-war Zouave regiments and, in 1868, the Sixth Maryland Regiment paraded through Baltimore with turbans wound round their fezzes to celebrate the opening of a new steamship line to Bremen, Germany. Civil War Zouave regiments formed veteran associations who proudly paraded in their uniforms, carrying their bullet-torn colours, well into the 20th century. Glasgow-born Andrew Coates, a private with the 5th New York, emigrated to America in 1855 and continued his activities in veterans affairs until his death in 1921 at the age of 81, while English-born Private Robert Sadler, who was wounded at Manassas with the 5th, died in Los Angeles in 1923 at the age of 83.

The Chiricahua Apache under Geronimo

'Fierce as so many tigers'

For generations, the Apache had resisted European settlers taking over their homeland in New Mexico and Arizona. In the 1860s, Cochise led the Chiricahua on the warpath. After he surrendered in 1872 and retired to the reservation, the Chiricahua turned to Geronimo under whose leadership they managed to run rings around a huge Federal force.

Apache chief Geronimo, photographed in 1887, adopts a warlike stance. However, by this time he and his warriors had surrendered and were again housed in a reservation.

By 1872, Lieutenant Colonel George F. Crook, commander of the Department of Arizona, had succeeded in establishing relative peace in the territory and was sent to the Department of the Platte – Nebraska – to subdue the Sioux. With the death of Cochise in 1874, some 4000 Apache were forcibly moved to a reservation at San Carlos, a barren wasteland in east-central Arizona. Deprived of traditional tribal rights, short on rations and homesick, they revolted. Led by Geronimo, hundreds of Apache left the reservation to resume their war against the incoming settlers.

THE HUNT FOR GERONIMO

In 1882, Crook was recalled to Arizona to conduct a campaign against the Apache. Geronimo surrendered in January 1884, but took flight from the San Carlos reservation again in May 1885, accompanied by 35 men, 8 boys and 101 women. With stolen weapons, horses and stores, they fled eastwards, towards the trails that run southwards into Mexico and the Sierra Madre country. Their escape signalled the beginning of a new Apache uprising.

Crook, along with scouts Al Sieber, Tom Horn and Mickey Free – a white child Cochise had been falsely accused of abducting – set out in pursuit. He put 20 troops of cavalry in the field with more than 100 scouts. Two columns were sent across the border under a treaty the United States had signed with the Mexican government. The Mexican army joined the hunt for Geronimo in the Sierra Madre. Civilian posses also took up the chase.

Although pursued relentlessly by the US and Mexican forces, the Chiricahua struck back repeatedly. In hit-and-run raids and clever ambushes, they killed dozens of settlers and troopers in the US and an unknown number in Mexico. In a raid on their own reservation, they killed 12 Apache who had refused to join the breakout and stole horses, supplies, weapons and ammunition. Afterwards, they simply disappeared into the rugged landscape.

FAILED PEACE AND ESCAPE

During November and December 1885, one band of ten Apache swept 1200 miles (1930 km) across New Mexico and Arizona, killing 38 people and stealing some 250 horses and mules, before escaping into Mexico. Crook's troopers managed to win some minor skirmishes, even striking at Geronimo's camp in the Sierra Madre, but the Apache recovered quickly and the troops chasing them would be left exhausted. Crook complained that the Apache were: 'so scattered that it is almost impossible to follow them, particularly over rocks, which often delays the party following trails for several hours.'

Nevertheless, Geronimo put out peace feelers. On 25 March 1886, ten months after the breakout, he met Crook at Cañon de Los Embudos in the Sierra Madre, a few miles south of the US border. Crook noted that the

Members of the US army, led by George Crook, are shown seated with Geronimo at the close of the Apache war at the end of March 1886. (Wood engraving after a contemporary photograph.)

COCHISE

Cochise lived peacefully as a woodcutter until 1861, when a raiding party drove off cattle belonging to a white rancher and abducted the son of a ranch hand. An inexperienced army officer named Lieutenant George Bascom ordered his men to seize Cochise and five other Apache. In the ensuing struggle, one Apache was killed. Cochise suffered three bullet wounds, but escaped by cutting through the side of a tent. He then abducted a stagecoach driver and two passengers to exchange for the Apache captives, but Bascom retaliated by hanging the prisoners, including Cochise's brother and two nephews.

To avenge their deaths, Cochise went on the warpath, attacking dozens of settlements and killing over 150 settlers in two months. Others fled. During the Civil War, Cochise had joined his uncle Mangas Coloradas. In July 1862, the two chiefs led 700 braves to ambush Union troops in Apache Pass, but were put to flight by howitzers. Mangas Coloradas surrendered and was murdered the following year; Cochise became the leader of the Apache. With 200 followers, he eluded capture for more than ten years, waging a hit-and-run campaign from mountain strongholds. However, when 128 unarmed Apache were slaughtered by Arizonans in 1871, General George Crook was brought in to stop the killing. Cochise surrendered, but escaped again in the spring of 1872.

In September 1872, Cochise agreed to return to the reservation provided his friend Thomas Jeffords was made Indian agent. He had already cost the United

This is the only known authentic portrait of the Apache leader Cochise. He was born around 1812. Cochise County, Arizona, is named after him.

States 1000 dead and $40 million. Cochise died on the Chiricahua Apache Reservation on 8 June 1874 with Jeffords by his side.

Chiricahua were 'in superb physical condition, armed to the teeth, and with an abundance of ammunition', adding later they were 'fierce as so many tigers – knowing what pitiless brutes they are themselves, they mistrust everyone else'.

Two days later, the Chiricahua surrendered on the understanding that, after two years exile, they would be allowed to return to Arizona. But as they approached the border, the Apache became afraid that they would be murdered once they were back in the United States, and Geronimo and his small band made a run for it. Having lost his prize prisoner, Crook was replaced by Brigadier General Nelson A. Miles.

For five months, Geronimo pitted his handful of fighters against an overwhelming force in the last campaign of the Indian wars. He terrorized both sides of the border, eluding capture in what is the largest manhunt in the history of the region. His fighters struck at settlements and ranches across northern Sonora. They killed miners and cowboys, and shot up a detachment of US cavalry. Reports, inflated by panic and rumour, said that Geronimo had a force of 150 Apache warriors, though the number was more like 15.

A BROKEN PROMISE AND FINAL SURRENDER

While Crook had the reputation of being a great Indian fighter, Miles was altogether a different type of strategist. He began by sending any Chiricahua rebels he caught into exile in Florida. In fact, he planned to send the whole tribe there, including those who had stayed on the reservation – even those who had worked as scouts for the army. He organized a system of heliographs – signalling devices – to send messages from mountaintop to mountaintop across the country and put 5000 US troopers in the field. But still they failed to track down Geronimo. Eventually Miles sent 33-year-old Lieutenant Charles B. Gatewood, along with two Apache scouts, Ki-eta and Martine, to find Geronimo and open peace talks.

Geronimo knew and trusted Gatewood, who located Geronimo's camp near the village of Fronteras, in the Sonora Mountains, a few miles south of the border. Gatewood approached under a white flag of truce and Geronimo agreed to surrender. On 3 September 1886, Geronimo met General Miles at Skeleton Canyon in Arizona. Miles promised once again, after exile in Florida, that he and his men would be permitted to return to Arizona. This promise was never kept.

On 5 September 1886, Miles assembled Geronimo and his followers at Fort Apache and sent them east. In Florida, they found not the reservation in a land of timber and water they had been expecting, but a prison camp where Geronimo and his men were put to hard labour. It was May 1887 before Geronimo saw his family again. In 1894, they were moved back west, not to Arizona, but to a reservation at Fort Sill in the Oklahoma Territory.

There Geronimo attempted to 'take the white man's road'. He farmed and joined the Dutch Reformed Church, which expelled him over his gambling. He never saw Arizona again. Neither did Ki-eta or Martine, who were also exiled. By special permission of the War Department, Geronimo was allowed to sell photographs of himself, handiwork and crudely scrawled autographs to make money. He died near Fort Sill on 17 February 1909, after he lay, drunk, in the middle of a road all night in freezing rain.

THE CHIRICAHUA APACHE UNDER GERONIMO

1861 Cochise falsely accused and goes on the warpath

1862 The Apache attack the California volunteers, but are dispersed by howitzers

1863 Mangas Coloradas murdered in captivity, making Cochise leader of the Apache

1871 General George Crook sent in to end the Apache war

1872 Cochise surrenders to Crook

1874 Cochise dies on the Chiricahua Apache Reservation; Geronimo flees the reservation to restart the war

1882 Crook recalled

1884 Geronimo surrenders

1885 Geronimo takes flight from the reservation once more; the Apache sweep across Arizona and New Mexico

1886 Geronimo surrenders to Crook in Mexico once again, but escapes as they approach the border; Crook replaced by General Nelson A. Miles; after five months, Geronimo surrenders to Miles and is exiled to Florida

1894 Apache relocated to Oklahoma

1909 Geronimo dies

'I was born on the prairies where the wind blew free and there was nothing to break the light of the sun. I was born where there were no enclosures.'

GERONIMO (1829–1909)

The Zulu Impis

The regiments of Shaka and Cetewayo

The disciplined troops of Shaka established an empire that stretched from the Cape Colony to the borders of modern-day Tanzania. Under his nephew Cetewayo, they shocked the world, massacring a British column armed with the latest rifles and artillery.

Shaka was the father of the Zulu nation. Born the illegitimate son of the Zulu chief Senzangakona around 1787, he was driven out with his mother Nandi, a Langeni, which the Zulu considered an inferior clan. Even his name was an insult – '*Shaka*' was an intestinal parasite thought to be responsible for menstrual irregularities and said, by Zulu elders, to be the true cause of Nandi's pregnancy.

At 16 years of age, Shaka was taken under the protection of Dingiswayo, king of the Mtetwa, and was trained in his army, excelling in single combat. When Senzangakona died, Shaka returned to the Zulu – then numbering just 1500 – as their chief. He quickly reorganized his army. Any opposition resulted in instant death and the people who had made his childhood a misery were impaled on the sharpened stakes of their own kraal fences.

Before Shaka, the Zulu were armed with oxhide shields and throwing spears, and battles were desultory affairs which broke off before there were many casualties. Shaka armed his men with short-bladed assegais for stabbing at close quarters. He also developed a heavier shield that was used to force his opponent to expose his side to the thrust of his assegai. Some were also armed with knobkerries or cudgels.

The Zulu warrior Utimuni, the nephew of Shaka, in full costume. The long shield, made from cow or goat skin, was no defence against British army gunfire. The long-handled spears were intended to be thrown at an enemy.

THE IMPI REGIMENTAL SYSTEM

Shaka instituted a regimental system, with each regiment or impi composed of men roughly the same age and housed in their own separate kraal. They were distinguished by different head-dresses and coloured markings on their shields. Officers directed battles by hand

signals, while Shaka sent instructions by runner. He also developed the famous 'buffalo' formation, with the men forming the 'chest' pinning the enemy down while the 'horns' encircled them. The 'loins' were the reserve, who sat looking away from the action to prevent them from becoming unduly excited.

Zulu males were raised as warriors from the age of six. They dispensed with their traditional oxhide sandals and were trained to outrun a horse, covering as much as 50 miles (80 km) a day on foot. They swore loyalty to the Zulu king and were not allowed to marry before they had proved their courage in some way. In wartime, warriors painted their upper bodies and faces with chalk and red ochre. They were also famous for their custom of 'washing of spears' in their enemy's blood. They cut open the belly of their victims – sometimes, allegedly, while they were still living. This was supposed to allow the release of the enemy's spirit so it could not haunt the killer.

Shaka set about destroying all the tribes around him, integrating any survivors into the Zulu nation which, within a year, had quadrupled in number. Soon he was fielding impis 1000 strong, accompanied by young boys who carried cooking pots and sleeping mats.

ESTABLISHING AN EMPIRE

When Dingiswayo died, Shaka took over the Mtetwa empire. Fighting against the Ndwandwe, he introduced a tactic new to Africa: scorched earth. The Ndwandwe were

The Battle of Isandhlwana on 22 January 1879 was the last stand of the 24th Regiment of Foot (South Welsh Borderers) during the Zulu War. The troops can be seen here forming a British Square – facing the enemy on four sides. (Oil painting by English artist Charles Edwin Fripp (1854–1906).)

'A magnificent people, the Zulus. They convert our bishops, beat our generals and write "finis" to a French dynasty.'

BRITISH PRIME MINISTER, BENJAMIN DISRAELI, 1879

finally defeated in a two-day battle at the Mhlatuzi fords. In 1820, Shaka began the *Mfecane* – 'the Crushing' – arbitrarily wiping out clans across the plateau of Natal. The devastation was so complete that the Boer's Great Trek of the 1830s passed through uninhabited land. The Zulu nation grew to 250,000 with an army of 40,000 and occupied territory that stretched from the Cape nearly 2000 (3218 km) miles to the north. To create this empire, it is estimated that Shaka killed over two million people, often in mass executions.

When Shaka was wounded in 1824, he was treated by a visiting Englishman. In recompense, he allowed English traders to operate out of Port Natal and a kraal 100 miles (160 km) to the north at Bulawayo, and even tried to exchange ambassadors with George IV. In 1827, Shaka's mother died. In grief, he killed 7000 Zulu. No crops were planted for a year and milk – a Zulu staple – was banned. Milking cows were slain so that calves could know what it felt like to lose a mother and pregnant women were slain with their husbands. Enforced chastity had already dispirited Shaka's army. When they were sent further and further from home to find more lands to conqueror, they rebelled. Two of Shaka's half-brothers murdered him in 1828. He died without dignity, begging for mercy.

THE RISE OF CETEWAYO

The last great king of the Zulu was Shaka's nephew Cetewayo. Born in 1826, he began taking part in raids on European settlers at the age of 12, distinguishing himself in the war against the Swazis of 1853–4. Polygamy ensured he had many rivals for the throne and he had to wait until six of his half-brothers were killed and two were forced into exile before he was proclaimed king in 1872.

In 1877, the British decided to annex the Transvaal and the Boers began to encroach on Zulu land. In response, Cetewayo increased the size of his army. The British High Commissioner, Sir Bartle Frere, decided to eradicate the menace. In December 1878, he sent an ultimatum, insisting Cetewayo disband his army. When he refused, the British invaded. But on 22 January 1879, the Zulu, armed only with spears, but vastly outnumbering their enemy, wiped out an entire British regiment at Isandhlwana. Near the end of the battle, about 4000 warriors, after cutting off the retreat of the survivors to the Buffalo river southwest of Isandlwana, attacked the fortified mission station at Rorke's Drift.

The British recovered and defeated the Zulu at Kambula on 29 March 1879 and took the Zulu capital Ulundi on 4 July 1879. During the battle the only son of Napoleon III, then exiled in England, was killed. Cetewayo was captured. However, he was allowed to visit Queen Victoria in England and was restored as ruler of Zululand in 1883. But those who had ruled in the meantime refused to accept him. Defeated by a rival, he sought refuge with the British resident in Eshowe, where he died of a heart attack in 1884.

Isandhlwana and Rorke's Drift

British forces under the command of Lord Chelmsford had crossed the Buffalo river at Rorke's Drift on 11 January 1879 and encamped below a rocky hill known to the Zulu as Isandhlwana. Chelmsford then set out with roughly 2500 men to search for the Zulu army, leaving behind a force of 950 Europeans, 850 natives and two field guns under the command of Lieutenant Colonel Henry Pulleine.

At roughly 11 a.m. on 22 January, a scouting force on the nearby Nqutu plateau spotted a group of Zulu herding cattle up a ridge. One trooper reaching the crest saw below him 20–25,000 Zulu warriors. Under the senior *indunas* – regimental commanders – Dabulamanzi, Mavumengwana and Tshingwayo, they formed themselves into the classic buffalo's horn formation. British morale was high as disciplined volleys of Martini-Henry rifle fire thinned the encircling Zulu. But soon the ammunition began to dwindle and rifles began to jam in the heat. As the fire slackened, the Zulu charged. Within 20 minutes, the entire perimeter was obliterated. The Zulu overran the camp and hundreds of native and imperial troops died as they

This 1880 oil painting of the Defence of Rorke's Drift is by the French artist Alphonse Marie de Neuville (1835–85). At Rorke's Drift, a small British contingent held off a Zulu army of over 4000 warriors.

fled back towards the Buffalo river. By 4 p.m., it was all over. Every living thing in the camp – including the horses, dogs and mules – had been killed. In accordance with Zulu tradition, the dead British soldiers were stripped and disembowelled.

Some 50 European and 300 native troops survived. Zulu casualties were estimated at 3000–4000 killed. The world was shocked that a modern European army equipped with the latest rifles and artillery could be defeated, let alone massacred, by spear-wielding tribesmen.

Consequently, British propaganda concentrated on the action at Rorke's Drift where – forewarned – 120 men in fortified positions saw off 4000–5000 of the Zulu rear guard. But this was of no consequence, since the Zulu commander had been ordered not to cross the river into British territory and the Zulu had already crushed the British force at Isandhlwana.

THE
FIRST & SECOND
WORLD WARS

Painting of British soldiers recovering a field gun during a First World War battle. Few of the original British Expeditionary Force (the Old Contemptibles) survived the war.

The Old Contemptibles

The British Expeditionary Force of 1914

The 'Old Contemptibles' was the name given to the British Expeditionary Force sent to defend Belgium and France at the beginning of the First World War. By the end of 1914, it was replaced by fresh armies. Few of the original force survived, but those who did relished the name the 'Old Contemptibles', as they held their ground against a German army that regarded them with contempt.

The British Expeditionary Force was formed in 1908 by the British secretary of state for war, Richard Haldane. Following the Second Boer War of 1899–1902, it was decided that the British should have a standing army, ready to be sent on foreign adventures. Before that, the British army had been organized in a more *ad hoc* fashion. When trouble arose, individual units had been shipped off, which were then organized into brigades or larger units when they arrived in the theatre of operations.

Britain had also taken on responsibilities on the Continent that would bring her into conflict with Germany, which was rapidly becoming a great power. In 1904, the British had signed the *Entente Cordiale* with France, which ended almost a millennium of intermittent conflict between the two nations, addressed concerns on colonial expansion, and critically created an alliance against Germany. And since the creation of Belgium in 1831, Britain had guaranteed her neutrality.

A group of British army veterans known as the Old Contemptibles enjoy a brief moment of relaxation in the trenches during the First World War.

THE CONTEMPTIBLES GET THEIR NAME

As the threat of a German attack on France grew, it was clear that the British should organize and train an army against such an eventuality before it actually took place. So Haldane organized the units of the British army stationed at home in Britain into an expeditionary force of six infantry divisions, comprising 72 infantry battalions, and one cavalry division of 14 cavalry regiments.

With the outbreak of the First World War on 4 August 1914, four of these infantry divisions and the one cavalry division were sent to France, along with engineers, artillery, medical, supply and signal units, and four squadrons of the newly formed Royal Flying Corps. Two divisions of infantry were held back for home defence since, at the time, it was feared that Germany might send a landing force to Britain. That threat soon passed, and one division was sent to France at the end of August and the other in early September.

The commander-in-chief of the British Expeditionary Force was Field Marshal Sir John French. The rumour circulated that, in an order of the day

ostensibly issued on 19 August 1914, Kaiser Wilhelm had ordered German forces to 'walk over French's contemptibly small army'. The words 'contemptibly small' were reported, perhaps through mistranslation, as 'contemptible, small'. However, no such order had been found in the German archives, Kaiser Wilhelm denied saying it, and there are indications that it was made up by the British War Office for propaganda purposes. Whatever the truth was, British Tommies soon embraced it, rejoicing in being regarded as 'contemptible'.

British troops attempt to stop Germans from getting through Landrecries during the retreat from Mons. (Painting by English artist William Barnes Wollen (1857–1936).)

THE OLD CONTEMPTIBLES

1908 The British Expeditionary Force set up

AUGUST 1914 The First World War begins; the British Expeditionary Force sent to France; thought to have been dismissed as 'contemptible' by the Kaiser; fight the Battle of Mons

SEPTEMBER 1914 The Old Contemptibles fight in the First Battle of the Marne

OCTOBER–NOVEMBER 1914 The Old Contemptibles fight in the First Battle of Ypres

DECEMBER 1914 British Expeditionary Force disbanded; surviving members of the Old Contemptibles join the newly formed 1st and 2nd British Armies

THE GERMAN ADVANCE HALTED

The initial British Expeditionary Force, 70,000 strong, had arrived in France on 14 August 1914. The II Corps was on its way to meet the French army at Charleroi when it met the advancing German army at Mons. Eight German infantry battalions, supported by artillery, attacked in close formation and were cut down by the marksmen of the 4th Middlesex Regiment and 4th Royal Fusiliers. The fire was so intense that the German commander General von Kluck thought they were using machine guns.

After five hours of fighting, German artillery began to force the Middlesex Regiment and Royal Fusiliers back. By then, the whole of the German 1st Army – 150,000 men – had arrived and the British were hopelessly outnumbered. The French on their eastern flank had withdrawn and they risked being encircled. The Belgian army then withdrew from Mons and the British were forced to follow suit.

To halt the advancing Germans, a group of Royal Fusiliers was ordered to destroy the bridges over the Mons–Condé Canal. The men came under heavy German fire and, during the operation, Private Sidney Godley, Captain Theodore Wright, Corporal Charles Jarvis and Lieutenant Maurice Dease were among those who won the Victoria Cross, Britain's highest award for gallantry. Lieutenant Dease was the medal's first posthumous recipient.

On 25 August, the British fell back to Le Cateau and set up defensive positions. Early the next morning, the Germans attacked. The British flanks began to crumble and only the arrival of French cavalry kept the line together. That night, the British pulled back to St Quentin. They had suffered 7800 casualties. Several regiments had vanished from the rolls and II Corps was in a seriously depleted condition.

By the end of August, three German armies were sweeping south towards Paris. The French and the British Expeditionary Force were in full retreat. To prevent the encirclement of Paris, General Joseph Joffre, the commander-in-chief of the French forces, planned to attack the German 1st Army along the River Marne on 6 September. Sir John French agreed to join the attack. General von Kluck sent his entire force to meet the Allied forces, opening

'A' Company of the 4th Battalion Royal Fusiliers rest in the square at Mons, Belgium, on 22 August 1914 – the day before the Battle of Mons. Minutes after the picture was taken the company moved into position at Nimy on the banks of the Mons–Condé Canal.

a 30-mile (48-km) gap between his 1st Army and the German 2nd Army led by General Karl von Bülow. The British Expeditionary Force and the French 5th Army advanced into the gap, dividing the two German armies.

For the next three days the German forces were unable to break through the Allied lines, though at one point the French 6th Army was only saved when Paris taxis rushed 6000 reserve troops to the front line. Then on 9 September, German commander-in-chief General Helmuth von Moltke ordered von Kluck and von Bülow to retreat. The British and French now crossed the Marne. By the evening of the 10th, the First Battle of the Marne was over. The British had lost 12,733 men, the French 250,000. They had ended German hopes of a swift victory, leading to a prolonged war that cost over eight million lives.

THE MONS STAR

The survivors of the Old Contemptibles were awarded a medal known as the 1914 Star – nicknamed the Mons Star because the recipients had taken part in the retreat from Mons. Struck in 1917, it was issued to the officers and men of the British Expeditionary Forces who had served in France and Belgium between 5 August and midnight on 22 November 1914 – that is, the outbreak of war and the end of the First Battle of Ypres. Some 365,622 soldiers were awarded the medal. The last known living recipient of the medal, Alfred Anderson, died in 2005, aged 109.

THE FIRST BATTLE OF YPRES

By early October, the British Expeditionary Force had recaptured the town of Ypres in Belgium. The first major German attempt to regain it began on 15 October. Again the experienced British Expeditionary Force held its positions despite heavy losses. German attacks continued for the next four weeks but, with the arrival of the French army, the line held. With the weather deteriorating, the Germans abandoned the Ypres offensive on 22 November. Some 135,000 Germans were killed or wounded during the action. The British Expeditionary Force lost around 75,000 men and was effectively destroyed as a fighting force. The British Expeditionary Force was officially stood down on 26 December 1914 when it was divided into the 1st and 2nd Armies – the 3rd, 4th and 5th Armies were created later in the war. There were two more major battles at Ypres: the Second Battle of Ypres in April–May 1915 and Passchendaele (also known as the Third Battle of Ypres) in July–October 1917. Total casualties exceeded 850,000 men.

Few of the original British Expeditionary Force survived the war. However, in 1925, those still alive formed the Old Contemptible Association. Britain sent another British Expeditionary Force to defend France during the Second World War. This time they failed to hold the German army back.

'It is my Royal and Imperial command that you concentrate your energies for the immediate present upon one single purpose, and that is that you address your skill and all the valour of my soldiers to exterminate the treacherous English, and walk over French's contemptibly small army.'

ATTRIBUTED TO KAISER WILHELM II, 1914

The Few

RAF Fighter Command pilots of the Battle of Britain

In the summer of 1940, Adolf Hitler was massing his forces on the French coast, ready to launch a seaborne invasion of Britain. All that stood between Britain and Nazi occupation were the pilots of the RAF's Fighter Command – the men British Prime Minister Winston Churchill would famously dub 'The Few'.

On 1 August 1940, German leader Adolf Hitler signed Führer Directive No. 17, ordering Germany's airforce, the Luftwaffe, to smash the Royal Air Force (RAF). The Luftwaffe were to take on the RAF in the air and attack their ground facilities and supply centres. British cities, though, were not to be terror bombed without the express order of Hitler himself.

This painting shows British Spitfires and Hurricanes engaging with a wave of German Heinkel bombers during the Battle of Britain.

The Germans had 2442 aircraft – 969 heavy bombers, 336 dive bombers, 869 single-engined fighters and 268 twin-engined fighters. The RAF's Fighter Command had just 620 planes. However, fighter production had risen from 157 in January 1940 to 496 in July. There was a shortage of trained pilots though. The RAF only had 1134 in all, but they also formed four Polish, one Czech and one French squadron with experienced pilots who had escaped from occupied Europe.

Spitfires and Hurricanes

The RAF's Spitfires and Hurricanes were much faster and more manoeuvrable than the twin-engined Messerschmitt Bf 110 'destroyer' – also known as 'Göring's folly', after the Luftwaffe's commander Reichsmarschall Hermann Göring. On the other hand, the single-seater Messerschmitt Bf 109E was faster than the Mark I Hurricane and about as fast as the Mark II Spitfires that were just appearing in front-line squadrons. The Bf 109E could also climb faster than the British fighters, though the British fighters were still much more manoeuvrable and, with eight machines guns, could outshoot their German adversaries. And it is generally reckoned that the Spitfire, though in short supply, was unrivalled as an interceptor aircraft at that time.

German heavy bombers were easily vulnerable to attack from both Hurricanes and Spitfires, particularly in daylight. German dive bombers were also easily shot down, and German fighters could only give them partial protection over targets in England because they were at the limit of their flying range.

GROUP CAPTAIN MALAN'S TEN RULES OF AIR FIGHTING

1. Wait until you see the whites of their eyes. Fire short bursts of one to two seconds and only when your sights are definitely 'on'.

2. While shooting think of nothing else, brace the whole of the body, have both hands on the stick, concentrate on your ring sight.

3. Always keep a sharp lookout. 'Keep your finger out'.

4. Height gives you the initiative.

5. Always turn and face the attack.

6. Make your decisions promptly. It is better to act quickly even though your tactics are not the best.

7. Never fly straight and level for more than thirty seconds in the combat area.

8. When diving to attack always leave a proportion of your formation above to act as a top guard.

9. INITIATIVE, AGGRESSION, AIR DISCIPLINE and TEAMWORK are words that MEAN something in air fighting.

10. Go in quickly – Punch hard – Get out.

THE FEW

22 June 1940 France surrenders to Germany

1 August 1940 Hitler orders the destruction of the RAF in preparation for Germany's invasion of Britain

24 August 1940 German plane accidentally bombs civilian target in London

26 August 1940 The RAF bomb Berlin

7 September 1940 German bombers switch from bombing RAF airfields to blitzing London

19 September 1940 Hitler cancels invasion of England

HOME ADVANTAGE

The British had an advance radar defence network. Incoming German planes could be detected in time for the British to get their fighters airborne. Control centres could then direct the fighters by radio to intercept the enemy. And as the battle was fought over British soil, downed British pilots could be returned to their units, while the German aircrew who survived were taken prisoner. On 15 August 1940, for example, 70 German planes were shot down. That day, 28 Hurricanes and Spitfires were also lost, but over half of their pilots eventually returned to their squadrons.

Although there had been preliminary attacks in June and July, the air war began in earnest on 8 August with the Germans sending up to 1500 aircraft a day to bomb the British airfields and radar stations. During fighting on 8, 11, 12 and 13 August, the RAF lost 88 planes, while the Luftwaffe lost 145 aircraft. Between 13 and 17 August, the RAF had lost 184 aircraft, against the Luftwaffe's 255. However, in late August the Luftwaffe was close to winning. Essential airfields were riddled with bomb craters. The RAF's effectiveness was curtailed by bomb damage to its radar stations and operations centres. Aircraft were being destroyed on the ground and losses began to turn in the Germans' favour.

Between 24 August and 6 September, the Luftwaffe lost 378 planes, against the RAF's 262. Although this appeared to give the British the edge, the German losses included both bombers and fighters, while the British were losing all-important fighters and experienced pilots. Fighter Command had less than 1000 pilots, seeing action several times a day. With 15 to 20 pilots killed or wounded daily, Fighter Command was reaching its last gasp.

A TIMELY ACCIDENT

Late in the evening of 24 August, a German plane accidentally bombed a non-military target in London. Churchill immediately ordered a retaliatory attack on Berlin. On 26 August, 81 twin-engined bombers took off for the German capital. Only 29 planes made it to their target, and the damage to Berlin was slight. But Hitler had promised the German people that such a thing would never happen. Infuriated, he abandoned the 1 August directive and ordered the terror bombing of London.

The German bombing campaign that followed was called the Blitz. It began on 7 September with 330 tons of bombs being dropped on London. The terror bombing campaign was later extended to Liverpool, Coventry and other cities. Although the population suffered terribly from these attacks, the switch of the Luftwaffe's objective gave Fighter Command the breathing space to recover. Between 7 and 30 September, the RAF downed 380 German aircraft for the loss of 178 of its own. The German air offensive reached a peak on 15 September with a series of attacks where British air defences claimed to have downed 185 German planes. The figure was later revised to 56. But it hardly mattered. The British were now shooting down bombers faster than German factories could produce them. By 31 October, the Germans had lost 1733 planes against Britain's 1379. But Fighter Command had only lost 414 airmen, including a number from Poland. So Churchill was not exaggerating when he told the House of Commons at the height of the battle on 20 August 1940: 'Never in the field of human conflict has so much been owed by so many to so few.'

Hitler repeatedly postponed his invasion. On 19 September, the invasion fleet was dispersed. During the following months, the Luftwaffe continued its Blitz with night-time

THE SPITFIRE

The weapon that won the Battle of Britain was a new plane called the Spitfire, and it became a symbol of British and Allied resistance to Hitler. It was designed by Reginald Mitchell, who died of cancer a year before the plane went into service with the RAF. The distinctive elliptical shape of the wings allowed them to be very thin, reducing drag. This gave the Spitfire a top speed higher than that of the Hawker Hurricane. The Spitfire became the plane most closely associated with the Battle of Britain, though more Hurricanes fought and bore the brunt of the battle against the Messerschmitt Bf 109E.

Designed to fly at over 250 miles per hour (402 kph), the Spitfire was one of a new generation of all-metal, low-wing fighters. Taking advantage of the techniques of monocoque construction, it was built around 19 separate frames. Powered by a powerful Rolls-Royce Merlin engine, it had a closed cockpit, oxygen equipment and four wing-mounted machine guns. The prototype took to the air on 6 March 1936. Production facilities were set up across the Britain, but by May 1940 not a single Spitfire had been completed and the Air Ministry stepped in to get things moving. In June, the first ten Spitfires rolled off the production line, just in time for the Battle of Britain, which began the following month. The plane continued in service in all theatres throughout the war.

The Mark IX Spitfire entered service in 1942 and over 5000 of this variant were built. In 1944, it was the first aircraft to shoot down a Messerschmitt Me 262 jet.

bombing raids on Britain's cities. Some 10,000 sorties were flown. However, the Luftwaffe never turned its attention back to British airfields. By the time spring weather had made a fresh invasion possible, Hitler had turned his eyes eastwards and was planning his attack on Soviet Russia. Fighter Command had won the Battle of Britain. Victory for the Luftwaffe would inevitably have led to the invasion and occupation of Britain, but Fighter Command had denied Hitler the air superiority he needed. It had created the conditions for Britain's survival, for the continuation of the war and for the eventual defeat of Nazi Germany.

'The gratitude of every home in our Island, in our Empire, and indeed throughout the world, except in the abodes of the guilty, goes out to the British airmen who, undaunted by odds, unwearied in their constant challenge and mortal danger, are turning the tide of the world war by their prowess and by their devotion. Never in the field of human conflict was so much owed by so many to so few.'

BRITISH PRIME MINISTER WINSTON CHURCHILL, HOUSE OF COMMONS, 20 AUGUST 1940

The Waffen-SS

Hitler's 'death's head' élite

The Waffen-SS – literally the 'Weapons SS' – was the combat arm of Hitler's personal protection squad, the *Schutzstaffel*, or SS. They were selected on a racial basis and for their commitment to Nazi ideology. Outside the command of the Wehrmacht, they were answerable only to SS chief Reichsführer Heinrich Himmler and Hitler himself. Wearing the *totenkopf*, or 'death's head' insignia of the SS, they were known for their cruelty.

The SS – the black-uniformed élite of the Nazi Party – was founded by Hitler in 1925 as a small personal bodyguard. From 1929, it was headed by Heinrich Himmler, who built up their number from under 300 to over 50,000 by the time the Nazis came to power in Germany in 1933. In 1934, on Hitler's orders, they carried out a bloody purge of the regular brown-shirted members of the Nazi Party in a bloodbath called the 'Night of the Long Knives'. The SS executed over a dozen of the leaders of the *Sturmabteilung*, or SA – the 'Assault Battalion' – whose loyalty to Hitler could not be assured. Accruing new police and military powers, the SS became practically a state within a state.

An armed branch called the *SS-Verfügungstruppen*, or SS-VT, had been formed in 1933. On *Kristallnacht*, 9 November 1938, when Jews and Jewish property were attacked thoughout Nazi Germany, the SS-VT helped burn down synagogues in Vienna. Then with the outbreak of the Second World War, the four SS-VT regiments were redesignated the Waffen-SS so that they could accompany the German army into battle. With the SA sidelined, former members were keen to join the SS and their numbers swelled.

FOREIGN RECRUITS

Recruits had to be over 1.8 metres (5 feet 11 in) tall, fit and of Aryan appearance. Unlike the *Wehrmacht*, the Waffen-SS was allowed to recruit people who were suitably Germanic from the occupied territories. Danish, Belgian, Norwegian, Swedish, Finnish and Dutch *Freiwilligen* (volunteer) units were formed. Hitler was against this, preferring that foreign recruits who believed in a greater Germany should be integrated in regular German formations. Despite the Führer's misgivings, later in the war, Bosnian, Latvian, Estonian and Ukrainian divisions were formed. There were plans for a Greek division, too, but these were abandoned when Greek partisans blew up the party's headquarters. However, Greek volunteers were allowed to join Ukrainian Waffen-SS units. French and Albanians also volunteered, and some Estonians were conscripted. There was also the British Free Corps,

A German recruiting poster for the Waffen-SS from 1941. The SS insignia are clearly visible on the helmet and on the collar of the uniform, as well as on the flag in the background.

THE WAFFEN-SS

1925 The *Schutzstaffel*, or SS, founded by Hitler

1929 Himmler takes command

1933 The armed *SS-Verfügungstruppen*, or SS-VT, formed

1934 The SS consolidate their élite status in the 'Night of the Long Knives'

1938 The SS-VT burn synagogues in Vienna during *Kristallnacht*

1939 The SS-VT go to war as the Waffen-SS

1940 Atrocities at Le Paradis and Tulle in France

1943 The Waffen-SS distinguish themselves at the Third Battle of Kharkov and the Battle of Kursk

1944 Atrocities at Oradour-sur-Glane and Ardenne Abbey in France; Marzabotto, Grizzana, Monzuno, Ardeatine and Sant'Anna di Stazzema in Italy; Malmedy in Belgium; and Distomo in Greece

1945 The Waffen-SS make last stand at the Reichstag

formed by British citizens (usually prisoners of war), but it never numbered more than 27 men.

Basic training consisted of several months of small arms and physical training, and political indoctrination. After that, recruits were sent to specialist schools. Training was extended after the Waffen-SS proved itself on the Eastern Front and its premier divisions were upgraded to armoured *panzergrenadier*, then full panzer divisions.

The *SS-Panzerkorps* distinguished itself at the Third Battle of Kharkov in 1943. The II *SS-Panzerkorps* recaptured the city and blunted the Soviet offensive, saving General Erich von Manstein's Army Group South from being cut off. The city was abandoned soon afterwards.

When operating under army command, the Waffen-SS was frequently criticized for its reckless disregard of casualties. It was also implicated in atrocities in both Eastern and Western Europe.

German Waffen-SS infantry advance along a road in Holland during the invasion of the country in May 1940.

THE BATTLE OF KURSK

Later in 1943, the II *SS-Panzerkorps* took part in Operation Citadel, the attack on the Soviet salient at Kursk, which precipitated the largest tank battle ever staged and ended any hope of German victory on the Russian front. The *Leibstandarte*, *Das Reich* and *Totenkopf* – now SS *panzergrenadier* divisions – took part in the immense armoured battles near Prokhorovka on the southern flank of the Kursk salient.

In the wake of the defeat at Kursk, divisions of the Waffen-SS – particularly those considered 'élite', such as the *Leibstandarte* and the *Wiking* – were increasingly deployed in the most crucial sectors of the German theatres of operation. Hitler came increasingly to rely on the Waffen-SS during the final years of the war. While he began to suspect the loyalty of the Wehrmacht – particularly after the 'Valkyrie' assassination plot of 20 July 1940 – he knew the devotion of the SS was unwavering. The Waffen-SS was prominent in the last operations of the war, including the Battle of Normandy, the Battle of the Bulge and Operation Spring Awakening – the last German offensive on the Western front in March 1945.

By the end of the war, the Waffen-SS had 40 fully mechanized divisions in the field, though there was nothing they could do to stop the Allies who were pouring into Germany from both the east and the west. Although the situation became increasingly hopeless, they fought on. Remnants of the 11th *SS-Freiwilligen-Panzergrenadier-Division Nordland* fought in the final defence of the Reichstag in April 1945.

'I face death without fear or complaint. I want you to be able to talk about your only son, that he faced death as an upstanding German man should … I wish you everything good until we meet again after this life.'

WAFFEN-SS MEMBER ARNO KRAUSE, IN A LETTER TO HIS PARENTS AFTER BEING CONDEMNED TO DEATH FOR THE MASSACRE AT MALMEDY

WAFFEN-SS WAR CRIMES

Members of the Waffen-SS were accused of a number of war crimes, including:

• On 27 May 1940, SS Division *Totenkopf* machine-gunned 97 soldiers of the Royal Norfolk Regiment who had surrendered at Le Paradis in France.

• On 28 May 1940, 80 British prisoners of war were killed by SS *Leibstandarte* Adolf Hitler at Wormhout in the Pas-de-Calais.

• On 24 March 1944, Waffen SS officers murdered 335 Italian civilians in caves near Rome in reprisals for an attack on a column of German policemen.

• On 7 June 1944, members of the 12th SS Panzer Division took 18 captured Canadian soldiers of The North Nova Scotia Highlanders and the 27th Canadian Armoured Regiment (Sherbrooke Fusilier Regiment) to Ardenne Abbey near Caen in France and murdered them.

• On 8 June 1944, the Second SS Division *Das Reich* hanged 97 civilians in the French village of Tulle and 321 were sent to Germany as forced labour in retaliation for an attack on a German column by the Maquis.

• On 10 June 1944, 642 inhabitants of Oradour-sur-Glane in Haute-Vienne, France, were killed by the men of SS *Das Reich*.

• On 10 June 1944, Waffen-SS troops of the 4th *SS Polizei Panzergrenadier* Division went door to door for two hours at Distomo in Greece, massacring 218 men, women and children.

• On 12 August 1944, retreating SS-men of II Battalion of *SS-Panzergrenadier*-Regiment 35 of 16th *SS Panzergrenadier* Division *Reichsführer-SS*, commanded by *SS-Hauptsturmführer* Anton Galler, rounded up 560 villagers and refugees in the Italian village of Sant'Anna di Stazzema – mostly women, children and older men – shot them and burned their bodies.

• Between 29 September and 5 October 1944, soldiers of the 16th *SS Panzergrenadier* Division *Reichsführer-SS*, led by *SS-Sturmbannführer* Walter Reder, systematically killed hundreds of civilians in Marzabotto, Grizzana and Monzuno near Bologna in Italy.

• On 17 December 1944, *Kampfgruppe Peiper*, part of the 1st SS Panzer Division, massacred 90 US prisoners of war at Malmedy during the Battle of the Bulge.

The Waffen-SS were often recruited from concentration camp guards. In Eastern Europe, they were used to round up Jews for deportation to death camps. Waffen-SS units were used in the brutal suppression of the Warsaw Uprising and were known for their barbaric reprisals against partisans.

At the Nuremberg Trials in 1946, the Waffen-SS was declared a criminal organization, along with the leadership of the Nazi Party, the SS, the SA, the Gestapo, the High Command of the German armed forces and the *Sicherheitsdienst*, or SD, the Nazi's security force.

Special Operations Executive

The Baker Street irregulars

When France surrendered to Nazi Germany on 22 June 1940, the British government sought to help those people in occupied France who wanted to continue the fight. On 2 July, Hugh Dalton, Britain's Minister of Economic Warfare, said what was needed was 'a new organization to co-ordinate, inspire, control and assist the nationals of the oppressed countries who must themselves be the direct participants'.

O n 16 July 1940, Prime Minister Winston Churchill set up the Special Operations Executive (SOE) with Hugh Dalton at its head. Churchill's orders could not have been more straightforward. He told them: 'Now set Europe ablaze.'

At the height of the Blitz, SOE set up its headquarters at 64 Baker Street in London, giving them their nickname 'the Baker Street irregulars'. Recruits were sent out to training bases across the UK where they were taught the arts of camouflage and disguise, how to derail a train, how to get out of a pair of handcuffs and how to kill with their bare hands. After parachute and survival courses, they were ready to be dropped into occupied Europe.

The Special Operations Executive had diagrams showing how to make and use explosives and other sabotage devices. They also had booklets showing the silhouettes of ships together with the places where mines would prove most effective against them.

SPECIAL EQUIPMENT AND OPPOSITION

Agents were given special equipment, dreamt up by a team at The Frythe, a secluded house near Welwyn Garden City in Hertfordshire, who developed portable radios, explosive devices, booby traps, unusual weapons such as a single-shot pistol disguised as a cigarette – even a submersible canoe called Sleeping Beauty. In the Thatched Barn in North London, a team of ex-propmakers under movie director Elder Wills disguised explosives designed to blow the tyre off an enemy truck as dead rats or cow dung.

Workshops produced abrasive grease that would seize an engine, or put a locomotive out of action. There was a False Documents Section that gave agents bogus identities, providing fake ID cards, ration books and travel documents. Outfitters produced clothes in Continental styles. French cigarettes and other everyday items were provided. No detail was considered too trivial. The slightest slip could give a British agent away. As they were operating behind enemy lines, field agents faced the possibility of capture, torture and execution, so each agent was issued with a suicide pill usually concealed in a button.

There was considerable opposition to the SOE in other branches of the service. The Secret Intelligence Service, MI6, considered it 'amateur, dangerous and bogus',

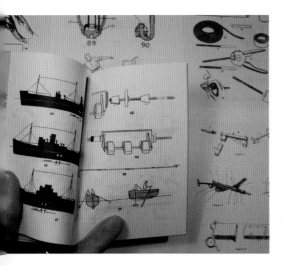

and were concerned that acts such as blowing up bridges would hinder their intelligence-gathering operations. Air Chief Marshal Charles Portal said: 'I think that the dropping of men dressed in civilian clothes for the purpose of attempting to kill members of the opposing forces is not an operation with which the Royal Air Force should be associated.'

The commander-in-chief of Bomber Command, Air Marshal Sir Arthur 'Bomber' Harris, was also opposed to SOE operations, since he did not want his planes to be diverted from the task of carpet-bombing Germany. He was overruled. Likewise, the Royal Navy were unwilling to allow their submarines and motor torpedo boats to be used on SOE operations, so the SOE often resorted to requisitioning fishing boats and caiques.

The aftermath of a train derailment caused by the French Resistance. As well as engaging in acts of sabotage and carrying out assassinations, the French Resistance played a vital role in providing military intelligence to the Allies.

SPECIAL OPERATIONS EXECUTIVE

1940 SOE set up by Winston Churchill

1941 SOE blow up power station in Bordeaux, France

1942 Agents kill Reinhard Heydrich in Prague; blow up Gorgopotamos bridge, Greece

1943 Agents blow up heavy water plant in Norway

1944 SOE organize sabotage and ambush behind German lines during the invasion of Normandy

1946 SOE disbanded

'The disruption of enemy rail communications, the harassing of German road moves and the continual and increasing strain placed on German security services throughout occupied Europe by the organized forces of Resistance, played a very considerable part in our complete and final victory.'

General Dwight D. Eisenhower, May 1945

STRIKING SOME VITAL BLOWS

SOE's first serious blow against the enemy came in June 1941 when agents blew up the Pessac power station in France. The blast crippled work at the U-boat base in Bordeaux and brought the all-electric railways in this region to a total halt. After that, many hundreds more SOE operations were mounted both in Europe and in the Far East after Japan entered the war in 1942.

Each occupied country was assigned to a 'section' within SOE, though more sections were assigned if the country had more than one, often antagonistic, resistance organization. France had six. SOE operated in France, Belgium, the Netherlands, Denmark, Norway, Germany, Italy, Hungary, Czechoslovakia, Poland, Romania, Albania, Yugoslavia, Greece and Southeast Asia.

On 4 June 1942, under the codename 'Operation Anthropoid', SOE agents assassinated SS chief Heinrich Himmler's deputy, Reinhard Heydrich, in Prague. In reprisals, the SS killed 5000 men, women and children in two Czech villages, including the total destruction of Lidice. To avoid similar incidents, SOE then concentrated on carrying out 'invisible sabotage', which left no trace and implicated nobody. In one case, an agent sent a supply train, loaded with tanks, to the wrong destination, using only a forged document.

In Greece on 14 November 1942, SOE agents blew up the Gorgopotamos rail bridge, which carried vital supplies for Rommel's army in North Africa. Then on 16 February 1943, the SOE pulled off what it considered to be its most successful operation of the war. It knocked out the heavy water plant at Vemork in Norway, putting an end to the Nazi programme to build an atomic bomb.

An agent's life was fraught with danger. It was estimated that SOE wireless operators working in occupied France had a life expectancy of just six weeks. The agents had to lug around a short-wave transceiver that weighed 13.6 kilograms (30 lb) and which fitted into a suitcase 0.6 metres (2 ft) long. To send and receive messages from London, they needed a 21-metre (70-ft) aerial. It was estimated that it would take German detector vans around 30 minutes to discover where the transceiver was being used. Where possible, therefore, operators sent and received their radio communications in isolated areas. The agents were also under strict instructions to keep transmissions brief. But because of the need to code and decode messages – and to send and receive them one letter at a time in Morse code – they often had no choice but to overrun the 30 minute time limit.

Women in the SOE

In 1940, SOE contacted the commandant of the First Aid Nursing Yeomanry to provide personnel for the SOE. At first the women were used to produce passports, ration cards and other forged documents needed in occupied Europe. They were also employed to transmit, encode and decode messages to and from agents in the field. However, in April 1942, Churchill gave his approval for women in the SOE to be sent into occupied Europe. Women, it was thought, would be less conspicuous than men. In occupied countries, women went about their business relatively normally, while the Gestapo were suspicious of men on the streets. Women were used as couriers and wireless operators. One woman, Pearl Witherington, took over as leader of the Wrestler Network after senior SOE agent Maurice Southgate was arrested in May 1944. She organized over 1500 members of the Maquis operating behind German lines during the D-Day landings.

Violette Szabo organized resistance operations and provided vital information to the Allies. Captured and interrogated, she was executed in 1945.

Wireless operators were instructed to always spell certain words incorrectly. That way, London could tell if an operator had been captured and a German had taken over. Agents were taught that, when captured, they must try to stay silent for 48 hours, even under torture. In that time all the people working with them were supposed to move house. However, by controlling the wireless traffic of a captured SOE operator, dozens of new agents fell directly into German hands. Most were eventually shot.

D-Day and beyond

SOE made its greatest contribution during the invasion of Normandy in 1944, organizing the French Resistance to sabotage bridges and railways, preventing men and materials getting to the front. One target was the Das Reich Second SS Panzer Division. SOE agents siphoned off all the axle oil from the division's rail transport cars, replacing it with abrasive grease. All of them seized up. Then when Das Reich's armour took to the roads, their columns were ambushed, delaying them or keeping them out in the open while Allied planes wreaked havoc. The Das Reich Division was seven days late reaching the coast. By that time the Allies had established a firm foothold on French soil. SOE also operated in the mountains of Yugoslavia and northern Italy. Under SOE direction, 600 partisans took the surrender of 12,000 German troops in Genoa. But when the war ended, there was no further role for SOE. In January 1946, it was disbanded forever.

Office of Strategic Services
The Jedburgh teams

Before the Second World War, the US had no central intelligence agency. Each branch of the service and government, including the FBI and the Treasury, did its own foreign intelligence gathering. Then the Office of Strategic Services (OSS) – the forerunner of the CIA – was set up. Seeking a more active role, it recruited service personnel. Like Britain's Special Operations Executive, they were trained to organize resistance behind the lines in occupied areas. During the invasion of Western Europe, specialist Jedburgh teams were dropped behind enemy lines.

Members of the OSS, known as Jedburghs, performed acts of sabotage and guerrilla warfare in occupied Europe. Here a team receives operations instructions from a briefing officer in a London flat.

When America entered the Second World War in December, Canadian spymaster William Stephenson, Britain's senior intelligence officer in the US, suggested to President Franklin Delano Roosevelt that the US set up an intelligence organization along British lines. On 13 June 1942, the Office of Strategic Services was set up under William J. 'Wild Bill' Donovan, a veteran of the First World War. Its job was to collect and analyze intelligence for the joint chiefs of staff and undertake operations not assigned to other agencies. It recruited personnel from all branches of the armed forces as well as civilians.

Its military personnel trained, armed and supplied the nationalist forces fighting the Japanese in China and Southeast Asia. These included Mao Tse-tung's Red Army and the Viet Minh under the command of Ho Chi Min in French Indochina. The OSS also recruited German spies, trained agents to work in Germany and Austria, and even spied on the Soviet Union, then America's ally. Its biggest intelligence-gathering exercise operating in Nazi-controlled Europe, known as the Dogwood chain, was run through an office in Istanbul. However, much of the information it produced was found to be unreliable and it was shut down.

In September 1942, OSS Special Operations branch joined the British Special Operations Executive to create a combined office known as SOE/SO in Baker Street, London. They began developing plans for their part in the invasion of Normandy that would take place in June 1944. It was decided to drop three-man teams behind enemy lines to sabotage the railway and communications system, arm and organize the local resistance, supply guides to the landing force, and relay intelligence back to London. Unlike the civilian operatives of SOE, these men would be in uniform. Each team

would consist of two officers – one from the country where they were operating – along with an NCO wireless operator who was supposed to have a passing knowledge of the local language. They would be called Jedburgh teams, after the town of Jedburgh near the border between England and Scotland – the name seems to have been picked at random from a list, since the British avoided giving their operations meaningful names for security reasons.

Behind enemy lines

In March 1943, the Jedburgh concept was tested in a simulation of a breakout from a Normandy beachhead. It was concluded that the teams should be dropped at least 40 miles (66 km) behind enemy lines where they would be most effective running small-scale guerrilla actions against enemy lines of communication. Each army and army group set up a special forces detachment to co-ordinate these guerrilla actions with those of the main invasion force. Naturally, it was necessary to secure French co-operation and Pierre Koenig, head of the French Forces of the Interior, joined SOE/SO.

After about two weeks of paramilitary training in the Scottish Highlands, Jedburghs moved to Milton Hall, nearer London, to continue their training. It included obstacle courses such as these high bars.

TEAM AUGUSTUS

On 15 August 1944, Team Augustus was sent to the Aisne region of northeast France, where it was to assist the local Maquis and serve as an additional communication link to London. Major John H. Bonsall of the US army was the team leader. With him were Captain Jean Delwiche, who was French, and Technical Sergeant Roger E. Cotea, also from the US. Landing near Colonfay, they were taken to a farm near the village of Clary. On 17 August, they radioed SFHQ – Special Forces Headquarters – saying that the reception had gone perfectly. Already the Resistance in the Aisne Department had 1100 armed and trained men, along with a further 4900 unarmed volunteers. Between 21 and 24 August, the Team Augustus sent several reports to London detailing specific targets for the Allied air forces, mostly large German troop columns. There were so many German troops in the area that it was thought unwise for the Maquis to undertake any operations against them. They also reported that the Germans were constructing field fortifications behind the Aisne river, although there were no minefields.

On 28 August, they learned that American tanks were in the area and moved to Soissons where they briefed staff officers of the US Third Armored Division on German defences in the vicinity. They then received orders from SFHQ telling them to try and prevent the enemy destroying the bridges over the River Somme. However, on the night of 30 August,

Between June and September 1944, teams of Jedburghs were flown from Harrington Aerodrome in England (seen here as night falls) and dropped into France to assist the Allied advance from behind German lines.

German troops stopped a horse-drawn cart and found the three occupants. They were in civilian clothes with false French identity cards and were carrying weapons and a radio. The Germans shot the team, leaving the horse, still towing its cart, to return on its own to its stable where armed FFI volunteers were waiting. They found the bodies of Team Augustus the following morning. The three men were buried at the Bareriton-sur-Serre cemetery where a memorial has been erected there in their honour.

In mid-September 1943, OSS and SOE recruited officers and non-commissioned officers who could speak French. Both were to provide enough men to field 35 Jedburgh teams, plus 15 reserve teams – a total of 300 men in 100 teams. The American volunteers arrived in Britain in late December 1943. They were given two weeks psychological testing. Then they were sent on communications courses, practised their marksmanship, received

> *'Officers recruited as leaders and seconds in command should be picked for qualities of leadership and daring, ability to speak and understand French, and all-round physical condition. They should be experienced in handling men, preferably in an active theatre of operations, and be prepared to be parachuted in uniform behind enemy lines and operate on their own for some time. They must have had at least basic military training and preferably have aptitude for small arms weapons.'*

OSS, Jedburgh requirements, 1943

physical training and were taught self-defence by former members of the Shanghai Police. In late January 1944, they trained in parachute jumping through the small hole – known as the Joe hole – cut in the bottom of the fuselage of a bomber. The training was so tough that, of the 55 officers sent to England from the US, 20 dropped out and additional volunteers had to be recruited from the American invasion force already assembling in Britain.

The Jedburghs were then gathered at a training school at Milton Hall, near Peterborough, England. There they were give operational training in guerrilla warfare tactics, demolitions, the use of enemy weapons, map reading, night navigation, agent circuit operations, intelligence, sabotage, escape and evasion, counter-espionage, ambushes, security, the use of couriers and hand-to-hand combat. They also received briefings on the history and organization of the Resistance in France and other European countries. From 31 May to 8 June 1944, they took part in a large-scale exercise in Charnwood Forest, Leicestershire, where the teams rehearsed receiving orders, linking up with Resistance groups and leading attacks against targets designated by radio.

JEDBURGH MISSIONS

The first Jedburgh team was dropped into Brittany in France just before D-Day (6 June 1944). Carried in specially converted bombers, they parachuted in under cover of darkness and were met by the local Maquis or Resistance group. SOE agents, already in place, organized liaison. The Jedburghs provided expertise, advice, military leadership and a vital link between the guerrillas and the Allied command. More importantly, for the guerrillas, the Jedburghs could arrange airdrops of ammunition and arms, and relay messages back to Special Forces headquarters in Britain.

In all, 91 Jedburgh teams operated in 54 French *départements* between June and December 1944. They also operated in Belgium and Holland, where they were less effective since the SOE operation there had been blown after a wireless operator had been captured. Like all Allied forces who operated behind Nazi lines, the Jedburghs were subject to torture and summarily executed, if captured, under Hitler's 'Commando Order', which authorized the summary execution of any commando captured. But as the Jedburghs normally operated in uniform, this constituted a war crime. When the war in Europe was over, there were further Jedburgh operations in the Far East.

OFFICE OF STRATEGIC SERVICES

JUNE 1942 The Office of Strategic Services set up

SEPTEMBER 1942 OSS join SOE in London

MARCH 1943 Simulation of Normandy breakout proves Jedburgh concept

SEPTEMBER 1943 Personnel recruited for Jedburgh teams

DECEMBER 1943 US volunteers arrive in Britain

JANUARY 1944 Training begins

MAY-JUNE 1944 Full-scale exercise takes place in England

JUNE 1944 First Jedburgh teams dropped in France

The Screaming Eagles

101st Airborne in Normandy

The 101st Airborne Division was dubbed the 'Screaming Eagles' for its airborne assault behind the beaches on D-Day. It rose to prominence again during the Battle of the Bulge and the final assault on Germany. Since then it has fought with distinction in Vietnam, the Gulf War, Iraq and Afghanistan.

Soldiers of the 101st Airborne 'Screaming Eagles' disembark from a Chinook helicopter during Operation Swarmer in Iraq, 16 March 2006. Operation Swarmer was a joint US-Iraqi air assault offensive targeting insurgents, near the central city of Samarra – it was the largest air assault in Iraq since the US invasion in 2003.

When the 101st Airborne Division was formed in August 1942 at Camp Claiborne, Louisiana, it was decided that only the toughest would serve. Men were needed who could survive being dropped from an aeroplane behind enemy lines and go on to fight and win. Only one in three men passed the selection, which included rigorous airborne training and a 140-mile (225-km) march to be covered in three days. However, rivalry soon broke out between the division's parachute and glider elements. The paratroopers considered themselves the élite as they received 'parachute pay', while the glider troops, whose duties were just as dangerous, got no extra money.

On its first large-scale manoeuvre in Tennessee on 10 June 1943, the 101st Airborne Division's first commanding officer, Major General William C. Lee, was injured in a glider. He later remarked: 'Next time I'll take a parachute.' The incident gave the glider troops some small measure of satisfaction.

In September 1943, the 101st moved to England to prepare for the Normandy invasion. In February 1944, General Lee suffered a heart attack and was replaced by General Maxwell D. Taylor, who would go on to lead the 101st until the end of the Second World War.

FIRST COMBAT MISSION

On the night of 5 June 1944, the 101st prepared for its first combat operation. Some 6700 soldiers would be dropped behind enemy lines before the main body of the Allied invasion force landed on the beaches. Jumping in the dark before H-Hour, they were to seize positions west of Utah Beach and eliminate the Germans' secondary beach defences. Then they were to capture the causeways and bridges that ran behind the beach, allowing the seaborne forces of the 4th Infantry Division free passage inland.

However, when the planes carrying the 101st reached France, they hit fog and also encountered anti-aircraft fire. The pilots broke formation to avoid collisions. Instead of jumping at the planned 100 miles per hour at 700 feet (160 km/h at 210 m), the 101st found themselves jumping at 200 miles per hour at 300 feet (322 km/h at 91 m). As a result, the division was scattered all over the countryside. Men landed far from their units. Many were killed before they hit the ground. The paratroopers were expecting reinforcements at dawn, when 51 gliders were scheduled to land. However, many of the gliders crashed, killing those on board. A second wave of gliders landing at dusk that day produced even more casualties. Some 1500 men were killed or captured. By the end of the first day, only one in three of the 101st had found their unit. Even those units that had assembled had difficulty in identifying their locations and their objectives.

GLORY AND MEDALS

However, the scattered jump into Normandy confused the German defenders just as much as it confused the 101st, who quickly got the better of the enemy in small unit actions. They captured the four elevated roads leading inland from Utah Beach, made contact with the 4th Infantry Division and secured various key terrain objectives behind the east coast of the Cotentin Peninsula.

General Dwight D. Eisenhower, Supreme Allied Commander Europe during the Second World War, gives a rousing briefing to paratroopers of the 502nd Parachute Infantry Regiment, 101st Airborne Division, at Greenham Common Airfield in England on June 5 1944 – the eve of the D-Day landings. The order of the day was: 'Full victory – nothing else.'

THE SCREAMING EAGLES

AUGUST 1942 The 101st Airborne Division formed

JUNE 1943 First large-scale manoeuvre

SEPTEMBER 1943 The division moves to England

JUNE 1944 The Screaming Eagles land in Normandy

SEPTEMBER 1944 Operation Market Garden

DECEMBER 1944 The 101st holds off the Germans at Bastogne

NOVEMBER 1945 The division deactivated in France

MAY 1954 The 101st is reactivated

1965 The division goes into Vietnam

1972 The 101st is the last US combat division to leave Vietnam

1991 The division leads Gulf War

2001 The 101st joins Operation Enduring Freedom

2003 The Screaming Eagles join Operation Iraqi Freedom

The 101st then turned south towards Carentan, which was key to controlling the peninsula. It was also the vital link between the Utah and Omaha beachheads, and taking it would help prevent the Germans from driving through to the coast and dividing the Allied landings. The Germans there had been ordered to fight to the last man. After heavy fighting, the 101st took Carentan. The division then held the town for two more days under a heavy German counter-attack until reinforcements arrived.

The battle to secure the road into Carentan from the north was so costly it became known as 'Purple Heart Lane'. In one action, the men of the 502nd Regiment were advancing along the causeway with no cover, facing steady fire. When they reached the bridge on the Madeleine river, they ran into a strong enemy position concentrated in an old farmhouse and the adjoining hedgerows. Lieutenant Colonel Robert G. Cole, the battalion commander, called for artillery fire on the position, but it had no effect. Pinned down, he ordered a charge with fixed bayonets. But when Colonel Cole leapt up to lead the charge, not all his men had received the word. Cole continued with the soldiers he had. The Germans withdrew from the farmhouse, and the charging soldiers cleared the hedgerow positions. Colonel Cole was awarded the Medal of Honour for his efforts that day. Unfortunately, he was killed before he received his medal.

Three weeks after landing in Europe, the 101st's mission in Normandy was over. The division was withdrawn from the lines in late June and sailed back to England on landing craft in July. By then one in four of the men had been killed or wounded.

THE PUSH INTO GERMANY

The 101st Airborne Division was back in action in September 1944 when it jumped into Holland during Operation Market Garden, the ill-fated race for the German border. The division's mission was to seize what became knows as 'Hell's Highway' – a section of road running north to the Rhine – so Allied tanks could advance into Germany. Six hundred gliders brought in half the division. The remainder landed by parachute. In two days, the 101st had completed its mission. However, British armour failed to reach Arnhem in time to relieve the paratroopers there.

During the Battle of the Bulge in December 1944, over 12,000 men of the 101st were sent south, arriving in the town of Bastogne just ahead of the Germans, who surrounded the town. The division was cut off, and it became a sitting target for German artillery. Because they had been deployed in haste, many of the men did not have clothing suitable for the freezing conditions.

For five days the 101st withstood German attacks without reinforcements or supplies. Then two German officers arrived at the American headquarters with a letter demanding that the 101st surrender. Their commander General Anthony McAuliffe gave a famous one-word reply – 'Nuts'. The division held out for another five days until relieved by General Patton's 3rd Army on 26 December.

The 101st continued to fight, pushing the Germans back into Germany itself and eventually ending up in Berchtesgaden where Hitler had his fortified residence known as 'The Eagle's Nest'. The war was over before the 101st could be sent to the Pacific. The division was stood down in France in November 1945. Most of the survivors had been discharged before they could take part in the victory parade in New York in 1946.

GENERAL ORDER NUMBER FIVE

'The 101st Airborne Division, activated at Camp Claiborne, Louisiana, has no history, but it has a rendezvous with destiny. Like the early American pioneers whose invincible courage was the foundation stone of this nation, we have broken with the past and its traditions in order to establish our claim to the future. Due to the nature of our armament, and the tactics in which we shall perfect ourselves, we shall be called upon to carry out operations of far-reaching military importance and we shall habitually go into action when the need is immediate and extreme. Let me call your attention to the fact that our badge is the great American eagle. This is a fitting emblem for a division that will crush its enemies by falling upon them like a thunderbolt from the skies. The history we shall make, the record of high achievement we hope to write in the annals of the American Army and the American people, depends wholly and completely on the men of this division. Each individual, each officer and each enlisted man, must therefore regard himself as a necessary part of a complex and powerful instrument for the overcoming of the enemies of the nation. Each, in his own job, must realize that he is not only a means, but an indispensable means for obtaining the goal of victory. It is, therefore, not too much to say that the future itself, in whose moulding we expect to have our share, is in the hands of the soldiers of the 101st Airborne Division.'

MAJOR GENERAL WILLIAM C. LEE, 19 AUGUST 1942

101st Airborne Division shoulder sleeve insignia (the 'Screaming Eagle'), depicts the head of the bald eagle. Many different companies made screaming eagle patches for the US government in the Second World War, each having its own minor sub-variations.

DIVISION REACTIVATED

In May 1954, the 101st was reactivated as a training unit at Fort Jackson, South Carolina, then reorganized as a combat division at Fort Campbell, Kentucky. In 1965, the division was sent to Vietnam. In almost seven years of combat in Vietnam, elements of the 101st participated in 15 campaigns. But now, however, it deployed by helicopter instead of parachute and glider. In 1972, the 101st was the last US combat division to leave Vietnam. It had suffered twice as many casualties in Vietnam as it had in the Second World War.

In January 1991, the 101st is thought to have fired the first shot in the Gulf War. In 2001, it went into Afghanistan as part of Operation Enduring Freedom and, in 2003, it joined Operation Iraqi Freedom. It returned to Iraq for a second tour in 2005. As an élite fighting force, it is in action to this day.

'I only spent five days in Normandy before being seriously wounded, but it was five days of my life that I can never forget.'

PRIVATE DOUG GARRETT OF B/502 WRITING ABOUT HIS FIRST COMBAT IN NORMANDY, 1944

The Old Breed

The 1st Marine Division

The 1st Marine Division was formed in the run-up to the Second World War and fought its way across the Pacific in a series of victorious, though costly, engagements. The troops' expertise in amphibious landings was again needed in the Korean War. The 1st Marine Division fought for six years in Vietnam. Then in the Middle East it was in the front line in Desert Storm and Operation Iraqi Freedom.

A Marine of the 1st Marine Division shouts instructions to soldiers of the Iraqi Civil Defense Corps during a firefight while on a joint patrol in Nasir Waal Salaam, Iraq, on 5 June 2004. During 2004, the 1st Marine Division was involved in two battles in the Iraqi insurgency stronghold of Fallujah.

The first of the regiments that made up the 1st Marine Division – the 1st Marine Regiment – was formed in Guantanamo Bay, Cuba, on 8 March 1911 and was in action throughout the Caribbean over the next seven years. The 10th Marines was formed in Quantico, Virginia, on 25 April 1914 as an artillery battalion. The 5th was formed in Vera Cruz, Mexico, on 13 July 1914 and saw action in 15 major engagements in the First World War. The 7th was formed in Philadelphia on 11 August 1917 and spent the war in Cuba, while the 11th was formed as a light artillery regiment in Quantico on 3 January 1918 and was sent to France. The 7th and the 10th were decommissioned between the wars, but they were recommissioned in the run-up to the Second World War.

On 1 February 1941, the 1st Marine Division was activated on board the battleship USS *Texas*. To the earlier regiments were added the 1st Reconnaissance Battalion, 1st and 3rd Light Armoured Reconnaissance Battalions, 1st Tank Battalion and 3rd Assault Amphibian Battalion, giving a combat-ready force of more than 22,000 men. On 7 August 1942, the 1st Marine Regiment landed on the Japanese-occupied island of Guadalcanal in the first major land engagement of the Pacific War. As the fighting intensified, the whole division would join in the campaign in the Solomon Islands until it was relieved by the Americal Division on 9 December 1942. By then, the division had lost 650 killed, 1278 wounded and 31 missing with a further 8580 suffering from malaria. However, it had won the first of the Presidential Unit Citations it was to earn during the Second World War.

During 1943 and 1944, the division would see action during Operation Cartwheel, the codename for the campaigns in Eastern New Guinea and New Britain. It came ashore at the Battle of Cape Gloucester on 26 December 1943, taking the airstrip there four days later, and fought on New Britain until February 1944 at such places as Suicide Creek and Ajar Ridge. During the campaign, the division lost 310 killed and 1083 wounded. Afterwards, it was sent to Pavuvu in the Russell Islands for rest and re-equipping.

PELELIU AND OKINAWA

The division won its second Presidential Unit Citation during the Battle of Peleliu. The division's commander, Major General William H. Rupertus, predicted the fighting would be 'tough but short'. He said: 'It'll be over in three of four days – a fight like Tarawa. Rough but fast. Then we can go back to a rest area.' He was wrong. The first week of the battle alone cost the division 3946 casualties as they secured the key airfield sites. The division fought on Peleliu for one month before being relieved, suffering over 6500 casualties in all – over a third of the division's manpower. It was out of action until the landings on Okinawa on 1 April 1945, the last American land campaign of the Second World War, and fought until the island was secured on 21 June 1945. By then it had lost 1155 killed in action and won its

American Marines coming ashore from landing craft at Guadalcanal on 5 September 1942. The island was the scene of fierce fighting between Allied and Japanese forces. Eventually, the Japanese were outnumbered and defeated there.

GUADALCANAL

On 6 July 1942, the Japanese had landed on the island of Guadalcanal, a British protectorate in the Solomon Islands, and began building an airfield there. In the Allies' first major offensive in the Pacific, 6000 marines made an amphibious landing on 7 August, taking the 2000 Japanese defenders by surprise. Both sides then began reinforcing, and a bitter fight in the island's jungles ensued. US forces quickly finished the airfield, naming it Henderson Field after a marine aviator killed at the Battle of Midway. Marine, army, navy and Allied aircraft defended the airfield and threatened any Japanese ships that ventured into the vicinity during daylight hours. However, at night, Japanese naval forces were able to shell the airfield and land reinforcements and supplies. The fast ships used to make these runs became known as the Tokyo Express. By October, some 36,000 Japanese troops were surrounding the marines'

The insignia of the 1st Marine Division, celebrating the division's victory over the Japanese forces at the battle of Guadalcanal.

small enclave, but their attempts to overwhelm the perimeter failed. Six separate naval engagements were fought off Guadalcanal. America lost eight cruisers, two heavy cruisers and 14 destroyers, while the Japanese lost two battleships, four cruisers, one light carrier, 11 destroyers and six submarines. So many ships sank that the surrounding waters were referred to as Ironbottom Sound. However, America won the battle of supply. By January 1943, there were 44,000 US troops on the island. Badly outnumbered and starved of food and ammunition, the Japanese were forced to withdraw their remaining 12,000 men in early February. They had lost 24,000 men killed. The US lost 1592 killed and 4200 wounded – though more perished from malaria and other diseases.

third Presidential Unit Citation. After the surrender of Japan, it was sent as an occupation force to North China, where it first encountered the Chinese Communists.

By the time the Korean War broke out in June 1950, the division had become known as 'The Old Breed'. Because of the division's expertise in amphibious landings, it was chosen to join General MacArthur's landing at Inchon on 15 September 1950. After the liberation of Seoul, the 1st Marine Division was put back aboard ships and landed on the eastern side of the Wonsan Peninsula. As it moved north towards the Yalu River, the division was confronted by seven Chinese divisions on 27 November 1950.

'I would pick either Midway or our retreat from Guadalcanal as the turning point, after which I was certain there was no chance of success.'

ADMIRAL YONAI, JAPANESE NAVY MINISTER, 1945

FROZEN CHOSIN

Fighting in the mountains around the Chosin Reservoir, the Old Breed lost over 900 killed and 3500 wounded, and suffered over 6500 non-battle casualties – mostly from frostbite. However, the Chinese 9th Army suffered more than 37,500 casualties trying to block the 1st Marine Division's march out of 'Frozen Chosin'. In these battles, and those that followed between April and September, the division earned its fourth, fifth and sixth Presidential Unit Citations. During the Korean War, the division lost 4004 dead and 25,864 wounded.

In 1962, the 2nd Battalion, 1st Marines were sent to Guantanamo Bay for two months during the Cuban Missile Crisis, when US president John F. Kennedy demanded the removal of Russian missiles from Cuba. More than 11,000 men of the 5th Marine Expeditionary Brigade participated in the naval blockade which forced the withdrawal of the missiles.

VIETNAM AND IRAQ

In 1965, the 7th Marine Regiment participated in the first major engagements for American ground troops in South Vietnam. By March 1966, the 1st Marine Division headquarters were established at Chu Lai. By June, the entire division was in South Vietnam. Between March 1966 and May 1967, it conducted 44 operations. During the 1968 Tet Offensive, the division was involved in fierce fighting, successfully beating back the enemy. By the time it withdrew in 1971, the 1st Marine Division had won its seventh and eighth Presidential Unit Citations.

In 1990, the division was sent to Saudi Arabia as the nucleus of Desert Shield. In Desert Storm, it helped smash the Iraqi army and liberate Kuwait. It returned to Iraq in 2003 as the land component of the 1st Marine Expeditionary Force that took the Rumaylah oil fields. After making a feint towards Basra, it took An Nasiriyah, fighting its way on to Baghdad and north to Tikrit, the home town of Saddam Hussein.

Troops and a tank of the 1st Marine Division move through snow-covered communist Chinese lines during the Allies' successful breakout from the Chosin Reservoir in North Korea in 1950. This feat was achieved despite them being hugely outnumbered.

THE OLD BREED

FEBRUARY 1941 The 1st Marine Division formed

AUGUST 1942 Lands on Guadalcanal

1943–4 Sees action during Operation Cartwheel on Eastern New Guinea and New Britain

SEPTEMBER 1944 Lands on Peleliu in the Caroline Islands

APRIL 1945 Lands on Okinawa

SEPTEMBER 1950 Lands at Inchon

NOVEMBER 1950 Defeats seven Chinese divisions around Chosin

AUGUST 1965 Arrives in Vietnam

MARCH 1966 Division headquarters established at Chu Lai

JUNE 1966 Entire division in Vietnam

JANUARY 1968 Fights in Tet Offensive

AUGUST 1990 Joins Desert Shield

JANUARY 1991 Leads Desert Storm

MARCH 2003 Joins Operation Iraqi Freedom

The US Army Rangers

'Rangers lead the way'

Units using Ranger tactics and designated as Rangers were employed on the American frontier as early as 1670. A band of Rangers under Captain Benjamin Church brought the Indian conflict known as 'King Phillip's War' to a conclusion in 1676. Nearly 350 years later, the Rangers are still an élite unit.

I n 1756, Major Robert Rogers recruited nine companies of Rangers to fight alongside British redcoats during the French and Indian War of 1754–63. Rogers was the first to introduce the methods of frontiersmen into a permanent fighting force. However, during the War of Independence he sided with the British.

In 1777, George Washington formed his own 'Corps of Rangers', also known as the Continental Rifles. British General John Burgoyne said they were: 'the most famous corps of the Continental Army, all of them crack shots.' Then Thomas Knowlton organized a reconnaissance force of some 150 hand-picked men from New England, known as 'Knowlton's Rangers' – the Special Forces of their day.

In the Civil War, Confederate Colonel John Singleton Mosby employed raiding parties of 20 to 50 men. One one occasion, nine Mosby's Rangers routed an entire Union regiment. Rangers under Colonel Turner Ashby played a vital role during Jackson's Shenandoah Valley Campaign of 1862. On the Union side, disaffected Virginians formed the Loudoun Rangers who captured Longstreet's ammunition train, and even took on Mosby's force.

THE RANGERS REACTIVATED

The Rangers were resurrected in the Second World War with the activation of the 1st US Army Ranger Battalion in Northern Ireland on 19 June 1942 under Captain – soon Major – William Darby. The Rangers were then sent to the British Commando Training Centre in Scotland. Of the 600 volunteers, 500 passed Commando training.

In August 1942, five officers and 44 enlisted men took part in the disastrous Dieppe Raid. They were the first US ground troops to see action in occupied Europe. Three Rangers were killed and several were captured. The 1st Ranger Battalion then spearheaded the US landings in North Africa. In Algeria they made a night landing, silenced two gun batteries and opened the way for the 1st Infantry Division to capture Oran. On 31 March 1943, the Rangers led General Patton's drive to capture the heights of El Guettar with a 12-mile (19-km) night march across mountainous terrain. At dawn they swooped on the Italians from the rear, clearing the pass and capturing 200 prisoners.

The 3rd and 4th Ranger Battalions were formed from volunteers in North Africa. The three battalions then led the landings in south Sicily. They were the first ashore at Salerno

Troops in a landing craft approach Omaha Beach on D-Day. The 2nd Ranger Battalion was tasked with the vital mission of destroying German gun emplacements that could have decimated Allied troops attempting to come ashore. The Rangers brought into use the tactics for which the regiment was created – fast deployment of men and the application of special skills against both conventional and special operations targets.

in the invasion of Italy. Seizing the strategic heights at Chinuzi Pass, they fought off eight German counter-attacks. Then they joined the bitter winter mountain fighting near San Pietro, Venafro and Cassino.

ANNIHILATION AT ANZIO

The 6615th Ranger Force spearheaded the night landings at Anzio on 22 January 1944, capturing two gun batteries and seizing the port. A week later, the 1st and 3rd Battalions infiltrated 5 miles (8 km) behind the German lines, while the 4th fought to clear the road towards Cisterna. But the Germans had reinforced the night before. The Rangers were surrounded and outnumbered, and soon ammunition was running low.

THE RANGER'S CREED

Recognizing that I volunteered as a Ranger, fully knowing the hazards of my chosen profession, I will always endeavour to uphold the prestige, honour and high esprit de corps of the Rangers.

Acknowledging the fact that a Ranger is a more élite soldier who arrives at the cutting edge of battle by land, sea or air, I accept the fact that as a Ranger my country expects me to move further, faster and fight harder than any other soldier.

Never shall I fail my comrades. I will always keep myself mentally alert, physically strong and morally straight, and I will shoulder more than my share of the task whatever it may be, one hundred percent and then some.

Gallantly will I show the world that I am a specially selected and well trained soldier. My courtesy to superior officers, neatness of dress and care of equipment shall set the example for others to follow.

Energetically will I meet the enemies of my country. I shall defeat them on the field of battle for I am better trained and will fight with all my might. Surrender is not a Ranger word. I will never leave a fallen comrade to fall into the hands of the enemy and under no circumstances will I ever embarrass my country.

Readily will I display the intestinal fortitude required to fight on to the Ranger objective and complete the mission, though I be the lone survivor.

However, intelligence later revealed they had thwarted a planned German counter-attack intended to push the Allies into the sea.

All three battalions had been virtually destroyed and disbanded. However, two more had been formed in the United States. The 2nd Ranger Battalion carried out the most dangerous mission of the Normandy landings on 6 June 1944. Three companies assaulted the cliffs of Point du Hoc overlooking Omaha Beach while under intense machine-gun, mortar and artillery fire. They then succeeded in destroying a large gun battery that could have wreaked havoc on the Allied landing fleets offshore.

For two days and nights they fought without relief until the other new Ranger battalion, the 5th, linked up with them. It had landed on Omaha Beach with three companies of the 2nd Battalion and were pinned down by murderous crossfire and mortars from the heights above. It was there that General Norman D. Cota gave the now famous order that has become the motto of the modern-day 75th Ranger Regiment: 'Rangers lead the way.'

The 5th, along with A and B Companies of the 2nd, broke through the German defences and opened a breach for others to follow. Meanwhile, due to rough seas, C Company landed west of Vierville. They suffered 50 percent casualties during the landing, but still scaled a 27-metre (90-ft) cliff using ropes and bayonets to knock out an enemy position that was sweeping the beach with deadly fire.

The Rangers went on to distinguish themselves in the hard-fought battle of Brest. The 5th fought in the Battle of the Bulge and Huertgen Forest, while the 2nd fought through the central Europe campaign and won commendations for its actions in the battle of Hill 400. The 2nd and 5th were deactivated in 1945.

RANGERS IN THE PACIFIC

The 6th Ranger Battalion was activated at Port Moresby, New Guinea, in September 1944. It was the first American fighting force to return to the Philippines, destroying the coastal defences on the islands off Leyte, three days before the main landing. It landed on Luzon, making behind-the-lines raids. On 30 January 1944, C Company, supported by a platoon from F Company, struck 30 miles (38 km) behind enemy lines and rescued some 500 emaciated and ailing prisoners of war, survivors of the Bataan Death March. The Rangers killed over 200 of the garrison and, carrying prisoners on their backs, evaded two Japanese regiments to reach the safety of American lines. After the capture of Manila and Aparri, the 6th was to spearhead the invasion of Japan. But the war was over and the unit deactivated.

With the outbreak of war in Korea in June 1950, the all-white 4th Ranger Company and the all-black 2nd Ranger Infantry Company (Airborne) were formed – the US army was still racially segregated at this time. Training included amphibious and airborne operations – including low-level night parachute jumps – demolition, sabotage, close combat, and the use of foreign maps and weapons.

In the winter of 1950 and the spring of 1951, more Ranger companies were attached to infantry divisions in Korea, performing their duties in front of the lines. The 1st Ranger Infantry Company (Airborne) began with a daring night raid 9 miles (14 km) behind enemy lines, destroying the headquarters of the 12th North Korean Division. The 1st was in the middle of the first mass assault by the Chinese. In the ensuing bloodbath, the communists suffered 10,000 casualties.

The 2nd and 4th Ranger Companies made a combat jump, landing behind enemy lines north of the 38th parallel. The 2nd plugged a critical gap, while the 3rd earned the motto 'Die, Bastard, Die!' The 4th Ranger Company executed an amphibious assault on the Hwachon Dam and the 5th, attached to the 25th Infantry Division, absorbed the onslaught of four Chinese armies totalling 125,000 men. To hold the line, Ranger sergeants were put in command of infantry units.

The 8th Ranger Infantry Company (Airborne) earned their nickname the 'Devils' when A 33-man platoon fought a between-the-lines battle with two Chinese reconnaissance companies. Seventy Chinese were killed. The Rangers suffered two dead and three wounded, all of whom were brought back to friendly lines.

Some of the members of the US Army's 6th Ranger Battalion, led by Lieutenant John F. Murphy (centre), who took part in a daring raid on Cabanatuan prison camp to rescue American and Filipino prisoners held there.

'The Ranger battalion is to be an élite, light, and most proficient infantry battalion in the world; a battalion that can do things with its hands and weapons better than anyone. The battalion will not contain any 'hoodlums' or 'brigands' and if the battalion is formed of such persons, it will be disbanded. Wherever the battalion goes, it will be apparent that it is the best.'

GENERAL CREIGHTON ABRAMS, 1973, AUTHORIZING THE FIRST BATTALION-SIZED RANGER UNIT, ACTIVATED 1974

Merrill's Marauders

5307th Composite Unit (Provisional)

Merrill's Marauders was the name given to Lieutenant Colonel Frank D.
Merrill's 3,000-man force that fought the Japanese in the jungles of Burma,
beating them in five major battles as well as in 30 smaller skirmishes. One of
the Marauders' greatest feats was their march of 65 miles (105 km) through
thick Burmese jungle to capture the airfield at Myitkyina. This feat would be an
inspiration to US soldiers when they returned to the jungles of Asia some
20 years later during the Vietnam War.

*Frank D. Merrill, commander
of Merrill's Marauders. The
special forces unit enjoyed the
rare distinction of having each
soldier awarded the Bronze
Star in recognition of their
achievements during the Second
World War.*

At the Quebec Conference of August 1943, Franklin D. Roosevelt, Winston Churchill
and other Allied leaders conceived the idea of having an American ground unit
spearhead the Chinese army, another ally, on long-range penetration missions behind enemy
lines in Burma. Its goal would be the destruction of Japanese communications and supply
lines and generally to play havoc with enemy forces while an attempt was made to
reopen the Burma Road, the Allied supply route into China.

A presidential call for volunteers for 'a dangerous and
hazardous mission' was issued, and some 2900 American
soldiers responded to the call. Officially designated as the
5307th Composite Unit (Provisional) and codenamed
'Galahad', the unit later became popularly known as
Merrill's Marauders, after its leader, Frank D.
Merrill. Marauder volunteers came from a variety
of theatres of operation. Some came from stateside
cadres; some from the jungles of Panama and
Trinidad; and the remainder were battle-
hardened veterans of Guadalcanal, Solomon
Island and New Guinea campaigns. In
India some Signal Corps and Air Corps
personnel were added, along with pack
troops with mules. They were organized
into six 400-man combat teams, two to
each battalion, colour-coded Red, White,
Blue, Green, Orange and Khaki.

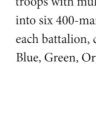

OPERATIONS IN BURMA

After preliminary training by British general Charles Orde Wingate in great secrecy in the jungles of India, about 250 men were detached to form a rear echelon headquarters that remained behind in India to organize the vital air-drop co-ordination between the Air Transport Command and the six Marauder combat teams. The other 2750 Marauders then began their march up the Ledo Road that led from India over the outlying ranges of the Himalayas into Burma. The Marauders walked over 1000 miles (1609 km) through dense jungle, carrying their own food rations and fighting as they went. With no tanks or heavy artillery to support them, and vastly outnumbered, they defeated the veteran soldiers of the Japanese 8th Division that had conquered Malaya and Singapore.

Always moving to the rear of the Japanese main forces, they completely disrupted enemy supply and communication lines. Near Walawbum on the Chindwin river, they cut off the Japanese rearguard, killing between 400 and 500 of them and severing the Japanese supply lines up the Hukawng Valley. By then the Marauders had already lost 550 men.

Merrill's Marauders march through a jungle stream in North Burma. In this operation they were fighting alongside American-trained Chinese troops to drive the Japanese from the Ledo Road, built as an alternative supply route to the Burma Road into China.

In April 1944, General 'Vinegar Joe' Stilwell, US commander of the Chinese forces in Burma, ordered Merrill's men to take up a blocking position at Nhpum Ga. Ill-equipped for such a task, the Marauders found themselves surrounded, but by co-ordinated action managed to break out, killing 400 of the enemy at a cost of 57 dead, 302 wounded and 379 incapacitated due to illness and exhaustion. They also lost 75 of their 200 mules.

After an outbreak of amoebic dysentery, the Marauders were down to 1300 men when they began a 65-mile (105-km) trek over the 1830-metre (6000-ft) Kumon Mountains to Myitkyina, on 17 May 1944. American intelligence put the number of defenders in Myitkyina at around 1000. In fact, there were 4600. Meanwhile, the Japanese overestimated the number of attackers, due to the speed and ferocity of their assaults. Medical staff who had moved up to tend the wounded said:

'Many of them were seriously ill and they were so tired, dirty, and hungry that they looked more dead than alive. They suffered from exhaustion, malnutrition, typhus, malaria, amoebic dysentery, jungle sores and many other diseases resulting from months of hardship in the tropical jungle.'

Nevertheless, on 3 August 1944, Myitkyina fell. Only 600 of the Japanese escaped and 187 were taken prisoner. The Marauders lost 272 killed, 955 wounded and 980 evacuated due to sickness. For the action, they won a Distinguished Unit Citation.

BEHIND THE LINES IN THE PHILIPPINES

In the Second World War, there were other US irregular units, led by idiosyncratic and charismatic individuals, that fought alongside the main formations. In the Pacific, Lieutenant-General Walter Krueger, a native of San Antonio, set up a small élite volunteer force called Alamo Scouts. Famously, the Scouts led American Rangers and Filipino guerrillas in an attack on a Japanese prison camp at Cabanatuan on Luzon, freeing all 511 of the Allied prisoners held there and returning them to American lines. Never numbering more than 70 men, the Alamo Scouts earned 44 Silver Stars, 33 Bronze Stars and four Soldier's Medals. In just under 80 dangerous missions, they never lost a man in action.

A number of US Army officers also conducted their own guerrilla operations behind enemy lines in the Philippines. Colonel Russell Volckmann, who would later play an important role in the formation of the Green Berets, escaped when Bataan fell in 1942, took to the hills and formed a Filipino guerrilla band in northern Luzon. By 1945, he had five regiments under his command. When US forces returned to Luzon, Volckmann and his band had already cleared the Japanese from a large portion of northwestern Luzon's mountains. Then, with air support, they swept along the western and northern coasts.

MERRILL'S MARAUDERS

AUGUST 1943 Proposal made for a US ground unit to be sent to Burma

SEPTEMBER 1943 Unit organized

OCTOBER 1943 5307th Composite Unit (Provisional) sent to India to be trained by General Orde Wingate, commander of the Chindits

JANUARY 1944 Marauders organized as light infantry assault units

FEBRUARY 1944 Marauders begin their march into Burma

APRIL 1944 Ordered to take up conventional blocking position at Nhpum Ga

MAY 1944 Deploy for attack on Myitkyina

AUGUST 1944 Myitkyina falls; Marauders disbanded

Members of Merrill's Marauders are decorated with the Distinguished Unit Citation by US General 'Vinegar Joe' Stilwell after the capture of Myitkyina in August 1944.

> ## FIGHTING IN THE JUNGLES OF BURMA
>
> *'By now my dysentery was so violent I was draining blood. Every one of the men was sick from one cause or another. My shoulders were worn raw from the pack straps, and I left the pack behind ... The boys with me weren't in much better shape ... A scout moving ahead suddenly held his rifle high in the air. That meant Enemy sighted ... Then at last we saw them, coming down the railroad four abreast ... The gunner crouched low over his tommy-gun and tightened down. Then the gun spoke. Down flopped a half-dozen Japs, then another half dozen. The [Japanese] column spewed from their marching formation into the bush. We grabbed up the gun and slid back into the jungle. Sometimes staggering, sometimes running, sometimes dragging, I made it back to camp. I was so sick I didn't care whether the Japs broke through or not; so sick I didn't worry any more about letting the colonel down. All I wanted was unconsciousness.'*
>
> CAPTAIN FRED O. LYONS, MERRILL'S MARAUDERS, 1945

Captain Wendell Fertig, a reservist, also raised his own guerrilla force of Filipinos, warlike tribes, escaped prisoners of war and men who refused to surrender. His USFIP – United States Forces in the Philippines – eventually totalled 40,000 men. Between 1942 and 1944, USFIP conducted numerous raids against the Japanese occupation forces on Mindanao, capturing supplies and harassing the enemy. To inspire faith in his Filipino followers he promoted himself to Brigadier-General, a move that did not endear him to General MacArthur. Shortly before the return of MacArthur, the Japanese had 150,000 men trying to find Fertig. His guerrilla force took part in the Battle of Mindanao, which ended the Japanese hold on the island. A week after the fall of Myitkyina, the survivors of Merrill's Marauders were consolidated with the 475th Infantry.

THE MARAUDERS' LEGACY

On 21 June 1954, the 475th was redesignated the 75th Infantry. During the Vietnam War, they became the 75th Ranger Regiment. In 1974, they became a new Ranger battalion which served in the invasion of Grenada in 1983 and Panama in 1989. Since then, they have seen action in Desert Storm and the 'Black Hawk Down' incident in Mogadishu, Operation Enduring Freedom in Afghanistan and Operation Iraqi Freedom, and are trained as a rapid-reaction force in the 'War on Terror'.

> *'The unit must display such gallantry, determination, and esprit de corps in accomplishing its mission under extremely difficult and hazardous conditions as to set it apart and above other units participating in the same campaign.'*
>
> DISTINGUISHED UNIT CITATION, 1944

The Devil's Brigade

The 1st Special Service Force

The Devil's Brigade was known formally as the 1st Special Service Force (1SSF). It was a joint American-Canadian unit created on 9 July 1942 at Fort William Henry Harrison, Montana. Parachute-trained, the Devil's Brigade saw most of its action in Italy, but it also fought in southern France. Its forte was close-quarter combat against numerically superior forces.

RIGHT *Remote, mountainous territory, such as here, where US forces are seen marching, was exactly the kind of arduous terrain in which the Devil's Brigade was designed to operate.*

BELOW *Troops of the 1st Special Service Force are briefed before setting out on a patrol at Anzio, Italy. It was at Anzio, following the 1SSF's aggressive raids on enemy positions, that the Germans first dubbed them 'the Devil's Brigade'.*

The idea for the unit initially came from a British spymaster and inventor named Geoffrey Pyke. He planned to create a small force of commandos to sabotage oil fields in Romania, hydroelectric plants in Italy and heavy water plants in Norway. He even developed a tracked troop carrier to transport commandos quickly across the snow. However, the British commandos were overburdened with other military commitments at the time, so the idea was handed to the US Army.

Initially a winter warfare unit was to have been made up of Americans, Canadians and Norwegians, but no suitable Norwegians were available. Its commanding officer, Lieutenant Colonel Robert T. Frederick, advertised for personnel at army posts. He promised 'vigorous training, hazardous duty'. He asked for men who had previously been hunters, game wardens, forest rangers and lumberjacks – people already inured to the cold – and he called his new unit the 1st Special Service Force. They mustered at Fort William Henry Harrison in Helena, Montana, in July 1942. Their shoulder badge was a red spearhead with USA embroidered horizontally and Canada vertically.

Although the 1SSF was the only dual-national Allied unit during the Second World War, there was little friction between the Americans and Canadians. In the original recruitment, Canadians formed just one-third of the unit's strength, but they provided a disproportionate number of the officers. Most of the senior appointments – company, battalion and regimental commanders – were, at least initially, Canadians. Canada also established a special depot to provide trained replacements.

AT THE DOUBLE

Training was arduous. Recruits were taught parachuting, skiing and mountain climbing. Everything was done 'at the double' and their physical conditioning was brought to a peak by calisthenics, obstacle courses and long marches with 45-kilogram (100-lb) packs. Each man learned how to handle explosives and to use every weapon in the Force's extensive arsenal. The 1SSF's weapon of choice was the M1941 Johnson machine gun and V-42 combat knife that was designed

by Colonel Frederick and made exclusively for the Force. They were also taught how to use captured enemy weapons, along with hand-to-hand combat and night fighting. These specialized skills were necessary as they were used as shock troops, raiding strategic positions and often parachuting behind enemy lines. Men who did not make the grade were quickly returned to their original units.

As SOE (Special Operations Executive) had already knocked out the heavy water plant in Norway, on 10 July 1943, 1SSF sailed for the Aleutians where their specialist training in harsh conditions was to be put to the test as part of the invasion force for the island of Kiska. They were expecting a fierce fight after the ferocious defence the Japanese had put up on neighbouring Attu, but when they arrived on Kiska they found that the Japanese had left.

THE TAKING OF MONTE LA DEFENSA

In November 1943, the 1SSF arrived in Naples and quickly established its reputation, taking a seemingly impregnable enemy stronghold on the Monte la Defensa that had already cost many British and American lives in failed attempts to dislodge the enemy. The Germans' strategic fortress was perched on top of a mountain, surrounded by sheer cliffs. At night, in the depths of winter, 1SSF scaled the cliffs and caught the enemy by surprise. It went on to attack the nearby Monte la Remetana on 6 December 1943, then Monte Sammurco and Monte Vischiataro, before being relieved in early January 1944. In one month's fighting it had suffered 77 percent casualties, including many cases of frostbite and exposure. Any other unit that had suffered such devastating casualties would have been unfit for further duty for some time. The 1SSF were back in action within a month.

The survivors were sent to Anzio to take over from the Rangers after their catastrophic losses at Cisterna. Many of the casualties managed to get themselves out of hospital to join in. Colonel Frederick had been a classmate of the Rangers' commanding officer Colonel Darby, and the surviving Rangers were seconded into the Brigade. The 1SSF was assigned a sector that should have been held by a division with five times as many men. The 1SSF went on the offensive. Their aggressive patrolling forced the Germans to withdraw, and this is where they earned their nickname 'the Devil's Brigade'. It is said that they captured a German officer's diary which called them *Die schwarzen Teufel* – 'the Black Devils' – as they often attacked at night with blackened faces. Enemy morale was further undermined when the 1SSF began leaving cards on the bodies of dead Germans that carried the red spearhead and the words *'Das Dicke Ende kommt noch'* – 'The worse is yet to come.'

FIRST INTO ROME

The 1SSF led the breakout from Anzio, then went behind enemy lines to take seven bridges around Rome before the enemy could destroy them. On the night of 4 June 1944, they were among the first Allied troops into Rome. This was all the more remarkable as they had never officially been issued with vehicles – apart from Pyke's snowmobile that never left Montana. By the time the 1SSF reached Rome, it had more vehicles than a unit twice its size, mostly as the result of 'midnight requisitions'. After securing the bridges across the Tiber, they drove on northwards in pursuit of the retreating Germans.

On 14 August 1944, elements of the Force captured the three fortified islands of Îles d'Hyères, in preparation for Operation Dragoon, the Allied invasion of southern France.

THE DEVIL'S BRIGADE

JULY 1942 1st Special Service Force created at Fort William Henry Harrison, Montana

JULY 1943 1SSF ships out to the Aleutian Islands

NOVEMBER 1943 1SSF lands in Naples

DECEMBER 1943 1SSF takes Monte la Defensa

FEBRUARY 1944 1SSF lands at Anzio

MAY 1944 Devil's Brigade leads the breakout from the beachhead at Anzio

JUNE 1944 Devil's Brigade among the first Allied troops into Rome

AUGUST 1944 Devil's Brigade captures Îles d'Hyères in preparation for Operation Dragoon

DECEMBER 1944 1SSF disbanded

THE V-42 STILETTO

Designed by Lieutenant Colonel Robert T. Frederick, the V-42 Stiletto was the trademark weapon of the Devil's Brigade. It had a sharp, narrow 18-centimetre (7-inch) blade and a 14-centimetre (5.5-inch handle) with a pointed metal end for cracking skulls. Troops reinforced the end of the leather sheath with metal. This was to prevent the sharp tip penetrating the leather and cutting them. The sheath was worn low on the leg so the knife could be drawn easily. In the field, the Devil's Brigade began to dull the tip after they found that the sharp point embedded in the victim's bone and made the knife difficult to withdraw from the corpse. The 'V' in the name stood for Victory and the '42' for 1942, the year the knife was first manufactured. A profile of the V-42 knife now appears on the crest of the US Army Special Forces.

The V-42's blade had a ground-in thumbprint that ensured the knife was orientated 'on edge', ensuring a thinner profile for thrusting between the ribs.

Once the main force had landed on 22 August 1944, the 1SSF was attached to the 7th Army as part of the First Airborne Taskforce and continued advancing through southern France towards the Italian border. On 5 December 1944, after capturing the village of Villeneuve-Loubet near Antibes, the unit was disbanded. The fighting in southern France was coming to an end and the men were returned to Canadian and American airborne units.

During its brief existence, the 1800 men of the 1SSF inflicted some 12,000 casualties on the Germans and captured 7000 prisoners. While doing so they sustained a casualty and attrition rate of 600 percent.

The 1SSF would leave its legacy in the Canadian Airborne Regiment, established in 1968, and in Canada's Special Service Force, established in 1976 – a quick reaction force that also incorporated the Airborne Regiment. South of the border, Colonel Aaron Bank, a veteran of the wartime OSS (Office of Strategic Services), used the 1SSF as a model for his new special forces unit that would become the Green Berets.

'... the Force never in all its service yielded an inch of ground nor left a battle with an indecisive conclusion. The Force won everything it fought for ...'

THE INDEPENDENT RECORD, HELENA, MONTANA, 7 AUGUST 1955

'Honour and Fidelity'

The French Foreign Legion

The French Foreign Legion is an integral part of the French army. It is a professional fighting unit that uses the same equipment and is sent on the same missions as any other infantry, tank or engineer unit. However, it takes volunteers of any nationality, race or creed ready to serve France and has a unique *esprit de corps*, taking as its mottos 'the Legion is our homeland' and 'march or die'.

The French Foreign Legion has inherited the traditions of foreign troops who have served France since the Middle Ages. Scottish Guards served Charles VII (1422–61); Louis XIV and his descendants had their Irish 'Wild Geese'; and Napoleon had his Polish Lancers. After Louis-Philippe took the throne in the July Revolution of 1830, he created the French Foreign Legion.

Established on 10 March 1831, the Legion was composed of foreign volunteers commanded by French officers. Recruits were aged between 18 and 40. They often turned up without any means of identification, and the Legion became a convenient refuge for displaced foreigners, many of whom were thought to have revolutionary political beliefs. To get these dangerous radicals out of the country, the Legion was immediately employed in the conquest of Algeria, a project the French government also used to occupy the veterans of Napoleon's *Grande Armée*.

In August 1835, some 4000 Légionnaires landed in Spain to support Isabella II's claim to the throne over that of her uncle Carlos. They found themselves involved in a savage war, and on 8 December 1838, when the Foreign Legion was disbanded, there were only 500 survivors. These made their way back to France. When a second Foreign Legion was formed, they re-enlisted alongside the Carlists, their former enemies who had sought refuge in France.

THE BATTLE OF CAMERONE

The Legion then returned to Algeria – an unpopular posting with the regular army. In 1855, they fought in the Crimea and, in 1859, fought the Austrians in Italy. But it was in Mexico that the Legion won its legendary status. On 30 April 1863, near Puebla, two officers and 62 Légionnaires under Captain Jean Danjou were attacked by 2000 men of the Mexican army. While retreating, the Legion formed up into a square and drove off several cavalry charges, inflicting heavy casualties.

One of the Legion's most celebrated exploits occurred when about 60 Légionnaires, led by Captain Jean Danjou, held off 2000 troops of the Mexican army at Camerone Hacienda in Mexico. All but three of the Legionnaires perished. (Painting by unknown artist.)

'What can I refuse to such men?
No, these are not men, they are devils.'

COLONEL MILAN, MEXICAN COMMANDER AT CAMERONE, 1863

Danjou decided to make a stand at Camerone Hacienda, an inn surrounded by a 3-metre (10-ft) wall. The Mexican commander demanded that they surrender as they were so greatly outnumbered. Danjou refused. Instead, he went around to each of his men with a bottle of wine and made them swear not to surrender. After a day of fighting, Danjou was dead and there were only five Légionnaires left alive. Down to their last bullet, they fixed bayonets and charged. Two were killed immediately. The Mexican commander, Colonel Milan, then ordered a ceasefire and the three surviving Légionnaires were returned to France. Since then, the name of Camerone adorns every Legion flag.

Under normal circumstances, the French Foreign Legion is not allowed to fight in Metropolitan France. But after the defeat of the French army in the Franco-Prussian War of 1870, they were deployed in an attempt to raise the siege of Paris. The Legion then took part in France's colonial expansion, fighting in the campaigns in Vietnam, Sudan, Dahomey, Madagascar and Morocco.

French army infantry, including units of the Foreign Legion, on board the aircraft carrier Le Foch *in the port of Split, Croatia, June 1995, prepare to disembark as part of a multi-national Rapid Reaction Force.*

After very heavy casualties in the First World War, disbanded regiments were merged into one – the Foreign Legion's '*Régiment de Marche*', headed by 'the Father of the Legion' Colonel Paul-Frédéric Rollet. With the end of the First World War, the Legion was involved in the pacification of Morocco and the Middle East, with the campaigns in the Rif and the Atlas Mountains, and in Syria against the Druze.

THE LEGION DIVIDES

During the Second World War, the Legion distinguished itself at Narvik during the Norwegian campaign of 1940. Before the fall of France in 1940, the 11th Regiment of the Foreign Legion had continued its heroic tradition, being decimated rather than retreat in the face of the enemy. But after the fall of France, the Legion was divided. Some joined the Free French, while others joined the Vichy government. They fought each other during the Syria-Lebanon Campaign of June 1941. The Legion's 13th Half-brigade, with Free French help, won a famous victory at Bir-Hakeim in Libya in 1942. The Legion went on to fight victorious campaigns in Tunisia, Italy, Provence, Alsace and Germany.

After fighting the Japanese, the 5th Foreign Infantry Regiment remained in Indochina. During the French-Indochina War, every Foreign Legion regiment was represented on the battlefield, fighting with distinction at Phu Tong Hoa, along Colonial Road 4 and at Dien Bien Phu, where they fought to the last man.

In 1954, the Legion returned to Algeria where it was put in charge of security. It was soon sending out major intervention forces to fight the National Liberation Front and other

THE LEGIONNAIRE'S CODE OF HONOUR

1. Légionnaire: you are a volunteer serving France faithfully and with honour.

2. Every Légionnaire is your brother-at-arms, irrespective of his nationality, race or creed. You will demonstrate this by an unwavering and straightforward solidarity which must always bind together members of the same family.

3. Respectful of the Legion's traditions, honouring your superiors, discipline and comradeship are your strength, courage and loyalty your virtues.

4. Proud of your status as a Légionnaire, you will display this pride, by your turnout, always impeccable, your behaviour, ever worthy, though modest, your living-quarters, always tidy.

5. An élite soldier: you will train vigorously, you will maintain your weapon as if it were your most precious possession, you will keep your body in the peak of condition, always fit.

6. A mission once given to you becomes sacred to you, you will accomplish it to the end and at all costs.

7. In combat: you will act without relish of your tasks, or hatred; you will respect the vanquished enemy and will never abandon neither your wounded nor your dead, nor will you under any circumstances surrender your arms.

smaller insurgent groups during the Algerian War of Independence of 1954–62. In 1956, the Legion was dispatched to Egypt for the Suez débâcle. Back in Algeria, the Legion fought in the Battle of Algiers in 1957. When the French withdrew from Algeria in 1962, the Legion's regiments regrouped in the south of France and Corsica, or overseas in Djibouti, Madagascar, Tahiti and French Guiana.

RAPID INTERVENTION FORCE

The French Foreign Legion remodelled itself as a rapid intervention force, particularly for use in France's former colonies in Africa. In 1969–70, the 1st Foreign Regiment and the 2nd Foreign Parachute Regiment took part in operations in Chad. In May 1978, the 2nd Foreign Parachute Regiment saved hundreds of European and African civilians in Kolwezi, during fighting in what was then Zaire. In 1990 and 1991, the Legion took part in Operation Desert Shield and Operation Desert Storm.

Since 1831, 902 of the Legion's officers, 3176 NCOs, and over 30,000 Légionnaires have died for France – one-third of them while fighting directly in defence of the country. After three years of service, a Légionnaire can apply for French nationality and may also be entitled to a French resident permit if he has obtained a certificate of satisfactory military service. The resident permit is valid for ten years and is renewable. Although foreigners by birth, many Légionnaires believe they have earned the right to become Frenchmen by the blood they have spilled.

'The Legion dies; it does not surrender!'

CAPTAIN JEAN DANJOU AT THE BATTLE OF CAMERONE, 1863

THE FRENCH FOREIGN LEGION

1831 French Foreign Legion is formed and sent to Algeria

1835 Legion lands in Spain to fight for Isabella II against the Carlists

1855 Legion fights in the Crimea

1859 Legion fights in Italy

1863 The Battle of Camerone

1871 Legion attempts to raise the siege of Paris

1884–5 Fights in the Sino-French War

1914–8 Fights in major engagements in the First World War, suffering massive casualties

1920S AND 1930S Fights in Algeria, Syria, Tunisia, Morocco and Indochina

1940 Fights at Narvik, Norway; with the fall of France the Legion divides

1941 Free French and Vichy Légionnaires fight each other

1942 Légionnaires victorious at Bir-Hakeim in Libya

1945 Legion's 11th Regiment is decimated rather than retreat

1946–54 Fights in French Indochina War

1954 Fights to last man at Dien Bien Phu

1954 – 62 Fights in Algerian War of Independence

1956 Fights at Suez

1969–70 Intervenes in Chad

1978 Saves civilians in Zaire

1990 Guards flank in Desert Shield

1991 Fights in Desert Storm

The Gurkhas

'Better to die than be a coward'

For almost 200 years, fearsome Nepalese fighters have been part of the British army. Along with all their modern equipment they still carry their time-honoured weapon, a 46-centimetre (18-in) long curved knife known as a kukri. Traditionally, once the kukri was drawn in battle, it had to 'taste blood' – even if its owner had to cut himself before returning it to its sheath.

A Gurkha officer inspecting kukris in 1942. The kukri – a large knife used for work such as slashing jungle foliage and preparing food as well as for hand-to-hand fighting – is the weapon with which the Gurkhas are most associated.

The Gurkhas come from Nepal and take their name from the eighth-century Hindu warrior-saint Guru Gorkhanath. As a youth, Bappa Rawal, founder of the royal house of Nepal, was out hunting when he came across Guru Gorkhanath meditating and stayed by him while the rest of the hunting party moved on. When the Guru awoke, he was impressed by the devotions of Bappa Rawal and gave him a kukri, then instructed him on how to stem the incursion of Muslims through Afghanistan. Bappa Rawal and his Gurkha followers went on to halt the initial Muslim invasion of India.

The Gurkhas established themselves in the area of Gorkha in central Nepal. The powerful Shah family then used Gurkha soldiers to conquer the region and establish the kingdom of Nepal. In 1769, a Gurkha dynasty took the throne. The British East India Company tried to invade Nepal in 1815, but they suffered so many casualties that they quickly signed a peace treaty. As the British took over the rest of the Indian subcontinent, Nepal became a protectorate and the British were granted permission to recruit Gurkhas to serve in the British Indian Army.

FIGHTING FOR THE BRITISH

From 1817, Gurkhas served under the East India Company, siding with the British during the Indian Rebellion of 1857. Gurkha regiments went on to serve in Burma, Afghanistan, Malaya, Cyprus, along the Northeast and the Northwest Frontiers of India, in Malta during the Russo-Turkish War of 1877–8, in China during the Boxer Rebellion of 1900 and in Tibet during the British invasion of 1904.

Between 1901 and 1906, Gurkhas were reorganized into ten regiments, numbering from the 1st to the 10th. These were the Gurkha Rifles. During the First World War, more than 100,000 Gurkhas served in the British army, suffering some 20,000 casualties in the process. By then there were 33 Gurkha battalions. They fought in France, along the Suez Canal, at Gallipoli and Salonika, in Persia and in Palestine and Mesopotamia alongside the legendary and eccentric British officer Lawrence of Arabia.

FIGHTING TO THE LAST MAN

At the Battle of Loos in September 1915, the 8th Gurkhas Rifles fought to the last man. At Gallipoli, the 1st Battalion of 6th Gurkhas Rifles captured 'Gurkha Bluff' and were the only Allied troops in the campaign to hold the crest line and look down on the Dardanelle Straits, which was the reason for the landings there. The 2nd Battalion of the 3rd Gurkha Rifles took part in the capture of Baghdad in 1917.

A photograph of a group of Gurkha soldiers and their British officer (with sword), taken during the Indian Mutiny or Great Sepoy Rebellion (1857–8). The first Gurkha regiments were incorporated into the British army around 1816.

'If there was a minute's silence for every Gurkha casualty from World War II alone, we would have to keep quiet for two weeks.'

GURKHA WELFARE TRUST, 1969

THE GURKHAS

1815 The British East India Company attempt to invade Nepal, but find the Gurkhas more than a match

1817 Gurkhas begin to fight for the British East India Company

1857 Side with the British during the Indian Rebellion

1857–1914 Serve as British colonial troops in the Far East and Malta

1914–18 The Gurkha Rifles fight in all major theatres of the First World War

1919 Fight in the Third Afghan War

1919–39 Garrison Waziristan

1939–45 Fight in Europe, the Middle East and the Far East during the Second World War

1947 Four Gurkha regiments transferred from the Indian army to the British army

1948–60 Fight against communist guerrillas in the Malayan Emergency

1962–6 Fight in the Brunei Revolt

1966 Transferred to Hong Kong for security operations during China's Cultural Revolution

1974 Defend the British base in Dhekelia in Cyprus during Turkish invasion

1982 Fight in the Falklands War

1990–1 Deployed to the Persian Gulf for the Gulf War

'As I write these last words, my thoughts return to you who were my comrades, the stubborn and indomitable peasants of Nepal. Once more I hear the laughter with which you greeted every hardship. Once more I see you in your bivouacs or about your fires, on forced march or in the trenches, now shivering with wet and cold, now scorched by a pitiless and burning sun. Uncomplaining you endure hunger and thirst and wounds; and at the last your unwavering lines disappear into the smoke and wrath of battle. Bravest of the brave, most generous of the generous, never had a country more faithful friends than you.'

Sir Ralph Turner MC, who served with the 3rd Queen Alexandra's Own Gurkha Rifles during the First World War

In 1919, Gurkhas fought in the Third Afghan War, then they were sent to garrison Waziristan, the troublesome tribal region of what is now Pakistan. With the outbreak of the Second World War, the number of battalions was increased to 41. Other Gurkhas were recruited as specialists in non-Gurkha units. Some 250,280 Gurkhas fought in Syria, North Africa, Italy and Greece, and against the Japanese in Singapore and in the jungles of Burma and northeast India. They also undertook peace-keeping duties in India. Suffering around 25,000 casualties in all theatres, they earned 2734 awards for bravery. In the two world wars, some 43,000 Gurkhas lost their lives.

With Indian independence in 1947, four Gurkha regiments were transferred from the Indian army into the British army, forming a Gurkha brigade. However, their numbers have been cut back from a peak of 112,000 men in the Second World War, to around 3500. Since then they have served in Hong Kong, Malaysia, Borneo, Cyprus, the Falklands, Kosovo, Bosnia, East Timor, Sierra Leone and now in Iraq and Afghanistan, winning 13 Victoria Crosses – Britain's highest award for gallantry.

TOUGH RECRUITMENT

Gurkhas are still selected from hopeful young men living in the foothills of Nepal. Each year around 28,000 youths compete for just over 200 army places. The selection process is one of the toughest in the world. Potential recruits have to run uphill for 40 minutes carrying a wicker basket filled with rocks weighing 32 kilograms (70 lb) on their backs. However, the prize is worth winning: a career in the British army means that the young soldier can earn for himself and his family much more money than he could by living in Nepal.

The ranks have always been dominated by four ethnic groups: the Gurungs and Magars from central Nepal, and the Rais and Limbus from the east, where they live as impoverished

LANCE-CORPORAL RAMBAHADUR LIMBU

Lance-Corporal Rambahadur Limbu was the last Gurkha to win the Victoria Cross. Born in 1939, his father had fought for the British against the Japanese in the Second World War. But his father and mother died, leaving three boys. Limbu joined up as a boy soldier, but became homesick and deserted. Later, escorting a recruitment party down into India, he got drunk and signed up again. After training, he boarded a ship at Calcutta. He had never seen the sea before.

In Malaya – now Malaysia – he was selected for the 2nd Battalion of the 10th Gurkha Rifles. In November 1964, he found himself in the jungles of Sarawak, hunting Indonesian guerrillas. They had several contacts with the enemy. On 20 November, Limbu and 15 other Gurkhas came across an enemy force that outnumbered Limbu's unit by two to one. The guerrillas were dug in on the top of a hill. The only approach was along a knife-edge ridge, guarded by a soldier in a slit trench with a machine gun. Limbu led the attack. The machine gun opened up

and one of Limbu's men fell. 'As soon as I saw his blood, my own blood began to boil,' Limbu said. 'I swore that the enemy would pay for this with their blood.' Rushing forward Limbu reached the trench and killed the sentry.

The enemy were now fully alerted and rained down heavy automatic fire on the trench. But Limbu led from the front. With complete disregard for his own safety, he left the shelter of the trench and encouraged his men forward to a better firing position some way ahead. Another Gurkha fell. After making two trips under fire to drag the fallen men to safety, Limbu went forward again. This time he seized the machine gun. 'Within an hour we killed all of them,' he said. 'At the end of the battle four of them tried to escape, but they could not escape from our bullets.'

After receiving the Victoria Cross from the Queen at Buckingham Palace, Limbu visited the London Stock Exchange where the trading floor stopped business for three minutes to give him a standing ovation – the only time this has ever happened.

hill farmers. The men in each battalion often have close family ties, which gives them a unique *esprit de corps*. Gurkhas are not only fighting for a cause or for their British officers, but also for their family and friends.

The Gurkhas are now based at Shorncliffe near Folkestone, Kent, in southeast England. Though they are an integral part of the British army, they maintain their Nepalese customs and beliefs. The brigade celebrates religious festivals such as Dashain, where in Nepal – though not in the UK – goats and buffaloes are sacrificed as part of the ceremony.

A unit of Gurkhas shown on patrol in Helmand Province, Afghanistan in March 2008. The first Gurkha soldier was killed fighting in Afghanistan in November 2008, when an explosive device struck his Warrior armoured vehicle.

151

The Chindits

'March divided but fight united'

The 77th Indian Infantry Brigade, later the Indian 3rd Infantry Division, was an irregular long-range penetration force of British, Gurkha and Burmese soldiers who were pitted against the Japanese during the Burma Campaign of 1942–5. Their badge was the mythical *chinthé* – the half-lion, half-griffin figure seen guarding Burmese pagodas. This also gave the force their name, and they became known as Chindits.

By April 1942, the Japanese had forced the British out of Burma and were threatening India. But the Allies had agreed a 'Europe first' strategy, so the British commander in the Far East, General Archibald Wavell, had few resources at his disposal to defend British India. However, when Wavell had been commander in the Middle East, he had met a young officer named Charles Orde Wingate who had led a group of Ethiopian irregulars in East Africa. Wavell sent for Wingate, believing that similar tactics might work against the Japanese in Burma.

In the summer of 1942, Wingate assembled the 77th Indian Infantry Brigade in Uttar Pradesh. It comprised some 3000 men from 142nd Commando Company from the Bush Warfare School in Burma, the newly raised 3rd Battalion of the 2nd Gurkha Rifles, the 2nd Burma Rifles and the 13th Battalion of the King's Liverpool Regiment – a second-line battalion comprising largely older men.

BEHIND JAPANESE LINES

Wingate trained his men in the jungles of central India during the rainy season. His plan was to form long-range penetration groups that moved through the Burmese jungle on foot. Behind Japanese lines, they would communicate by radio and be supplied from the air – innovations at the time. Relying on mobility and surprise, they would disrupt the enemy's lines of communication. It was a tactic that had worked well for the Japanese when they had taken Singapore and Burma. Without artillery, Wingate's group would depend on close air support.

On 13 February 1943, the Chindits crossed the Chindwin river into Burma in seven columns, each comprising three infantry platoons with one support platoon. Wingate and his men penetrated deep into Burma. Their objectives were to cut the main railway line between Mandalay and Myitkyina, harass the enemy in the Shwebo area and, if possible, cross the Irrawaddy and cut the railway line between Mandalay and Lashio.

Their first objective lay 150 miles (241 km) to the east, which they aimed to reach undetected. Two Gurkha columns crossed the Chindwin 50 miles (80 km) to the south of the main force to draw off the enemy, and a diversionary attack was made by the 23rd Indian Division at Kalewa. As a result, the main force of Chindits reached the railway in two weeks without encountering any Japanese forces. At the target they were also resupplied by the Royal Air Force. But two columns were then ambushed and suffered heavy casualties. However, the rest of the column managed to blow up the railway line in more than 76 places over a distance of 30 miles (48 km).

When this photograph was taken, Wingate's Chindit guerrilla force had been fighting the Japanese in the jungles of Burma for three months. Their missions included blowing up Japanese supply dumps, and destroying roads, railway lines and bridges to prevent Japanese troop movements.

THE CHINDITS

APRIL 1942 British ousted from Burma

SUMMER 1942 The Chindits formed in India under Orde Wingate

FEBRUARY 1943 Seven columns enter Burma; spend 12 weeks disrupting Japanese communications

AUGUST 1943 The Quebec Conference approves expansion of the Chindits

FEBRUARY 1944 Three brigades of Chindits set up bases 200 miles (322 km) behind Japanese lines

MARCH 1944 Wingate killed in plane crash

JUNE 1944 77th Brigade suffer 50 percent casualties taking Mogaung

AUGUST 1944 Chindits pulled out of Burma

FEBRUARY 1945 Disbanded

BOOST FOR MORALE

The Chindits then crossed the Irrawaddy, but the enemy were now aware of their presence and Wingate had to disperse his force. This made it nearly impossible to resupply them by air, and sickness and the heat began to take their toll. Before they could reach the Lashio-Mandalay line, Wingate ordered a withdrawal and the Chindits headed back to India. They had spent 12 weeks in the jungle and marched almost 1000 miles (1609 km). Out of the 3000 men, they had lost 883. Because of the harsh treatment the Japanese meted out to their prisoners, those too badly injured to survive the journey back to India had been shot.

Wingate judged the operation to have been a dismal failure. The railways had been disrupted for less than a week. However, it provided a great boost for morale. It had also demonstrated that it was possible to take on the seemingly invincible Japanese army on land. Churchill was so impressed that he took Wingate with him to the Quebec Conference. There Wingate received renewed backing for his force and the decision was made to create a similar American unit, which became Merrill's Marauders. Wingate returned from Quebec with the authority to mount a second, larger expedition into enemy territory. Two more Gurkha battalions were added to the 77th. The Indian army's 111th Brigade joined the Chindits, while the British 70th Infantry Division provided three more brigades. Along with another brigade from the British 81st West Africa Division, the Chindits were redesignated the 3rd Infantry Division, which now had its own dedicated air support in the form of the US First Air Commando.

On 5 February 1944, the 16th Brigade of the Chindits infiltrated Burma, crossing 600 miles (966 km) of particularly difficult terrain to avoid the Japanese. Their task was to establish three fortified bases with airstrips around Indaw, now Sagaing, in central Burma. Using gliders, the force of 1000 men, along with their equipment, supplies and 1000 mules, were landed behind enemy lines in the largest airborne operation until D-Day.

The Chindits failed to take Indaw, which was heavily defended by the Japanese. But they found the main supply dump for the Japanese forces in northern Burma and called in an airstrike to destroy it. They held off attacks on their fortified bases in fierce hand-to-hand fighting with bayonets and kukris pitted again Japanese swords. The Chindits succeeded in blocking roads and railways in the area, disrupting the whole of Japanese-held Burma. But then, at the height of the Chindits' achievement, Wingate was killed in a plane crash, leaving the unit demoralized.

Command of the Chindits passed to Brigadier Lentaigne, commander of the 111th Brigade. But control was handed over to US General 'Vinegar Joe' Stilwell. He ordered the Chindits to abandon their strongholds and move north to support his Chinese divisions. Chindit commanders opposed this, since Wingate had maintained that troops could only operate behind enemy lines for 90 days, and he had intended to relieve them. Ninety percent of Chindit casualties occurred after Stilwell took over.

The Chindits were now used, not as guerrillas, but as regular infantry. They were ordered to attack heavily defended Japanese positions without armour or artillery support.

> *'… just like an officers' mess guest night …'*
>
> BRIGADIER 'MAD MIKE' CALVERT, AFTER A BAYONET CHARGE AGAINST THE JAPANESE, 17 MARCH 1944

CHARLES ORDE WINGATE

Wingate was born in India, the son of a long-serving Indian army officer. After being commissioned in the Royal Artillery, he served on the Abyssinian front with the Sudan Defence Force, exploring the Libyan Desert in his spare time. In January 1941, with just 2000 men, he expelled a much larger Italian force from Ethiopia and returned Emperor Haile Selassie to the throne. In June 1942, he was sent to India where he created the Chindits. After their first operation, he trained a similar US force, Merrill's Marauders. Promoted to major-general, he was given a much larger force to command. Within three weeks, they controlled a wide area 200 miles (322 km) behind enemy lines. On 24 March 1944, Wingate was flying over the Naga jungles of northern Assam in a tropical storm when his plane crashed and he was killed. He is buried in Arlington National Cemetery, Virginia.

Orde Wingate (seen on the right with pointer) makes final plans before the beginning of the Chindits' march into Burma in May 1943.

Even their air support had been withdrawn. At Mogaung, 1000 Chindits drove out 4000 Japanese, but in the 19-day battle the Chindits suffered 50 percent casualties – and won two VCs. Meanwhile the 3rd, 14th and 111th Brigades took Hill 2171 to the west of Mogaung, where another VC was awarded.

END OF THE CHINDITS

With the 77th Brigade now down to just 300 men – a mere one-tenth of its original strength – Brigadier 'Mad Mike' Calvert, the leader of the Chindits in the field, risked court martial by shutting down his radios and withdrawing his men. After enduring 20 days of artillery attacks, heavy fighting and supplies interrupted due to the monsoon, the 111th Brigade also withdrew again, shooting the wounded who had no hope of surviving the journey. Exhaustion and illness had taken its toll. Only just over 100 men remained fit for duty and Lord Louis Mountbatten, then supreme allied commander in Southeast Asia, ordered Stilwell to pull out the rest of the Chindits.

The Chindits left Burma on 27 August 1944. Back in India, half the men were admitted to hospital and nearly all required rest and a special diet. Nevertheless, they received reinforcements and began training for yet another operation.

However, in February 1945 the Chindits were officially disbanded as General Slim's 14th Army were rapidly pushing the Japanese out of Burma. In two years, the Chindits had lost 944 men killed, 2434 wounded and 452 missing.

The Special Air Service (SAS)

'Who dares wins'

Britain's Special Air Service Regiment – better known as the SAS – is the precursor of all other modern special forces units. The Green Berets, Delta Force and the US Navy SEALs all drew their inspiration directly from the SAS. The SAS was founded in August 1941 and was the idea of a young lieutenant named David Stirling.

Memorial near Doune, Stirlingshire, Scotland, to Lieutenant Colonel David Stirling, who founded the Special Air Service at the height of Second World War. He was awarded the OBE and DSO for his actions in war and was knighted in 1990, but died a few months later.

He had volunteered as a commando and was sent to make amphibious raids in North Africa, but his unit was disbanded due to a shortage of boats. However, Stirling believed that the idea of hitting the enemy in the rear was a sound strategy. He joined forces with a like-minded Australian named 'Jock' Lewes. The two of them would become the nucleus of the Special Air Service Regiment.

Lewes scrounged some parachutes, and he and Stirling started to make training jumps. Injured in a fall, Stirling spent months in hospital. However, this turned out to be a blessing in disguise, for it gave him time to formulate plans for his new unit. Instead of making regular commando raids with a force of up to 200 men, with its inherent problem of securing the beachhead, he proposed inserting small teams by parachute who would be collected by a second unit in wheeled vehicles.

When he was released from hospital, Stirling decided to take his plan to the commander-in-chief in the Middle East, General Sir Claude Auchinleck, but was refused entry to Auchinleck's headquarters. Although he was on crutches, Stirling simply clambered over the perimeter fence and barged into the office of Auchinleck's chief-of-staff Major-General Neil Ritchie. Impressed with the young man's audacity, Ritchie presented Stirling's plan to Auchinleck, who quickly saw its virtue. Stirling was promoted to the rank of captain and he was ordered to raise a new unit of 60 men and six officers. It was to be called L Detachment of the Special Air Services Brigade – which existed only on paper.

DISASTROUS FIRST MISSION, THEN SUCCESS

On 16 November 1941, the SAS set out to attack five enemy airfields around Timimi and Gazala in Libya. But on the night of the mission a storm blew up and the planes carrying the SAS were blown off course. After the drop, none of the teams found their target. Of the 62 men sent out, only 22 returned. The SAS's first mission had been a disaster.

To persuade Auchinleck to let his unit continue, Stirling abandoned the idea of airborne insertion and turned to the Long

Range Desert Group (LRDG). They had been set up in July 1940, comprising mainly New Zealanders, and had carried out a number of successful operations. Now they would be the SAS's 'Libyan Desert Taxi Service', inserting and extracting them – and, ultimately, joining in the fighting.

On 8 December 1941, the SAS set out for the LRDG patrol base at Jalo, far behind enemy lines. From there, they attacked enemy airfields at Tamit and Agedabia, destroying 61 planes before disappearing back into the desert. A few days later they attacked the airfield at Tamit again, destroying another 27 planes. However, Jock Lewes was killed by a German plane that attacked the LRDG patrol as it returned from the mission.

The following month they staged another successful raid, hitting the port facility at Bouerat. Stirling was promoted to major in recognition of his achievements. The future of the SAS now seemed assured, and Stirling set about designing the unit's famous badge. It was

A Long Range Desert Group patrol moving through a hilly desert area. Patrols such as this were often used to deploy, and then recover, SAS units operating in the area. The group's actions against the enemy caused Germany's Field Marshal Erwin Rommel to say: 'The LRDG caused us more damage than any other unit of their size.'

A Special Forces (SAS) officer seen on 29 July 2005 at a cordon in London, after a raid linked to the failed terrorist bomb attack in London, 21 July 2005. The SAS are heavily involved in clandestine anti-terrorist activities in the United Kingdom.

The cap badge of the SAS shows a dagger striking downward surrounded by flames – originally intended to depict King Arthur's sword Excalibur. The badge also carries the SAS motto 'Who dares wins'.

supposed to have been Excalibur, the sword of King Arthur, but ended up looking more like a dagger with wings. Under it was the motto 'Who dares wins'. At the same time Stirling began expanding his force. Fifty Free French paratroopers, later known as the French Squadron SAS, joined, along with the Greek Sacred Squadron, the Special Interrogation Group of anti-Nazi Germans and more commandos.

GUNS BLAZING

In July 1942, the SAS got Vickers 'K' machine guns and American Willys Jeeps with mounted heavy-calibre Brownings and racks for extra jerry cans of petrol and water. These were fast and more manoeuvrable than LRDG trucks and Stirling developed the tactic of speeding down the lines of enemy aircraft, guns blazing. However, in January 1943, David Stirling was captured and ended up in Colditz Castle, the German prison for persistent escapers. Command was passed to 'Paddy' Mayne, who had been in the SAS since its inception. Numbers had swelled to 750 – regimental size – and L Detachment of the SAS Brigade became 1 SAS. In May 1943, Lieutenant Colonel William Stirling, David's brother, formed the second SAS regiment – 2 SAS – with men from 62 Commando.

With the surrender of all the Axis forces in North Africa, the SAS was reorganized. Now 1 SAS became the Special Raiding Squadron, or SRS. Their job was to attack coastal installations in the Mediterranean, while 2 SAS were to be dropped behind the lines to

THE LEWES BOMB

Jock Lewes worked out that the easiest way to destroy an aeroplane was to punch a hole in one of its wings and set fire to the fuel in the tanks inside. This required a bomb that was both an explosive and an incendiary. A specialist sapper told him this was impossible, but after experimenting for two weeks Lewes came up with a solution. He took 0.5 kilograms (1.1 lb) of plastic explosive and rolled it in thermite from an incendiary bomb, dousing the mixture with old engine oil to make sure the fire spread. The resulting device weighed just under a kilogram (1 lb), so one man could carry enough to destroy a whole squadron. It became standard issue for the SAS.

'I regard seventy troopers of the SAS as being as valuable to me as seven hundred infantry in the role of hearts and minds, border surveillance, early warning, stay behind, and eyes and ears with a sting.'

MAJOR-GENERAL WALTER WALKER, COMMANDER OF COMMONWEALTH FORCES IN BORNEO, 1964

THE SPECIAL AIR SERVICE (SAS)

JULY 1940 Formation of the Long Range Desert Group

AUGUST 1941 L Detachment of Special Air Services Brigade formed under David Stirling

SEPTEMBER 1941 Official founding of the first SAS regiment (backdated from 1943)

NOVEMBER 1941 SAS undertake disastrous first mission

DECEMBER 1941 SAS team up with LRDG for attack on airfields at Tamit and Agedabia

JULY 1942 SAS rearmed with specialist equipment

JANUARY 1943 Stirling captured; command passes to 'Paddy' Mayne

MAY 1943 2 SAS formed

JUNE 1944 SAS brigade lands behind the lines in Normandy

FEBRUARY 1945 SAS clear up pockets of resistance in Germany

NOVEMBER 1946 SAS disbanded

MAY 1947 SAS reinstituted as a territorial unit

NOVEMBER 1958 Fight in Oman

1963 Fight in Borneo

1970–6 Lead counter-insurgency campaign in Malaya

1972 Assigned anti-terrorist role

1980 Rescue hostages from Iranian Embassy in London

support the landings on Sicily. They were so successful that, during the Italian campaign, they were given a free hand to blow up bridges, hit airfields and co-ordinate local partisan groups.

During the run-up to D-Day, 1 SAS and 2 SAS returned to England to form a brigade as part of the 1st Airborne Division, along with 3 SAS and 4 SAS, comprising French troops, and a Belgian squadron which later became 5 SAS. In the four months following D-Day, some 2000 SAS men operated from 40 secret bases up to 250 miles (402 km) behind enemy lines, disrupting communications, raiding supply depots, blowing up railway lines and gathering intelligence for the Allies.

In February 1945, Major Michael Calvert – ex-Chindits – took over as brigade commander. With the Western Allies closing in on Germany, the SAS sped up to 70 miles (113 km) ahead of the front line to clear pockets of resistance. During the campaign in northwest Europe they had killed or wounded 8000 enemy soldiers, while suffering 350 casualties of their own – including 24 men who were executed by the Germans after being captured.

After disarming the German army in Norway, the SAS was broken up. The French and Belgian units returned to their own national armies, while 1 SAS and 2 SAS were trained for operations against Japan. But the war ended before they could be put into action, and the SAS was disbanded on 30 November 1946.

On 1 May 1947, the SAS were reinstituted as a territorial unit, the 21st SAS. By 1956, at the height of the Malayan Emergency, the SAS had 560 officers and men. They operated in four-man teams, penetrating deep into the jungle on assignments that could last up to three months. In November 1958, they returned to the desert when D Squadron of 22 SAS were sent to put down a rebellion in Oman.

ANTI-TERRORIST ROLE

In 1963, 23 SAS were sent to fight insurgents in Borneo. Between 1970 and 1976, the SAS were back in Oman to wage another counter-insurgency campaign. After the terrorist attack at the Munich Olympics in 1972, the SAS began training for an anti-terrorist role. In 1980, they staged a dramatic rescue of hostages taken in the Iranian Embassy in London, which brought them to worldwide attention.

With the Special Boat Service, they saw action behind enemy lines in the Falklands War. It was a role they would continue to great effect in the Gulf War, the Balkans, Sierra Leone, Afghanistan and Iraq.

The Royal Marine Commandos

'... trained troops of the hunter class ...'

Britain's Royal Marines were formed in 1664. Among their many actions, they took the Rock of Gibraltar from the Spanish in 1704 and held it during a nine-month siege. Over 200 years later, after the fall of France in the Second World War, Winston Churchill called for 'specially trained troops of the hunter class, who can develop a reign of terror down these coasts'. They would be the Royal Marine Commandos.

'M' Company of the 42 Commando Royal Marines in action in January 2007 clearing areas used by the Taliban in the Helmand Province of Afghanistan. Around 150 Royal Marines from 42 Commando became the first UK troops to enter Helmand Province.

The first Royal Marine Commando unit was formed on 14 February 1942. It was named 'A Commando' and was the forerunner of the current 40 Commando Royal Marines. In March 1942, commandos raided the dry dock at St Nazaire. Although the British lost over half of their raiding party, the port facility was put out of action, denying it to the German battleship *Tirpitz*, which never put to sea again.

'A Commando' also saw action at the disastrous Dieppe landings in August that year. Despite the failure of that raid, the commandos were considered such a threat that on 18 October 1942 Hitler issued his 'commando order' that all commandos should be killed on sight, even if they were in uniform or attempted to surrender.

In September 1943, the Royal Marine Commandos were formed into the 3rd Special Service Brigade and were shipped out to the Far East where they saw action in the Burma Campaign. In Europe, they took part in the campaigns along the Dalmatian coast and in Sicily and Italy, landing at Salerno, Anzio and Termoli. Five Royal Marine Commando units took part in the D-Day landings, the largest amphibious assault in history. Nearly two-thirds of the British landing craft were crewed by Royal Marines, who suffered heavily in the landings and overall D-Day battle.

AN EXCLUSIVE ROLE

At the end of the Second World War, while the British army commandos were being disbanded, the commando role was assigned exclusively to the Royal Marines, and 3 Special Service Brigade became 3 Commando Brigade Royal Marines in October 1946. Between 1945 and 1971, the brigade acted as the mobile reserve in the Mediterranean and the Far East, with their headquarters alternating between Hong Kong, Malta and Singapore. The

'I know of no other case in Navy or Military Annals of such effective damage being inflicted so swiftly with such economy of force.'

LORD LOUIS MOUNTBATTEN ON THE RAID ON ST NAZAIRE DOCKS, 1942

brigade provided the rearguard when the British pulled out of Palestine in 1948. Units also saw action in the Malayan Emergency, Brunei, Korea, Cyprus, Tanganyika – now Tanzania – and in Borneo's confrontation with Indonesia.

FROM SUEZ TO THE BALKANS

During the Suez Crisis of 1956, 3 Commando Brigade landed at Port Said by sea and air, with 45 Commando mounting the world's first helicopter assault, from Royal Navy aircraft carriers. Later, in 1961, Royal Marine Commandos were sent to the Gulf to prevent an Iraqi invasion of Kuwait. In 1971, after 28 years abroad, the brigade returned to England, with its headquarters at Stonehouse Barracks in Plymouth, where Royal Marines had been stationed since the barracks were built in 1783. However, units of the Royal Marines have since seen operational duty throughout the world on many occasions.

Between 1971 and 1978, 41 Commando Group was based in Malta defending NATO's southern flank and, in 1975, 40 and 41 Commando were sent to Cyprus after the Turkish invasion of the island. Meanwhile, during the 1970s, 45 Commando was assigned to NATO's northern flank, training in arctic Norway. By 1978, other units carried out their annual winter training there, too. Royal Marine Commando units were among the first troops drafted into Northern Ireland when the troubles began in 1969 and have served in the province almost every year since that time, particularly in the nationalist heartlands of West Belfast and South Armagh.

After Argentina invaded the British territory of the Falkland Islands in April 1982, 3 Commando Brigade, along with two battalions from the Parachute Regiment, sailed for the South Atlantic. They were among the first troops ashore, making an amphibious landing at San Carlos Bay and securing the beachhead there. During the six-week campaign, they crossed the island of East Falkland on foot and were preparing to attack Port Stanley when the Argentinian surrender came.

Trained in mountain warfare, the Royal Marine Commandos joined Operation Haven in 1991 to protect Kurdish refugees from being slaughtered by Saddam Hussein's state police, following the first Gulf War. In 1994, 45 Commando were sent to Kuwait as part of the Allied response to the threat of another Iraqi invasion.

Elements of the brigade have deployed to the Balkans following the break-up of the former Yugoslavia in 1991, and detachments of commandos led boarding parties to enforce United Nations sanctions in the Adriatic. The brigade deployed Tactical Air Control Parties and a commando battery in the region in 1995 and were among the leading elements of the multinational force which took over from the United Nations in 1996. Then brigade headquarters, along with 45 Commando and other commando units, were deployed in Kosovo in 2000.

COMMANDO RAID ON ST NAZAIRE

Known as Operation Chariot, the raid on St Nazaire was planned by Lord Louis Mountbatten, then chief of combined operations. An old destroyer laden with explosives was to be rammed into the lock gates of the dry dock there and blown up, while other men destroyed the harbour facilities. On 26 March 1942, HMS *Campbeltown* – the former USS *Buchanan* – along with one motor torpedo boat, a gun boat, 16 motor launches and 622 men set sail from Falmouth in Cornwall.

At 12:30 a.m. on 28 March, they reached the mouth of the Loire. Under heavy fire from the German guns, the *Campbeltown* reached the lock gate at 1:34 a.m. and the fuses were set to blow up the ship at 9:00 a.m.. The defenders were now fully alerted, however, and only three of the launches managed to put men ashore. They set about blowing up the harbour installations.

After fierce fighting, most of the landing party was rounded up and the *Campbeltown* was

A wounded British commando sergeant is helped by one of his comrades, as both are escorted by German troops following the raid on St Nazaire.

inspected, but the Germans failed to find the explosives. The time for detonation came and went. Senior German officers arrived and were taken to the docks along with two British commandos. Despite the risk to their own lives, they kept quiet about the explosives. At 10:35 a.m., they finally detonated, destroying the lock gates, killing the two officers and some 250 German soldiers and civilians in the area.

The British lost 144 men killed; some 200 more were captured. They spent the rest of the war in a prisoner of war camp. Five of the landing party managed to avoid capture and were able to reach the British base at Gibraltar. For the action at St Nazaire, five Victoria Crosses – the British military's highest award for valour – were awarded.

RAPID REACTION

Since 1996, 3 Commando has been one of the two core brigades in the Joint Rapid Deployment Force, now called the Joint Rapid Reaction Force (JRRF). This means the brigade maintains a Lead Commando Group ready to deploy worldwide at short notice. In 1998, 40 Commando and the 539 Assault Squadron were sent to the Congo as part of a JRRF contingency force to help evacuate foreign nationals from Kinshasa. Then, in 2000, 42 Commando intervened in the civil war in Sierra Leone.

In 2002, the brigade was sent into Afghanistan to help in the fight against the Taliban. Then in 2003, it led the assault on the Al Faw Peninsula to secure the oilfield there and they were the first conventional Allied troops on the ground in Iraq. They went on to join the British capture of Basra, Iraq's second city.

The Special Boat Service

'By strength and guile'

The idea for the Special Boat Service came from a young subaltern named Roger Courtney. To convince his superiors of the effectiveness of such an outfit, he staged a daring one-man raid on a British commando ship, kayaking up to it, climbing the anchor chain, stealing a gun casing and leaving the way he had come, undetected.

The modern cap badge of the Special Boat Service, introduced in 2001, depicts a dagger with two undulating blue lines and the motto 'By Strength and Guile'.

When he presented his trophy to a group of high-ranking commando officers in a nearby pub, Courtney was promoted to captain and, in July 1940, he was given command of 12 men – the first Special Boat Section. Their unique piece of equipment was a 4.8-metre- (16-ft-) long collapsible sports canoe. When dismantled, it folded into a pack 1.4 x 0.3 metres (4.5 x 1 ft) and weighed about 22 kilograms (48 lb). This could easily be stowed on board a submarine or hidden on a beach. The two-man crews used double-bladed paddles that broke down in two parts.

One crewman was the designated canoeist who was in charge of the vessel. The other was the 'swimmer', whose job was to attack the target. The fledgling unit trained on the Scottish island of Arran. Their principal tactic was to approach an enemy vessel under cover of darkness and attach a mine to its hull. A timing device on the mine allowed them to make a safe getaway before it detonated. On 3 March 1941, they were sent to do some demolition work on the Lofoten Islands off Norway. They destroyed fish-oil factories, petrol dumps and 11 ships. In another daring raid on 22 June 1941, they paddled ashore from a submarine and blew up a train in a railway tunnel in Italy.

HIGH-VALUE TARGETS

Courtney's command had increased to 15 by April 1942 when they were sent to the Middle East, joining the 1st Submarine Flotilla. Paddling ashore from submarine mother ships, the teams would seek out and sabotage high-value targets such as railway and communication

'It is important that SBS of sub-units avoid being engaged by superior forces. Success depends on detailed planning and rehearsals. It is essential therefore that all intelligence is made available and that adequate time is allowed for preparation before an operation is launched ...'

THE ORGANISATION AND EMPLOYMENT OF THE SPECIAL BOAT SECTIONS, SBS MANUAL

lines. They made attacks on Greece, Crete and Rhodes, using their canoes to sneak into harbours and plant limpet mines on the hulls of enemy ships.

In the autumn of 1942, the force was reorganized in preparation for its most famous raid of the Second World War – the 'Cockleshell Heroes' raid on Nazi-occupied Bordeaux. In the spring of 1943, the SBS joined the Special Air Service, making raids on Crete. The Special Boat Squadron then became the Special Boat Service (SBS), based at Athlit in northern Palestine. From there it conducted operations in the Mediterranean, Adriatic and Aegean Seas.

RAIDS ON GREEK ISLANDS

In May 1943, S Detachment under the command of Captain Sutherland made another daring raid on Crete, destroying three airfields in the attack. The SBS made further attacks on Sicily in the run-up to the Allied landings. Following the Italian capitulation in November 1943, it became involved in attempts to gain control of enemy-held islands

This painting of a Special Boat Service unit operating at night vividly illustrates the covert method by which they often go about their missions. The non-metallic two-man canoes, an integral part of SBS equipment, have changed little since the Second World War. The canoes can be launched from boats or submarines or even parachuted into the ocean.

in the eastern Mediterranean. Although several islands fell to small raiding parties, the Germans soon stiffened their defences. In early November 1943, the Germans dropped paratroopers on the island of Leros. The British surrendered after losing 400 dead in five days of fighting. Only a small SBS team escaped.

The SBS kept up raids on Leros, Kos and other Greek islands, forcing the Germans to maintain large garrisons there and preventing troops from being deployed elsewhere. Its last major operation in the Aegean took place on Simi, when 81 SBS men accompanied the Greek Sacred Squadron as they fought their way back onto the island.

In 1945, while the other special forces' units were disbanded altogether, the War Office decided to raise a shallow-penetration special force under the Royal Marines. Early in the following year, survivor of the Cockleshell Hero raid Herbert 'Blondie' Hasler opened the School of Combined Operations, Beach and Boat Section, at Fremington, Devon, giving training in beach surveying, intelligence gathering and sabotage. By the end of August, the two units of 39 men were installed at the Royal Marines base at Eastney, Portsmouth. Their first mission was to remove limpet mines from ships in Haifa harbour.

STAY-BEHIND PARTIES

As part of Cold War defences, 2 SBS joined the Royal Navy Rhine Flotilla on the Dutch border. In 1951, they were joined by 3 SBS. In the event of war, they were to form stay-behind parties to gather intelligence and harass Russian troops. The SBS was also used to insert and extract agents along Eastern Bloc coastlines and gather intelligence on Soviet naval capabilities. Along with the Special Air Service, the SBS would frequently play the role of the Soviet Spetsnaz – the Red Army's special forces unit – in mock attacks on NATO installations. Some military analysts believe that this resulted in the West overestimating the Spetsnaz's capabilities.

In the Korean War, the SBS joined 41 Independent Commando of the Royal Marines and the US Marines to lead sabotage teams blowing up railways and vital installations along the North Korean coastline. It also saw action in Borneo, joining the SAS in their 'hearts and minds' campaign. In 1965, the SBS had set up courses in Singapore to train Malaysian troops, along with men from the South Vietnamese army and, later, US Marines preparing to fight in Vietnam. Meanwhile, SBS teams turned up at many of the world's trouble spots, even joining drug enforcement patrols in the Caribbean. They worked in covert surveillance in Northern Ireland and intercepted gun runners along the coastline.

The SBS came to public attention in 1972, parachuting into the Atlantic 1000 miles (1609 km) from shore when blackmailers threatened to blow up the cruise liner *Queen Elizabeth 2*. By 1987, it had set up M Squadron, dedicated to maritime counter-terrorist operations. Given winter training in Norway, the SBS was in the frontline of covert operations during the Falklands War – though it was equally at home in Desert Storm. Following the terrorist attacks known as 9/11, it staged a daring night-time raid on a Mauritian cargo ship in the English Channel believed to be carrying 'terrorist materials'.

In 2000, the SBS were involved in a rescue mission deep in the jungles of war-torn Sierra Leone, while in 2001 teams were part of the early campaign to oust the Taleban and Al Qaeda from Afghanistan. In 2003, the SBS were at the vanguard of the invasion of Iraq, helping to secure the beaches of the Al Faw Peninsula.

THE COCKLESHELL HEROES

After the fall of France, merchant ships used the port at Bordeaux to supply the German military stationed in that part of the country. With German U-boats using the Atlantic ports as a base, there was little the Royal Navy could do to prevent this. A bombing raid on the port would have led to many French casualties and was consequently ruled out. A seaborne commando raid was the only option. The raiders would be Royal Marine Commandos serving with the SBS. They drew their nickname from the pet name they gave their canoes – 'cockleshells'. During their months of training, the 12 men selected for the raid were not told what their target was to be. They were only informed on board the submarine HMS *Tuna* when it had surfaced off the French coast on 7 December 1942.

The raid started badly when one of the canoes was holed as it was being made ready. Then as the canoes approached the mouth of the River Gironde, they hit a violent rip tide. One canoe and its crew were lost. The crews of two other canoes were caught by the Germans and shot. Hiding by day and paddling upstream by night, the two remaining canoes managed to elude the German patrols, who had now been alerted that a raid was in progress. As they reached the harbour, they were spotted by a sentry

Passing a limpet mine to a comrade wearing diving gear during a rehearsal for Operation Franklin in December 1942. Canoeing between ships, the commandos clamped on mines timed to explode nine hours later. The daring exploit gave rise to the name 'Cockleshell Heroes'.

who somehow failed to raise the alarm, possibly mistaking the flimsy canoes for driftwood. Using limpet mines, the crews succeeded in sinking one ship and severely damaging four others, putting the harbour out of action for months. Winston Churchill said that this helped to shorten the war by six months.

The raiders escaped on the tide. Once out of danger, they abandoned their canoes, hoping to escape into Spain on foot. One team was caught by the Germans and shot. But, with the help of the Resistance, the leader of the raid Major Herbert 'Blondie' Hasler and his shipmate Marine Bill Sparks reached Spain, then Gibraltar. However, all the raiders were assumed to be dead. Hasler used his rank to get transport back to Britain, but Sparks was arrested. However, back in London, he managed to give his military police escort the slip and, after visiting his father, made his way to the headquarters of Combined Operations.

1st Battalion, the Parachute Regiment

The Special Forces Support Group

Paratroopers have always seen themselves as an élite, and there is a rivalry between battalions of the British Parachute Regiment as to who is the toughest. However, when the Special Forces Support Group was set up in 2006, it was formed around the 1st Battalion, the Parachute Regiment – better known as 1 Para.

The 1st Battalion, the Parachute Regiment can trace its roots to 2 Independent Company of the Commando Force who were trained as parachutists and 11 Special Air Service Battalion of the Commando Force who were organized into parachute and glider wings. In 1941, it became part of the 1st Parachute Brigade, then the 1st Parachute Division. The following year they emerged as the 1st Battalion, the Parachute Regiment. In 1944, they took part in the disastrous Operation Market Garden. Since then it has seen service in Egypt, Cyprus, the Persian Gulf and Northern Ireland. In Northern Ireland it was involved in the Bloody Sunday incident in 1972 when 27 civil rights protesters were shot.

In 2000, 1 Para began to work closely with the Special Air Service (SAS), first on Operation Palliser where they went into Sierra Leone to evacuate UK, European Union and Commonwealth citizens. Later that year, a group of Royal Irish Rangers with the United Nations peacekeeping force in Sierra Leone were taken prisoner by a gang of rebels calling themselves 'the West Side Boys'. In Operation Barras, 1 Para went in with the SAS and Special Boat Service (SBS) to free the hostages. While the SAS and SBS attacked the small rebel camp at Geri Bana where the hostages were being held, 1 Para attacked the larger camp at Magbeni on the other side of the creek to prevent the rebels there joining the action.

While the SAS-SBS fire-teams went through their carefully rehearsed plan and the SAS hostage-rescue team found and secured the prisoners, 1 Para helicoptered in, set up mortars and pounded the rebel positions. The first wave of paras held the line until the second wave arrived on the returning Chinooks. Now at full strength, the paras pressed home their attack. The fighting was ferocious. Despite their lack of discipline or any real sense of tactics, the rebels seemed completely fearless. It is thought that many were high on drugs and believed that they were protected by magic amulets.

The battle raged for several hours before it was deemed safe enough to call in the Chinooks to extract the hostages. The fighting at Magbeni went on for another six hours. When the last British troops were withdrawn, they took the rebel leader Foday Kallay with them. He has subsequently been sentenced to 50 years in jail. The British suffered one dead, SAS Trooper Brad Tinnion. Twelve paras were wounded, one seriously.

THE RANGER ROLE

In December 2001, 1 Para was called in to support the SAS again. This time they were attacking the al-Qaeda cave complexes in the Tora Bora Mountains in the search for Osama

Troops from 1 Para carrying out exercises in Kuwait in March 2003 prior to Operation Telic – the British codename for the invasion of Iraq by America and its allies. The large helicopter is a Chinook, much used for transporting forces such as paratroopers.

1ST BATTALION, THE PARACHUTE REGIMENT

MAY 2000 Operation Palliser

SEPTEMBER 2000 Operation Barras

DECEMBER 2001 1 Para supports the SAS in the Battle of Tora Bora

MARCH 2003 Operation Telic, 1 Para sees action in Iraq

DECEMBER 2004 1 Para becomes designated support unit for UK special forces

JULY 2005 The SFSG assists the SAS in Operation Marlborough, which eliminates three suicide bombers

MARCH 2006 The SFSG aids the rescue of hostages Norman Kember, James Loney and Harmeet Sooden

APRIL 2006 Defence minister in British parliament admits the SFSG is operating alongside US special forces in Iraq

SEPTEMBER 2006 The SFSG supports the SBS in Operation Medusa against the Taliban in Afghanistan

Members of the Special Forces Support Group, a special operations unit based around 1 Para. The covert nature of the unit's work is indicated by the blacked-out faces of the men photographed here.

bin Laden. After 1 Para participated in Operation Telic – the British designation for the invasion of Iraq – to support UK special forces. This role was now formalized with 1 Para being used as a battalion of rangers, as the 75th Ranger Regiment operates alongside Delta Force.

In April 2005, the 1200-strong Special Forces Support Group (SFSG) was established at a base in St Athan, Wales. Three companies come from 1 Para. The Royal Marines supply a fourth, while the RAF Regiment provides one platoon and the support group's forward air controllers. One company was deployed to Afghanistan in support of the SBS, under the command of an SBS officer, and at least one company was deployed to Iraq to support the SAS. Its task is to provide a quick-reaction force for UK special forces, sealing off and guarding an area of operation. It also takes part in large scale assaults alongside SAS and SBS forces, carrying out secondary assaults and diversionary raids. In addition, it acts as a blocking force against counter-attacks and provides chemical, biological, radiological and nuclear detection and protection. And it supports domestic anti-terrorist operations.

Although much about the SFSG remains secret, the unit is believed to have the latest high-tech special forces equipment, including computerized satellite communications that will allow it to download intelligence from national agencies such as GCHQ and MI6, as well as the Soflam laser marking system that allows it to designate targets for RAF aircraft. The unit trains alongside the SAS or the SBS and comes under the direct control of the director of special forces, who is based in Regent's Park, north London.

TASK FORCE RED

In April 2006, the British secretary of state for defence reported that a company of SFSG soldiers was operating in Iraq as part of the US-led Task Force 145, whose primary task was to hunt down senior members of al-Qaeda operating in Iraq. Later renamed Task Force 88, this joint US-UK special operations unit was itself divided into smaller task forces. Task Force Orange was made up of the electronic intelligence gatherers. Task Force Green was provided by the 1st Special Forces Operational Detachment – that is, Delta Force. Task Force Blue was US Navy SEALs from the DEVGRU, formerly SEAL Team 6. Task Force Black was made up of an SAS sabre squadron operating initially in southern Iraq. Some SBS operators were thought to have been attached to Task Force Black, as are members of the British Special Reconnaissance Regiment. Task Force Black was also supported by 100 men from the SFSG, known as Task Force Red.

In July 2005, British intelligence identified a house in Baghdad used as a base by suicide bombers. The SAS considered storming the building, but it was decided this was too risky. If any of the insurgents detonated a bomb inside the building its blast would be amplified within the structure, killing civilians in adjoining buildings. So it was decided to engage the insurgents as they left the house. Just before the dawn rush hour in the Iraqi capital on 31

THE BADGE CONTROVERSY

The uniform of the new Special Forces Support Group caused problems. While all the troops in the unit continued to wear their own regimental cap badges, they were issued with a new shoulder insignia that depicts a silver dagger on a green background with red-lined black flashes of lightning running through it. It was pointed out that these elongated S-shaped flashes bore a more than passing resemblance to the insignia of Adolf Hitler's

SS. But this was not a problem to men seconded into Task Force Red, who wore US uniforms in Iraq since it was thought that the uniforms of British paratroopers would attract unwanted attention. However, they were armed with C7 Diemaco rifles – the Canadian version of the M16 favoured by the SAS.

The Special Forces Support Group's shoulder patch with its controversial insignia.

July, four SAS sniper teams set up in a building around 300 metres (984 ft) away. Troops from Task Force Red, the Special Forces Support Group quick-reaction force, were situated close by in case things went wrong. As it was, all three bombers were hit in the head and killed instantly the moment they stepped out of the door.

On 8 March 2006, Task Force Red set up a cordon around the house where peace activists Norman Kember, James Loney and Harmeet Sooden were being held by the Sword of Righteousness Brigade, who had previously killed US citizen Tom Fox. The SFSG were to keep the public away, while the SAS hostage-rescue team stormed the building.

In September 2006, the SFSG supported the SBS in the Canadian-led Operation Medusa in Afghanistan to drive the Taliban from the strategically important Panjwayi district of Kandahar province. While the SBS spearheaded the attacking force, the SFSG provided cut-off groups. SFSG personnel were among the 14 killed when an RAF Nimrod spy plane crashed during the operation. Generally, though, the activities of the SFSG remain clouded in secrecy, like those of the SAS and SBS.

The SFSG were also on hand when a 30-man SAS team raided a house that intelligence had pinpointed as the location of a senior al-Qaeda figure – possibly al-Zarqawi's successor – in Iraq on 5 September 2007. Unfortunately, they had underestimated the number of insurgents in the house and the scale of the likely resistance. Sergeant Eddie Collins, an SAS man who had joined from 3 Para, was the first in. He was shot in the head and died instantly.

'They are making a really good name for themselves with the Hereford blokes and the Americans. If the shit hits the fan and the SAS need them, the boys are there as a quick reaction force.'

DAILY TELEGRAPH, 24 APRIL 2006

MODERN

WARFARE

Special Forces troops training in the harshest of conditions. Because of the nature of modern conflicts, small units of special forces are used more and more often to undertake high-risk operations.

Special Reconnaissance Regiment

Britain's most secret special forces unit

The Special Reconnaissance Regiment (SRR) is a new special forces unit of the British army that specializes in surveillance and intelligence-gathering operations. It provides close-target reconnaissance and 'eyes-on' intelligence to the SAS and SBS. However, the secrecy surrounding the SRR is even greater than that around other special forces units. Very little information about the unit has leaked into the public domain.

Raised in 2005, the Special Reconnaissance Regiment can trace its history back to the early 1970s with the formation of the Mobile Reconnaissance Force (MRF) in Northern Ireland. After two MRF double-agents were discovered by the IRA and a covert operation was ambushed, it was replaced by the 14th Intelligence Company – also known as 14 Int or 'The Det' – manned by Special Air Service (SAS) and Special Boat Service (SBS) personnel.

As peace came to Northern Ireland, the 14th Intelligence Company was subsumed into the SRR, bringing with it the skills it had acquired during plain clothes surveillance operations against Republican and Loyalist terrorist organizations during the Troubles. The SRR's job was to relieve other UK special forces units of their surveillance duties and allow them to concentrate on offensive operations. It also joined the Special Forces anti-terrorist role the SAS had assumed after 9/11.

A US soldier (left) and a soldier of 1st Battalion, C Company, the Parachute Regiment (right) help to secure the town of AD Adyr, north of Basra in southern Iraq. Basra was the scene of a daring rescue of two SRR personnel by British forces.

SAS TRAINING

The Special Reconnaissance Regiment is half the size of the SAS, recruiting volunteers from all sections of the British armed forces, but the selection process is gruelling. SRR operatives need to be expert linguists. These days, they are required to be proficient in Middle Eastern languages such as Arabic and Farsi. On selection, they are taught the arts of surveillance, photography, close-quarters battle, and defensive and anti-ambush driving. They train alongside the SAS in Hereford. All personnel must maintain high levels of fitness as well as being capable of using a variety of rifles and hand guns to such a high degree that stripping and assembling can be carried out blindfolded. They must also be capable of attaining high levels of marksmanship with a wide variety of weapons. The SRR is the only UK special forces regiment to have women in operational roles.

ARREST IN BASRA

In Iraq, the SRR worked alongside Task Force Black. However, Special Forces operations do not necessarily go smoothly. On 19 September 2005, two SRR men, probably seconded from the SAS, had to be rescued after they were arrested in Basra. Dressed as Arabs, the two had been spotted at a police checkpoint. There was a chase. After an exchange of small-arms fire, the two men gave themselves up and identified themselves as British soldiers by showing a Union Jack. They were arrested and beaten up. It has not been revealed what mission they were on. At the time it was said that they were either on a surveillance operation to observe

SPECIAL RECONNAISSANCE REGIMENT

APRIL 2005 British defence minister announces the formation of the Special Reconnaissance Regiment

JULY 2005 SRR men thought to be involved in the killing of Jean Charles de Menezes after the 7/7 terrorist attack in London

SEPTEMBER 2005 Two SRR men rescued in Basra

the house of a colleague of Moqtada al-Sadr, leader of the Mahdi army, or that they were following an Iraqi police officer known to torture prisoners.

When the men were arrested, the police found weapons, explosives and communications equipment in their vehicle. They were accused of fomenting acts of terrorism, though an expert on special forces operations said that they were clearly involved in counter-terrorism since the SAS 'were in charge of hunting Iraqi extremists and neutralizing them'.

As soon as he heard about the arrests, the British commander in Basra, Brigadier John Lorimer, planned a rescue mission. He tried diplomatic means to secure the release of the two men, but these failed. Less than an hour later, a convoy of Warrior armoured cars pulled up outside the police station, backed by snipers and a Lynx helicopter. As the troops tried to negotiate their way in, a crowd gathered and started throwing petrol bombs. Three soldiers were injured. One of the Warriors then knocked down the wall into the police compound, but the two captured men were no longer there.

THE SAS TO THE RESCUE

In fact, the attack on the police compound had only been a diversion. While the compound wall was being knocked down, the SAS blew out the doors and windows of a suburban villa nearby with plastic explosive and hurled stun grenades at the Mahdi-army militiamen inside who were guarding the two undercover soldiers. A short, intense burst of automatic gunfire was heard before the men were freed and their captors were seen being dragged away, with hoods over their heads and their hands tied behind their backs. The entire operation took only a couple of minutes and proceeded unhindered, as the attention was focused on the army's invasion of the main police compound 100 metres away.

At least one SRR man has been killed in Afghanistan. On 27 June 2006, Captain David 'Pat' Patten of the Special Reconnaissance Regiment was with an SBS patrol that had snatched four Taliban rebels near Sangin in Helmand province. They were on their way back to base when one of their vehicles was hit by a rocket-propelled grenade. The men fled on foot to find cover in a drainage ditch. Captain Patten was hit in the chest by a bullet and fell.

'Pat got halfway across the field. You could see the round had hit him. He fell face first with the momentum of it,' his commander said at the inquest. 'As he lay there in the mud, with just his black rucksack showing, his left leg moved like it was an attempt to stand up. Then he went still. It was too difficult to cross the open field because the enemy were putting down some heavy fire, so myself and Paul headed north.'

Another special forces man was severely injured, and Sergeant Paul Bartlett of the SBS tried to make a break for it. He was killed by 12 bullets to the head, neck and chest. However, this allowed the remaining men to see where the enemy were and target them with a grenade. That held them off until a platoon of Gurkhas could reach the beleaguered men.

'I had good reason to believe the lives of the two soldiers were at risk.'

BRIGADIER JOHN LORIMER, BRITISH COMMANDING OFFICER BASRA, 20 SEPTEMBER 2005

DOMESTIC ANTI-TERRORIST ROLE

Since its formation in April 2005, the Special Reconnaissance Regiment has been involved in several controversial operations. In July 2005, following the London bombings, the SRR was deployed on the streets of the UK capital in a bid to counter the terrorist threat. It was reported that members from the SRR were involved in the surveillance operation involving Brazilian electrician Jean Charles de Menezes. He was mistakenly thought to be connected to the 7 July attacks and was trailed to Stockwell underground station by SRR operatives. As he boarded the train, he was shot in the head by the police and killed.

A CCTV camera shows the inside of Stockwell tube station and the position of undercover firearms officers some moments before Jean Charles de Menezes was shot.

The Ministry of Defence admitted that the army provided 'technical assistance' to the surveillance operation, but insisted the soldiers concerned were 'not directly involved' in the shooting. Press photographs of members of the armed response team taken in the immediate aftermath of the killing show at least one man carrying a special forces weapon that is not issued to SO19, the Metropolitan police firearms unit. The man, wearing civilian clothes with a blue cap marked 'Police', was carrying a specially modified Heckler & Koch G3K rifle with a shortened barrel and a butt from a PSG-1 sniper rifle fitted to it – a combination used by the SAS. Another man, dressed in a T-shirt, jeans and trainers, was carrying a Heckler & Koch G36C. Although this weapon is used on occasion by SO19 it appears to be fitted with a target illuminator purchased as an 'urgent operational requirement' for UK special forces

involved in the war on terror. Defence sources also said that the soldiers who took part in the surveillance operation that led to Jean Charles de Menezes's death included men from a secret undercover unit formed for operations in Northern Ireland.

The official Independent Police Complaints Commission report into the Stockwell incident does not mention the SRR, instead identifying the surveillance operatives involved as being from SO12 – Special Branch – and SO13 – the Anti-terrorist Branch. These have now been combined into SO15 Counter Terrorism Command.

The Spetsnaz

Russia's special purpose regiments

During the Cold War, the West became aware of the Soviet Spetsnaz, or special purpose regiments, who were trained in reconnaissance, sabotage and assassination. Since the collapse of the Soviet Union, their role has changed. Russia's Spetsnaz now mimic the US Navy SEALs, the SAS and Delta Force.

Russian military intelligence, the GRU, deployed special purpose units in Eastern Europe during the Cold War. Their job was to carry out reconnaissance and sabotage missions against NATO units in Europe in the event of war. The existence of Spetsnaz was a closely guarded secret within the Warsaw Pact. Troops were not allowed to admit they belonged to the Spetsnaz and wore standard airborne, or VDV, uniforms and insignia, while the naval Spetsnaz wore regular navy uniforms and insignia.

One Spetsnaz company was assigned to each of the Russian armies, with one regiment deployed in each theatre of operations. There was one Spetsnaz brigade in each of the four Soviet fleets and an independent Spetsnaz brigade in most military districts of the USSR. The Spetsnaz also had specialist intelligence units.

A Spetsnaz company was 135 strong, normally operating in 15 independent nine-man teams. A Spetsnaz brigade was 1000 to 1300 strong and consisted of a headquarters, three or four parachute battalions, a communications company and supporting troops. It also included an anti-VIP company, composed of some 70 to 80 men whose mission was to seek out, identify and kill the enemy's political and military leaders.

A Spetsnaz group prepares for a mission at Kabul airport in 1988 during the Soviet invasion of Afghanistan. During the time the Soviets were in the country, between 3000 and 5000 Spetsnaz were deployed there.

NAVY SPETSNAZ

In 1957, the Soviet navy set up its own Spetsnaz. The Black Sea Fleet followed suit in 1967. Two years later a marine counter-terrorist and counter-sabotage unit was created. A naval Spetsnaz brigade had a headquarters, two to three battalions of combat swimmers, a parachute battalion, supporting units and an anti-VIP company. It also had midget submarines to deliver combat swimmers to their targets.

The GRU first formed a top-secret reconnaissance and sabotage unit in 1970,

training combat swimmers for the KGB to carry out offensive operations against enemy ports and shipping. It also trained a special *Delfin*, or 'Dolphin', unit to spearhead seaborne assaults carried out by the Russian marines amphibious infantry.

The Ministry of the Interior, MVD, has its own Spetsnaz units trained in reconnaissance and house-to-house close-quarters battle assaults. They have been deployed in Chechnya, an area of the former USSR which has sought independence from Russia.

THE SECURITY SERVICE

The cream of the Spetsnaz work for the Federal Security Service of the Russian Federation, the FSB, who are the successor to the Soviet-era KGB and NKVD. *Stetzgruppa Alfa*, or special group A, was set up in 1974 as a counter-terrorist unit. They number between 1500 and 2000 men, and they are trained in armed response and intelligence gathering. Men showing toughness of character and the ability to use initiative are hand picked from conventional military units. Then recruits are submitted to an intense and deliberately brutal five-month induction period intended to instil the necessary toughness and resilience. All the Alfa recruits undergo airborne and firearms training. Around one-third have mountain training; another third are trained divers. Training can take up to five years.

Spetsnaz soldiers stand in front of Russia's White House in October 1993. They were ordered in by Russian president Boris Yeltsin to enforce fresh elections after the house had refused to dissolve parliament.

179

THE SPETSNAZ

1957 Soviet navy establishes Spetsnaz unit

1967 Spetsnaz unit attached to the Black Sea Fleet

1969 Marine counter-terrorism unit formed

1970 GRU sets up a top-secret reconnaissance and sabotage unit

1974 The élite Alfa unit set up by the security services

1979 Alfa assassinate Afghan president and his family

1980 Ministry of the Interior sets up its own 'black beret' anti-terrorist squad

2002 Alfa breaks siege at Moscow theatre

2004 FSB Spetsnaz unit ends siege at Beslan school with many casualties

Standard issue weapons for the Spetsnaz are 5.45mm AKS-74 assault rifles and 5.45mm PRI automatic pistols. They also carry NR-2 combat knives, which are specially designed for the Spetsnaz troops and incorporate a 7.62mm calibre barrel in the handle. They must also master a wide variety of foreign weapons,

On the battlefield, Spetsnaz soldiers have the reputation of being among the world's toughest and most ruthless soldiers. According to analysts, Spetsnaz tactics are far more improvised than those of Western special forces, with more emphasis placed on physical strength. Alfa is generally credited with attacking the presidential palace in Kabul on 27 December 1979 and murdering President Hafizullah Amin and his family.

Alfa tactics were much criticized after the siege in a Moscow theatre in 2002 and a school in North Ossetia two years later because of the high death toll among the hostages. However, in less high-profile hostage takings, it has done much better. In Sarapul City in 1981, it freed 25 boys held hostage at a school, and disarmed and arrested the hostage takers without loss of life. During a hijacking at Ilya Ufa City in 1986, five terrorists were killed and the plane was set on fire. Nine passengers were injured – some by the Spetsnaz – but the four dead appear to have been killed by the terrorists.

In Saratov in 1989, four escaped prisoners took refuge in an apartment with three men and one woman with a two-year-old child. After tossing a flash-bang grenade through the window, Alfa used a ram to break down the door, releasing the hostages unharmed and 'neutralizing' their captors.

In May 1990, it arrested the parties to a terrorist arms deal and, in August, in Armenia, Alfa took on an armed gang, killing three, wounding two and arresting another six. They thwarted a mass prison breakout in Sukhumi City that August, putting a delayed-action flash-bang in the bus the prisoners had demanded, then storming the jail. Less creditably, Alfa retook the TV tower in Vilnius from unarmed protesters at the cost of 14 dead and 700 injured.

In October 1993, Russian president Boris Yeltsin sent the FSB Spetsnaz into the parliament building in Moscow after the house refused to dissolve to make way for fresh elections. Within an hour of their arrival, parliament surrendered. However, fire from a house nearby prompted tanks to go to it, and a member of Alfa was killed by a sniper.

In June 1995, 80 Chechen terrorists led by Shamil Basayev stormed government buildings in the Russian city of Budyonnovsk, some 70 miles (113 km) north of the Chechen border, killing at least 20 policemen and soldiers. In the face of Russian reinforcements, the rebels retreated into Budyonnovsk hospital, taking around 1800 hostages, including 150 children and infants. After four days, Alfa stormed the hospital. Over 30 hostages were killed during this action. After a second failed assault, a ceasefire was called. In return for the hostages, the Russian government agreed to temporarily halt military actions in Chechnya and begin negotiations.

'We came in through specially made openings and just shot the sleeping terrorists at point-blank range.'

SPETSNAZ OFFICER, MOSCOW THEATRE SIEGE 2002

LIFTING SIEGES

In October 2002, some 200 men of the Spetsnaz Alfa forces ended the siege at a Moscow theatre where Chechen rebels had been holding around 900 people hostage for three days. After two hostages were shot, a full-scale assault began. There was an explosion, then gas was pumped in, followed by dozens of masked and heavily armed men. A gun battle began. One female terrorist was shot with a grenade in her hand. Others were shot at point-blank range while unconscious. Over 40 terrorists had died of gunshot wounds, while some 113 hostages had died due to the effects of the gas.

A heavily armed special forces soldier prepares to enter the Beslan school in North Ossetia in 2004.

FSB Spetsnaz troops also spearheaded the ending of a siege at Beslan school in North Ossetia when Chechens took over 1100 people hostage, including 777 children. On the third day, the FSB assaulted the school building with tanks, rockets and other heavy weapons. Hostages panicked and tried to flee. At least 200 were killed, along with 27 hostage takers. Over 700 hostages were injured, 92 of them critically. It was a terrible reminder of what can go wrong in a hostage-rescue mission.

'PENNANT' AND 'BLACK BERET' UNITS

Alongside Alfa is the *Vympel*, or 'pennant', which was formerly a Cold War-era sabotage, kidnap and assassination unit working under the direction of the KGB. With the collapse of the Soviet Union it was transferred to the MVD, and then to the FSB, where its members are trained in hostage rescue, counter-sabotage and counter-terrorism. They are also given specialist training to protect nuclear plants, hydroelectric dams and other industrial complexes. Every city that has a nuclear power station has a branch, though units are also rotated through Chechnya.

The MVD have its own Spetsnaz unit called the *Omon*, or 'black berets', that was originally raised to provide additional security at the 1980 Olympics in Moscow. It is now used in anti-terrorist operations, or to arrest armed criminals. Five MVD men were injured in the aftermath of a hijacking in 1994. Five terrorists were also killed, while four hostages were killed and six wounded.

The Ministry of Justice has a Spetsnaz unit, UIN, whose role is to suppress riots and deal with other problems in prisons. The Federal government also has a Spetsnaz unit called the GROM, unrelated to the Polish special forces unit of the same name. It recruits from other Spetsnaz units and its job is to guard airports, train stations, government buildings and government personnel. Altogether there are thought to be 20 Spetsnaz brigades, plus 41 additional companies, comprising over 30,000 men.

Team patch of the Vityaz unit of the Spetsnaz, which is assigned specifically to counter-terrorism duties and regularly conducts patrols in Chechnya and along the Caucasus border.

The Green Berets

From Vietnam to Afghanistan

In the 1960s, US Army special forces officially adopted their famous green berets – headgear they had originally borrowed from the British Royal Marines. During the decade, the number of special forces units more than doubled and the Green Berets headed the counter-insurgency operations in Vietnam and Latin America. They continue in that role to this day in Iraq and Afghanistan.

The shoulder sleeve insignia of the US Army Special Forces (Green Berets), which depicts a yellow dagger, its blade surmounted by three yellow lightning flashes, has been in use since 1955, with the words 'Airborne' added in 1958. The Special forces motto is De Oppresso Liber *('To Liberate the Oppressed').*

A designated American special forces unit was set up at Fort Bragg, North Carolina, in 1952. From 1953, special forces troops wore the distinctive green beret when they went into the field, although the army refused to authorize its official use. However, when President John F. Kennedy visited Fort Bragg on 12 October 1961, he sent word to the Special Warfare Center commander, Brigadier-General William P. Yarborough, that all special forces soldiers should wear their green berets during his inspection. Afterwards the president told the Pentagon that he considered the green beret to be: 'symbolic of one of the highest levels of courage and achievement of the United States military.' Soon, the green beret became synonymous with special forces and the two terms became interchangeable.

By 1961, there were already three special forces groups in existence, one based at Bad Tolz in West Germany, one in Fort Bragg and one in the Far East. A Green Beret, Captain Harry G. Cramer Jr of the 14th Special Forces Detachment, had become the first US soldier to die in Vietnam on 21 October 1956. Throughout the late 1950s and early 1960s, the number of special forces military advisers in Vietnam increased steadily. Their job was to train South Vietnamese soldiers in the art of counter-insurgency and to mould minority tribes into anti-communist forces. In September 1964, the Green Berets's 5th Group set up its headquarters in Nha Trang, where it remained until it returned to Fort Bragg in 1971, although some special forces teams stayed behind in Thailand from where they launched secret missions into Vietnam.

THE RAID ON SON TAY

The most high-profile operation undertaken by the Green Berets during the Vietnam War was their daring raid on Son Tay prison camp just 23 miles (37 km) from Hanoi, North Vietnam, on 18 November 1970. Militarily, this attack deep behind enemy lines was a brilliant success. The 60 guards were overwhelmed and the camp taken in a matter of minutes. However, as a rescue mission, it was a failure. The 70 American pilots held there had been moved shortly before and none was freed. Despite the mission's failure, it highlighted the inhumane way in which US prisoners were treated by the North Vietnamese.

Recruits of the 7th Group undergo an exercise in water training, learning how to approach a possibly hazardous situation without being detected. Their blackened faces help them to remain hidden in undergrowth.

By the time the 5th Group left Southeast Asia its soldiers had won 16 Medals of Honor, one Distinguished Service Medal, 90 Distinguished Service Crosses, 814 Silver Stars, 13,234 Bronze Stars, 235 Legions of Merit, 46 Distinguished Flying Crosses, 232 Soldier's Medals, 4891 Air Medals, 6908 Army Commendation Medals and 2658 Purple Hearts.

During the 1960s, other special forces training teams were operating in Bolivia, Venezuela, Guatemala, Columbia and the Dominican Republic. Counter-insurgency groups in Latin America carried out some 450 clandestine operations against guerrilla forces between 1965 and 1968. In 1968, the Green Berets were involved in tracking down and capturing the notorious revolutionary Che Guevara in the wilds of Bolivia.

THE GREEN BERETS

1952 US Army Special Forces set up at Fort Bragg, North Carolina

1956 A Green Beret is the first US soldier to die in Vietnam

1961 Special forces officially permitted to wear the green beret

1964 5th Special Forces Group set up headquarters in Nha Trang

1970 Raid on Son Tay

1971 Special forces officially pull out of Vietnam

1980 Operation Eagle Claw

1983 Operation Urgent Fury

1990 Operation Desert Shield

1991 Operation Desert Storm

2001 Operation Enduring Freedom

2003 Operation Iraqi Freedom

NATION BUILDING

Following Vietnam, three special forces groups were disbanded. The remaining Green Berets joined a programme called SPARTAN – Special Proficiency at Rugged Training and Nation-building. They worked with Native-American tribes in Florida, Arizona and Montana, building hospitals and roads.

The Green Berets were involved in Operation Eagle Claw, the failed mission to rescue the 52 hostages held in the US embassy in Tehran in 1980. When President Ronald Reagan took office in 1981, the army revitalized the Green Berets. The special forces qualification course was made longer and tougher. Only the highest-calibre soldiers were allowed to join, and training at Fort Bragg's John F. Kennedy Special Warfare School included freefall parachuting, escape missions and maritime operations. In October 1984, the army established a separate career field for special forces.

Special forces teams were once deployed to dozens of countries around the globe. Missions vary from training local armies and running counter-insurgency programmes to providing humanitarian aid and medical care. Special forces have been particularly successful in Honduras and El Salvador, where they prevented the civil war in neighbouring Nicaragua spreading beyond its borders. In October 1983, they took part in Operation Urgent Fury, the invasion of Grenada.

THE A-TEAM

One thing that remained unaltered was the fundamental building block of the Green Berets – the A-team. An Operational Detachment A, or ODA, is a 12-man team comprising two officers, two operations and intelligence sergeants, two weapons sergeants, two communications sergeants, two medics and two engineers, all trained in unconventional warfare and cross-trained in each others' specialities. Each must speak at least one foreign language.

'Ninety-one don't run'

MOTTO OF ODA 391 AT THE
DEBECKA PASS, 2003

They are equipped with high-powered communications systems such as tactical satellite communications, burst transmission devices, high-frequency radios, global positioning systems and sophisticated medical kits. Other key equipment includes individual and perimeter defence weapons as well as night-vision devices and demolitions explosives.

Currently, 4500 Green Berets are deployed around the world, tasked with undertaking seven specific missions: unconventional warfare, foreign internal defence, special reconnaissance, direct action, combating terrorism, counter-proliferation and information collecting. Other duties include combat search and rescue, security assistance, peacekeeping, humanitarian assistance, de-mining and counter-drug operations, and warfare alongside coalition partners.

The Green Berets were on hand for Operation Desert Shield in Saudi Arabia in 1990, Operation Desert Storm in Kuwait in 1991, Operation Restore Hope in Somalia in 1993, fighting in the Battle of Mogadishu in October of the same year, Operation Enduring Freedom in Afghanistan from 2001 and Operation Iraqi Freedom from 2003. In ongoing anti-terrorist operations in Iraq, they provide Task Force Green, while in remote areas of Afghanistan, the Green Berets have been building schools and providing help for the sick and injured.

THE BATTLE OF DEBECKA PASS

The Battle of Debecka Pass is sometimes referred to as the Alamo of the Iraq War. On 6 April 2003, two A-teams were given the task of securing a key crossroads near the town of Debecka in northern Iraq between the cities of Irbil and Kirkuk. They were to be assisted by 80 Kurdish Peshmerga militia, known to the Green Berets as 'the Pesh' or 'Peshies'. However, when they reached the intersection they found the Iraqi army dug in behind minefields and trenches. They called in a B-52 airstrike. But they still had to take the position, now hampered both by mines and unexploded bombs. While the Green Berets were involved in a firefight, Iraqi vehicles approached from the south and the A-team and their Peshie allies had to withdraw to a hill that they would call 'the Alamo'. Then a shell burst overhead, and they realized that they were under attack from an armoured column. The A-teams had recently been issued with Javelin anti-tank missiles, but had little chance to practise with them. There was a haze in the valley below, making the optical sights useless. They switched to infrared sights, but these took at least 45 seconds to cool down. While they waited, shells burst around them.

The first Javelin hit a troop truck and the Green Berets jumped in their vehicle to finish off the fleeing

A US soldier launches an FGM-148 Javelin anti-tank missile. Despite little previous experience in the use of the weapon, troops used it successfully to help achieve a victory in the Battle of Debecka Pass.

Iraqis. Then came the tanks. The Green Berets pulled their forces back behind the ridge and called for close air support. Meanwhile, another Javelin was loosed off. It hit an armoured personnel carrier (APC). Javelins took out two more trucks and two more APCs. The T-55 tanks had taken cover in defilade positions, making it impossible for the Javelins to get a lock on their heat signatures. Two US Navy F-14 Tomcats arrived. By then the Iraqi artillery had bracketed their position. The Green Berets had used half their ammunition and the Iraqis kept on coming. They were down to three Javelins when re-supply arrived. The Green Berets and the Peshmerga then held their position for two hours, while the enemy was bombed. Eventually the Iraqi soldiers abandoned their vehicles and fled the battlefield on foot. For the next two days Iraqi artillery and multiple rocket launchers continued to fire on the Green Berets' position. But the crossroads were secured and the Green Berets went on into Kirkuk to secure the oil facilities there.

The Lurps in Vietnam

Long Range Reconnaissance Patrols

Long Range Reconnaissance Patrols (LRRPs), commonly known as Lurps, were small teams that often penetrated as much as 40 miles (64 km) behind enemy lines during the Vietnam War – far beyond the reach of artillery support. They would walk, undetected, along the same jungle pathways as the enemy for days on end.

Long range reconnaissance became recognized as a task for a specialist unit in the Second World War with the formation of the British Long Range Desert Group. The SAS then inherited that tradition. The Finns also use long range units on reconnaissance and demolition operations behind enemy lines.

In Vietnam, US Army Special Forces formed the first Long Range Reconnaissance Patrol in May 1964. Working in five- or six-man teams, the Lurps, as they were nicknamed, began making patrols deep inside enemy territory. Although their role was primarily to gather intelligence, they often used more aggressive tactics, taking out enemy patrols where this could be done undetected.

The Lurps were a volunteer force, trained in fieldcraft and survival by the Green Berets; training was notoriously rigorous. And there were plenty of volunteers. The Lurps appealed to the independently minded who did not work well within a larger group. They were self-reliant and looked out for one another within small units, especially when they were deep inside 'Indian Country'.

TRAVELLING LIGHT

Usually a team would consist of one or two experienced leaders with a radio man, a medic and two scouts. They were heavily armed with M16 rifles, M26 hand-grenades, Claymore anti-personnel mines, .45 pistols and long killing knives. They also carried coloured smoke grenades for guiding helicopters to a pick-up zone. All this hardware weighed the men down. As they travelled on foot and had to carry everything they needed, they dispensed with flak jackets and steel helmets, substituting bandanas to stop the sweat running down into their eyes and donning the floppy jungle hats favoured by the SAS.

In 1964, special Lurps rations – nicknamed 'long rats' – were developed, since standard rations were too heavy to carry on extended missions on foot. They were lightweight, dehydrated pre-cooked meals that came in packs rather than bulky cans – a soldier from Okinawa had noticed that orientals could carry more food because it was dried and lighter. The new technique of freeze-drying was used to produce dehydrated stew, chilli and other tasty meals, plus crackers and dried fruit. All a man on patrol needed to do was add water.

THE LURPS IN VIETNAM

MAY 1964 First Long Range Reconnaissance Patrol set up in Vietnam; Lurps rations developed

OCTOBER 1964 Project Delta gets under way

SEPTEMBER 1966 Project Omega and Project Sigma extend Lurps mission throughout South Vietnam

OCTOBER 1967 Project Gamma extends Lurps missions into Cambodia

NOVEMBER 1967 Special Operations Group takes over Projects Omega and Sigma; patrols extend into Laos

JUNE 1972 Lurps teams wound up

The problem was that there was not much suitable water in the jungles of Vietnam, so Lurps would need to carry an extra six or seven pints of water to rehydrate them. Nevertheless the rations were much sought after, even by those who did not go out on patrols.

CHOPPERED INTO 'INDIAN COUNTRY'

A team would be dropped into a target area by helicopter. This was the most dangerous part of any operation, since the helicopter could be heard or seen for miles around. Once on the ground, the team would infiltrate quickly and hide themselves in a concealed observation post. Then they would look out for large troop movements. This information would be radioed back. They would also stalk well used Viet Cong or North Vietnamese army trails and try to ambush smaller formations, wiping out the whole enemy patrol or taking prisoners. If one of the Lurps team was injured, the man knew that his buddies would not leave him, despite the danger to themselves. However, a helicopter called in to transport an injured man out would draw attention to their position. The helicopter itself was also in danger if the Lurps team could not pin the enemy down with gunfire or grenades. Neither bad weather nor the cover of night were much of a help, either.

In 1967, a UH-1B multirole helicopter – nicknamed a 'Huey' – lands with US troops. One of the helicopter's main tasks in the Vietnam War was to insert and extract reconnaissance patrols.

Although enemy body counts during the Vietnam War are famously inexact – not to say over optimistic – it has been reported that 400 enemy died for every one Lurp killed. It has been estimated that, during the course of the war, Lurps conducted around 23,000 long range patrols. Of these, two-thirds resulted in sightings of the enemy. Lurps were also said to account for approximately 10,000 enemy killed in action through ambushes and sniping, or by calling in air strikes and artillery fire.

LURP OPERATIONS

The first LRRP project was originally named Leaping Lena which, in October 1964, became part of Project Delta run by special forces Detachment B-52 at Nha Trang in the south. Project Delta also assisted in the training of Detachment B-50 – known as Project Omega – which began operations in the central region of Vietnam in September 1966. At the same time, Detachment B-56, Project Sigma, was organized at Ho Ngoc Nau with II Field Force, the largest army corps in Vietnam which was based in the 11 provinces around the South Vietnamese capital, Saigon. Detachment B-57, Project Gamma, was established in October 1967 for operations inside neighbouring Cambodia. Projects Omega and Sigma were taken over by the Studies and Observation Group (SOG) in November 1967, but operated as independent LRRP units in such operations as Operation Daniel Boone, later Salem House, in Cambodia, and Operation Shining Brass, later Prairie Fire, in Laos.

Wading through the swampy Plain of Reeds region of South Vietnam in October 1969, this US Navy mobile strike force are on a mission to implant electronic sensors to detect the movement of enemy Viet Cong troops.

STAFF SERGEANT PATRICK TADINA

The record for the longest service in the Long Range Reconnaissance Patrol belongs to Staff Sergeant Patrick 'Tad' Tadina of the 173rd Airborne Brigade. He spent 60 months on continuous Lurps duty, from mid-1965 to October 1970. An ex-paratrooper from the 82nd Airborne Division, he was assigned to the 1st Infantry Division in Vietnam to help form its LRRP unit. After a year in Vietnam and eligible to be returned home, he extended his tour and rejoined the 173rd Airborne Brigade.

Short and fit, Tadina was of Hawaiian stock, which gave him an advantage; he was frequently mistaken for a Vietnamese. Instead of keeping his hair close-cropped like most paratroopers, he grew his hair long to look more oriental. Although he wore a red bandana like other Lurps, he topped it with a captured North Vietnamese army (NVA) hat. Confusing things further, Tadina carried

a Kalashnikov AK-47 rifle instead of an M16. On some missions, the enemy would call out greetings to him – until a burst of fire informed them that he was a foe not a friend.

On jungle patrol, Tadina always walked point, the lead position that most men avoided. However, he led more than 200 GIs on combat missions and brought every one of them back alive. He also claimed 111 kills in close-quarters action. Wounded three times, he was awarded 12 medals for valour, including five Bronze Stars and two Silver Stars.

One of his closest calls came when he led his patrol into an NVA ambush. 'They were very well camouflaged,' he recalled. 'One gook leaned out from his cover and stared at me. It was obvious that they thought I was NVA too. The only thing I could do was spray a 30-round burst into them.' Tadina took two bullets in the calf, but his patrol got away.

SPREADING THE KNOW-HOW

LRRP techniques were also taught to regular US forces and South Vietnamese ARVN Rangers, civilian irregular defence groups and special forces – known as LLDBs – at the Reconnaissance and Commando (Recondo) School at Nha Trang. As the popularity of the war began to wane at home in the United States, Congress began to place restrictions on cross-border activities, so there was less call for Lurps. Projects Delta, Gamma, Omega and Sigma had all been wound up by June 1972.

The Lurps ethos has continued in long range surveillance units, now trained to work up to 60 miles (98 km) ahead of the front line for up to four days. Long range surveillance troopers are often graduates of the US army's élite schools, including the US Army Sniper School, Special Operations Target Interdiction Course or SOTIC, Ranger School, Special Forces Combat Diver Qualification Course, HALO, RSLC, Pathfinder, Sabalauski Air Assault School, Jumpmaster and SERE. NATO had a Long Range Reconnaissance Patrol School in Germany. There are joint training exercises and exchange programmes with most US allies.

'We set up a hasty ambush and waited all day and part of the next, but it was busted. So the third day, we moved down the ridge line.'

SENIOR SPECIALIST 4, DOUG MILLER, LRRP PATROL LEADER DURING THE VIETNAM WAR

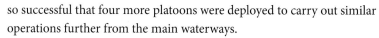

US Navy SEALs

Survivors of Hell Week

The acronym SEAL stands for Sea, Air, Land – all mediums US Navy SEALs use to enter combat. Clandestine naval units had their origins in the Second World War when skilled men were needed to reconnoitre enemy-held beaches and blow up underwater obstructions. But they came into their own with the rapid expansion of special forces during the Vietnam War.

A US Navy SEAL climbs into a SEAL Delivery Vehicle (SDV) before launching from the back of the attack submarine USS Philadelphia. SDVs carry SEALs from a submerged submarine to enemy targets, allowing them to remain under water and undetected.

When President John F. Kennedy came to office in 1961, he asked the armed forces to develop their unconventional warfare capabilities. The US Navy responded by establishing SEAL Teams 1 and 2 in January 1962, using experienced personnel from their wartime Underwater Demolition Teams. The mission of the SEALs was to conduct counter-guerrilla warfare and clandestine operations in the sea and up rivers. SEAL involvement in Vietnam began immediately. Advisers were sent to the South Vietnamese navy, and training courses for South Vietnamese commandos were begun in Danang.

In February 1966, a small detachment of SEAL Team 1 arrived in Vietnam to begin direct-action missions out of Nha Be in the Rung Sat Special Zone area, Saigon's outlet to the sea. Eventually there would be eight SEAL platoons permanently stationed in the country. Initially, SEAL reconnaissance teams were used to map Viet Cong infiltration networks in the Mekong Delta. Later they would go back and destroy them. These initial operations proved so successful that four more platoons were deployed to carry out similar operations further from the main waterways.

As the war escalated, SEAL Teams 1 and 2 deployed platoons along the Mekong, inserted and extracted by the so-called Brown Water Navy. By late 1966, the SEALs received further support, which included Helicopter Attack Squadron Light 3 (HAL-3) – also known as the 'Seawolves' – and the Special Boat Squadron with its 'swift boats', along with a Mobile Support Team.

SEARCH AND DESTROY

The SEALs carried out a number of search-and-destroy operations during their time in Vietnam. These included Operation Charlestown in December 1966, which involved the location and destruction of Viet Cong cells in the Rung Sat Special Zone; Operation Crimson Tide in September 1967, where the SEALs acted as scouts for large regular units during bigger operations; and Operation Bold Dragon III of March 1968,

where they destroyed a Viet Cong arms factory and bunkers on Tan Dinh Island. The SEALs also paid frequent visits to Haiphong Harbour, the main port of North Vietnam, on reconnaissance and sabotage missions.

SEALs took part in the Intelligence Coordination and Exploitation Program to neutralize the Viet Cong command structure, and later the Phoenix Counter-terrorist Program, eliminating potential Viet Cong recruits. Missions ranged from reconnaissance to ambush, and also included the kidnapping and assassination of Viet Cong political cadres, tax collectors and spies. Joint operations were also conducted with the Lien Doc Nguoi Nhia, the Vietnamese SEALs. These included raids on Viet Cong prisoner of war camps in the Mekong Delta. They also fought alongside the Republic of Korea's Marine Corps, most notably in Operation Van Buren and the Battle of Hoi An, where some 13 allied soldiers wiped out an élite North Vietnamese army regiment.

SEALs emerging from the water during tactical warfare training. The SEAL member in the foreground is carrying an M16 A1 rifle equipped with a grenade launcher.

SURVIVING HELL WEEK

To become a SEAL, recruits have to survive Hell Week. This is five and a half days of physical torment where the recruits are allowed to sleep for four hours – total. Soaked to the skin, they carry heavy boats over rocky beaches, crawl under barbed wire and clear obstacle courses while explosions are going off. Whistle drills punctuate the week.

Recruits also spend a lot of time in a mud-pit surrounded by barbed wire, where the physical exertion continues while they are hosed with sea water, promoting salt sores. They eat in the mud-pit and, when the whistle sounds, bury their heads in it. At the same time blank rounds are being fired, instructors bellow though bull horns and artillery

SEALs recruits in the mud during Hell Week. They are cold, exhausted, hungry and wet throughout this selection process.

simulators explode around them. The failure rate is typically between 70 and 80 percent.

As well as operating as a self-contained force, SEALs served as advisers for Provincial Reconnaissance Units and the Lien Doc Nguoi Nhia. The last SEAL platoon withdrew from Vietnam on 7 December 1971, and the last SEAL adviser left in March 1973.

PEACE-TIME DUTIES

After Vietnam, the SEALs undertook standard peace-time duties, such as instructing friendly troops in Central America, although it is thought that SEALs directed the mining of Nicaragua's main harbour under CIA authorization in 1984. On 1 May 1983, Underwater Demolition Teams from the Vietnam era were designated as SEAL Teams, and Special Boat Units, which had been around since the Second World War, were brought into the SEAL fold. Meanwhile, in November 1980, the United States Navy Special Warfare Development Group – SEAL Team 6 – was set up. Also known as 'the Mob' or DEVGRU, it is a special counter-terrorist combat swimmer unit, tasked with countering attacks on ships and oil rigs, as well as supporting Delta Force in conventional counter-terrorist operations.

Elements of Teams 4 and 6 saw action during Operation Urgent Fury, the invasion of Grenada, in 1983. The first American troops to land on the island were SEAL Team 4, whose mission included pre-landing beach reconnaissance. Team 6 was sent in to reconnoitre Point Salines airfield. Two teams of eight, each carrying the maximum combat load of over

27 kilograms (60 lb), made a hazardous night-time jump into the sea; four men did not resurface. Once on shore, they headed for the radio station, but came under fire from Soviet weaponry. Retreating into the surf a mile (1.6 km) offshore, they called in an air-strike.

More SEALs fast-roped from helicopters outside Government House, disarmed the police guard and released 14 hostages. They then came under fire. After four hours, an AC-130 Spectre gunship arrived, relieved the SEALs and evacuated the 14 staffers.

After Grenada, SEALs were also deployed on sabotage and raiding missions on Iranian ships and oil platforms in the Persian Gulf. SEAL Team 6 was put on alert when terrorists hijacked the Mediterranean cruise ship *Achille Lauro* in 1985 and murdered wheelchair-bound US citizen Leon Klinghoffer.

In Operation Just Cause, the invasion of Panama in 1989, SEAL Team 4 was tasked with cutting off General Noriega's possible escape routes. They closed the harbour and blew up the patrol boat *President Porras* tied up at Balboa Harbour.

Swimmers went ashore to reconnoitre the airfield at Paitilla, home to Noriega's Learjet. As nine SEALs crossed the airfield, the Panama Defence Force (PDF) opened fire, killing four SEALs and wounding several more. Three PDF troopers were killed and eight wounded. Meanwhile, a 40-mm grenade blasted a hole in the Learjet, rendering it useless.

During the Gulf War, the SEALs were the first to capture Iraqi prisoners after assaulting nine occupied Kuwaiti oil platforms on 19 January1991. They were also the first Western forces to arrive in Kuwait, infiltrating the city within hours of the invasion. Their mission was to provide intelligence reports and develop plans to rescue US embassy personnel. It is said that a SEAL sniper team on a reconnaissance mission had Saddam Hussein in their sights, but decided not to shoot as it fell outside their mission parameters.

FIRST ON THE GROUND

SEAL units have also conducted missions in the Lebanon, Somalia, Bosnia, Haiti and Liberia. Four men from SEAL Team 6 were part of the team assault involved in the Battle of Mogadishu in 1993. SEALs were the first men on the ground in Afghanistan in October 2001. During Operation Enduring Freedom, they carried out more than 75 special reconnaissance and direct action missions, destroying more than 226,800 kilograms (500,000 lb) of explosives and weapons.

The SEALs also played a significant role in Operation Iraqi Freedom, securing key oil facilities on the Al Faw Peninsula and the offshore gas and oil terminals. They helped clear the Khawr Abd Allah and Khawr Az Zubayr waterways. Conducting reconnaissance up the Shat Al Arab waterway, they captured high-value targets, raided suspected chemical, biological and radiological sites and rescued 19-year-old Private Jessica Lynch.

During the war on terror, the SEALs have also been involved in fighting in other global hot spots including the Philippines and the Horn of Africa. They are deployed from navy ships, submarines and planes. DEVGRU, or SEAL Team 6, makes up Task Force Blue in Iraq.

US NAVY SEALS

JANUARY 1962 SEAL Teams 1 and 2 formed

FEBRUARY 1966 SEAL Team 1 deploys to Vietnam

SEPTEMBER 1967 SEALs begin to scout for larger units

DECEMBER 1971 SEALs pull out of Vietnam

NOVEMBER 1980 SEAL Team 6, DEVGRU, formed

OCTOBER 1983 Operation Urgent Fury

OCTOBER 1985 *Achille Lauro* hijacking

DECEMBER 1989 Operation Just Cause

JANUARY 1991 SEALs take first prisoners in Gulf War

OCTOBER 1993 Battle of Mogadishu

OCTOBER 2001 SEALs first into Afghanistan

MARCH 2003 Operation Iraqi Freedom

'The more you sweat in peace, the less you bleed in war.'

INSCRIPTION OVER THE MAIN DOORWAY OF THE PHIL H. BUCKLEW CENTER FOR NAVAL SPECIAL WARFARE

Delta Force

The US Army's 1st Special Forces Operational Detachment-Delta

Along with SEAL Team 6, the US Army's 1st Special Forces Operational Detachment-Delta (SFOD-D) – more commonly known as Delta Force – is one of the US government's two principal special forces units who undertake counter-terrorist operations outside the United States. It is highly secretive, and the Pentagon has refused to comment publicly on the unit and its activities.

Colonel Charles A. Beckwith, commander of Delta Force and of the ill-fated 1980 mission to rescue the American embassy hostages in Iran, at the White House ceremony which finally welcomed them home.

Delta Force was created by US Army colonel Charles Beckwith in 1977 in direct response to the growing number of terrorist incidents that occurred in the 1970s. From its beginnings, Delta was heavily influenced by the British SAS as a result of Colonel Beckwith's year-long exchange tour with that unit in 1962–3. Like the SAS, Delta is organized into three operating squadrons – A, B and C Squadrons – each divided into three types of troops – assault, sniper and recce. As with the SAS, troops also develop other specialities: scuba, HALO (high altitude, low opening) parachute jumps, HAHO (high altitude, high opening) parachute jumps and other skills. Troops further break down into four or five, four- or five-man teams to fit the requirements of a particular mission.

Delta has an aviation platoon that uses aircraft with fake identification numbers painted in civilian colours. These work alongside the aircraft of the 160th Special Operations Aviation Regiment (Airborne) that supports Delta Force on military missions. Delta also have a 'Funny Platoon', an in-house intelligence arm that employs women – the only component of US special operations forces to do so. A clandestine technical unit runs eavesdropping equipment used to monitor terrorists. The unit's strength is around 2500, though only around 250 are trained to conduct direct action and reconnaissance missions.

Troopers are usually recruited from the US Rangers and special forces. Candidates are selected on the basis of a personal recommendation, though some are headhunted if they speak an obscure language or have some rare technical ability.

A scene from Black Hawk Down, *in which a Black Hawk helicopter supporting US forces crashes. They then face a desperate battle for survival until evacuated.*

BLACK HAWK DOWN

In October 1993, Delta Force joined a Task Force in Mogadishu that was tasked with capturing the warlord Mohamed Farrah Aidid. The operation went wrong from the beginning. As one of the Ranger teams was fast-roping from a Black Hawk, a soldier fell and was critically injured. Within minutes, the Rangers and Delta Force operatives found themselves in a vicious firefight with Somali militia. Nevertheless, the Delta Force team captured 20 of Aidid's top lieutenants, but the support convoy was ambushed. At the same time, the 160th SOAR MH-60 Black Hawk co-ordinating the attack from the air was hit by a rocket-propelled grenade and crashed. For the next five hours the Task Force fought for their lives in what was said to be 'the largest firefight since Vietnam'. Finally, with the help of Malaysian and Pakistani peacekeepers, the Task Force was evacuated. By then, 18 Rangers and Delta Force troopers were dead. The story is told in the movie 'Black Hawk Down'.

An example of a Standard United States Army Special Operations Command shoulder sleeve patch worn by Delta Force (SFOD-D) members based at Fort Bragg, North Carolina.

THE HOUSE OF HORRORS

The unit's headquarters at Fort Bragg, North Carolina, houses the CQB (close-quarters battle) indoor training range. Nicknamed 'The House of Horrors', this is where men are trained to assault buildings held by terrorists. The facility also comes equipped with mock-ups of trains and buses for practice assaults, and there is an 'aircraft room' containing a section of a wide-body jet. Delta also undertakes frequent exchanges with foreign counter-terrorist units, such as Britain's SAS, France's GIGN, Germany's GSG-9, Israel's Sayeret Matkal and Australia's Special Air Service Regiment.

The Delta Force is equipped with the most advanced weaponry and equipment in the US special operations arsenal. The choice of small-arms depends on the mission at hand and on personal preferences. Much of the unit's gear is highly customized and cannot be found anywhere outside Delta's lockers. Uniforms are rarely worn. When they are, they carry the standard insignia of US Army Special Operations Command. Civilian haircuts and facial hair are encouraged. In action, men wear hockey helmets and hiking boots rather than the standard-issue military footwear.

In July 1979, Delta Force deployed with the FBI at the Pan American Games in Puerto Rico as part of an anti-terrorist team. The following year it had its first taste of action in the ill-fated Operation Eagle Claw, the abortive attempt to rescue the hostages held in the US embassy in Tehran. Things went better for Delta Force in March 1981 when it was called in to storm an Indonesian aeroplane that had been hijacked by four terrorists at Bangkok airport. A Delta team was flown out and performed the rescue without a hitch, killing all four terrorists.

OPERATION URGENT FURY

During Operation Urgent Fury in 1983, Delta Force was deployed alongside SEAL Team 6 in Grenada and they assisted in the seizure of a key airfield. Later that year, a Delta Force operative died in the bombing of the US embassy in Beirut. In June 1985, it was deployed when TWA Flight 847 from Athens to Rome was hijacked by Hezbollah terrorists who killed a passenger, a US Navy diver named Robert Stethem. However, the Algerian government would not allow Delta Force to mount an assault on the plane at Algiers airport and as a result the terrorists escaped.

After the hijacking of the *Achille Lauro*, Delta Force and SEAL Team 6 were waiting on Sicily when the terrorists landed there, but the Italian authorities would not allow them to arrest the hijackers and the leader Abu Abbas escaped.

During Operation Just Cause in 1989, an eight-man Delta Force team burst into a brothel where Panamanian dictator Manuel Noriega was said to be hiding. Dashing upstairs, they caught a whiff of his characteristic cigars and the bed was still warm. Noriega had left less than an hour before. However, they succeeded in freeing from jail an American businessman who had been running an underground radio station in the city of Modelo.

THE GULF AND SOMALIA

In 1990, Delta Force joined the SAS in Operation Desert Shield, searching for mobile Scud missile launchers in the deserts of western Iraqi. Delta operatives also served as coalition commander General Norman Schwarzkopf's bodyguards. After Desert Shield, they moved on to Somalia as part of Task Force Ranger and took part in various operations to apprehend warlord Mohamed Farrah Aidid, which resulted in the Battle of Mogadishu.

Delta Force took part in Operation Uphold Democracy in Haiti in 1994. Delta operators served as bodyguards for visiting UN officials and diplomats, working together with the Polish counter-terrorist unit, GROM. In the mid- to late-1990s, Delta Force and SEAL Team 6 contingents were deployed again together in Bosnia to plan the capture of war criminal Radovan Karadzic. They carried out vital surveillance, but the arrest did not go ahead and Karadzic remained at large until 2008.

Anti-terrorist duties at the 1996 Olympics at Atlanta were carried out by Delta Force. A small team worked alongside the British SAS during a hostage crisis at the residence of the Japanese ambassador in Lima, Peru, that December. And in spring 1997, it was in Kosovo, in training for a mission to apprehend Serb president Slobodan Milosevic which, again, was aborted.

Delta Force was on hand for Operation Enduring Freedom in Afghanistan in 2001 and Operation Anaconda in 2002, as well as Operation Iraqi Freedom in 2003 and Operation Vigilant Resolve – also known at the Battle of Fallujah – in 2004. Since then, it has supplied Task Force Green in Iraq.

DELTA FORCE

1977 Delta Force founded by Colonel Charles Beckwith

JULY 1979 Joins anti-terrorism team at the Pan American Games in Puerto Rico

APRIL 1980 Operation Eagle Claw

MARCH 1981 Storm hijacked Indonesian plane at Bangkok airport

OCTOBER 1985 *Achille Lauro* hijacking

DECEMBER 1989 Rescues a jailed US businessman during Operation Just Cause

AUGUST 1990–JANUARY 1991 Searches for Scud launchers in Iraq during Operation Desert Shield

OCTOBER 1993 Battle of Mogadishu

SEPTEMBER 1994–MARCH 1995 Operation Uphold Democracy

OCTOBER 2001 Operation Enduring Freedom

MARCH 2003 Operation Iraqi Freedom

APRIL 2004 Battle of Fallujah

'Speed, surprise, and violence of action. Those were the keys to success and survival, those and the ability to shoot what we intended to shoot and nothing else. We were not just going in harm's way, we were going to charge down harm's throat, grab a handful of his guts, and turn him inside out.'

DELTA FORCE OPERATIVE ERIC L. HANEY FROM HIS BOOK *INSIDE DELTA FORCE*

US Air Force Special Operations Command

'All the Time, Everywhere'

Air Force Special Operations Command (AFSOC) was established on 22 May 1990 with headquarters at Hurlburt Field, Florida. AFSOC is the air force component of US Special Operations Command, whose command centre is at MacDill Air Force Base, Florida. Like other special operations units, it has a distinguished heritage.

In the European theatre of operations during the Second World War, regular US Army Air Force (USAAF) units were used to conduct special operations in high-threat areas under the direction of the Office of Strategic Services and British Intelligence Service. The first dedicated special operations unit was the Special Flight Section of the 12th Air Force's 5th Bombardment Wing in North Africa. From October 1943, this small, *ad hoc* unit flew highly modified and mission-specific B-17 Flying Fortresses, B-24 Liberators and B-25 twin-engined Mitchell bombers over occupied Europe.

The Special Flight Section later became known as the 885th Bombardment Squadron and flew Liberators out of Brindisi, once the Allies had occupied the heel of Italy. Its special operations transports flew 3769 sorties over the Balkans. They dropped 7149 tons of supplies to resistance groups, while the unit's C-47 Douglas Dakotas landed 989 times behind enemy lines, delivering another 1972 tons of supplies and evacuating thousands of Allied airmen and wounded partisans.

THE CARPETBAGGERS

The largest USAAF special operations effort in Europe was conducted by the 801st Bombardment Group. Nicknamed the 'Carpetbaggers', they were based in England. They specialized in the delivery of supplies, agents and propaganda leaflets behind enemy lines using B-24s specifically modified for their particular mission and painted black. In the summer of 1944, the 801st and units based in North Africa dropped Jedburgh teams behind enemy lines in France, and special operations crews became proficient in night-time, low-level, long range missions, often carried out in poor weather and over mountainous terrain. Later, Carpetbaggers airlifted fuel vital to keep up the momentum of General George S. Patton's armoured drive into Germany.

In the Far East, General Henry H. 'Hap' Arnold's fliers supplied the Chindits. By March 1944, this force was designated the 1st Air Commando Group. Its motto – 'Any Place, Any Time, Any Where' – has been adopted and updated by AFSOC. Its success led to the creation of the 2nd and 3rd Air Commando Groups that supported unconventional missions deep behind enemy lines in the Pacific. Air commandos are credited with the first combat aircrew rescue by helicopter, and the first combat use of air-to-ground rockets. They destroyed multiple ground targets and shot down a number of enemy aircraft.

After the war, air commandos were used on psychological warfare missions in the Philippines that led to the defeat of the Hukbo ng Bayan sa Hapon – or 'People's Anti-Japanese Army' – in 1954. Meanwhile in Korea, air commandos were flying low-level missions behind enemy lines in support of US army intelligence and CIA operations.

In April 1961, General Curtis E. LeMay, air force chief of staff, established the 4400th Combat Crew Training Squadron (CCTS). Nicknamed 'Jungle Jim', its two-fold mission was counter-insurgency training and combat operations. In November 1961, the 4400th CCTS

A group of Special Operations Weathermen of the US Air Force Special Operations Command are seen undergoing training near Hurlburt Field, Florida, their home base. On active duty, these 'Weathermen' collect and interpret meteorological data and provide air and ground forces commanders with timely, accurate intelligence.

Airmen from the 720th Special Tactics Group seen making a water rescue training jump from a C-130J Hercules over the coastline of Florida in 2007.

deployed a detachment to Bien Hoa, on Operation Farmgate, where they flew some of the first US combat missions in Vietnam.

As the Vietnam War expanded, the air force increased its counter-insurgency capability. The 4400th CCTS became a group in March 1962, and the following month it became part of the newly activated US Air Force Special Air Warfare Center at Eglin Air Force Base, Florida. In Vietnam, it was involved in Operation Ranch Hand, spraying the defoliant Agent Orange to deny the enemy the cover of the jungle.

By 1966 – the high-water mark for US air force special operations in Vietnam – the total special operations forces air contingent comprised 10,000 people and 550 aircraft in 19 squadrons. At the same time air commandos were also deployed in other countries including Malaysia, Greece, Saudi Arabia, Ethiopia, Iran and the Congo.

LEAVING VIETNAM AND AFTER

In 1968, the US Air Force Special Air Warfare Center became the USAF Special Operations Force, and in 1970 it supported the raid on Son Tay. In June 1974, the USAF Special Operations Force became the 834th Tactical Composite Wing in an attempt to play down the USAF's support for unconventional warfare. However, in April 1975, it was involved in Operation Eagle Pull, evacuating US embassy staff from Phnom Penh. Then came Operation Frequent Wind, where special operations helped in the evacuation from the American embassy in Saigon. In May that year, 41 special operations men were lost and over 50 were wounded in an attempt to rescue the crew of the US freighter *Mayaguez*, hijacked by the Khmer Rouge in the Gulf of Siam.

In July 1975, the 834th Tactical Composite Wing became the 1st Special Operations Wing, and by 1979 it was the only special operations wing in the air force. In December 1982, it was transferred from Tactical Air Command to Military Airlift Command as the 23rd Air Force. Its unique skills were called on in October 1983, in Operation Urgent Fury, where a 1st Special Operations Wing Combat Talon crew won the Mackay Trophy, instituted in 1911 for the 'most meritorious flight of the year', and a Spectre crew earned the Lieutenant General William H. Tunner Award for the most outstanding airlift crew.

In 1989, the air commandos joined Operation Just Cause in Panama. Spectre gunship crews of the 1st Special Operations Wing again won the Mackay Trophy and Tunner Award. A 919th Special Operations Group Spectre crew earned the President's Award, while a 1st Special Operations Wing Combat Talon crew won the greatest honour of all – ferrying the captured Panamanian president, Manuel Noriega, to prison in the United States.

US AIR FORCE SPECIAL OPERATIONS FORCES

On 13 December 2005, the US Air Force Special Operations Command at Hurlburt Field was redesignated the Air Force Special Operations Forces. It has about 12,900 active-duty, Air Force Reserve, Air National Guard and civilian personnel. It flies fixed and rotary-wing aircraft, including the CV-22, AC-130H/U, C-130, EC-130, MC-130E/H/W, MC-130P and MH-53. The 1st Special Operations Wing at Hurlburt Field is the air force's only active-duty special operations combat wing. The 352nd Special Operations Group, based at RAF Mildenhall in England, is the air force component for Special Operations Command Europe. The 353rd Special Operations Group, at Kadena Air Base, Japan, is the air force component for Special Operations Command Pacific. And the 720th Special Tactics Group at Hurlburt Field trains, organizes and equips more than 800 air combat controllers, special operations weathermen and para-rescue men for assignment to special tactics squadrons.

The 919th Special Operations Wing at Duke Field, Florida, is the command's reserve special operations wing. The 193rd Special Operations Wing, at Harrisburg International Airport, Pennsylvania, provides the only airborne psychological operations platform in the Department of Defense. The 123rd Special Tactics Squadron at Standiford Field, Kentucky, provides combat controllers and para-rescuemen worldwide, while the 227th Special Operations Flight at McGuire Air Force Base, New Jersey, provides support to airlift operations.

In an attempt to unify the command of special operations, the 23rd Air Force became the Air Force Special Operations Command under the US Special Operations Command (USSOCOM) at MacDill Air Force Base, Florida, on 22 May 1990. In January 1991, along with a nine-man team of US Navy SEALs, it evacuated 281 American and other foreign non-combatants from the US embassy in Mogadishu, flying in and out of the darkened embassy compound using night-vision goggles.

Under USSOCOM, it supported special forces operations during Desert Shield and Desert Storm, and joined bombing and psy-ops (psychological operations) missions. It then saw service in the Balkans, Haiti and Somalia. In March 1994, a 16th Special Operations Squadron AC-130H Spectre gunship suffered an in-flight explosion that forced it to ditch off the coast of Kenya. Eight crew members were killed; six survived.

Like other special operations forces units, the Air Force Special Operations Command was called on during Operations Enduring Freedom and Iraqi Freedom. It was also on call at other hot spots worldwide, in some cases assisting in humanitarian aid operations.

'The Air Commando concept was to have a self sufficient, self-contained force that could deploy anywhere in the world and conduct operations.'

BRIGADIER-GENERAL HARRY C. 'HEINIE' ADERHOLT, A COMMANDER OF AIR COMMANDOS IN SOUTHEAST ASIA DURING THE VIETNAM WAR

Israel's Sayeret Matkal

The raid on Entebbe

Israel's special forces, the Sayeret Matkal – the 'General Staff Reconnaissance Unit' – models itself on the British SAS, even sharing the motto 'Who Dares Wins'. The Sayeret Matkal is best known for Operation Thunderbolt, when it flew to Entebbe in Uganda to rescue more than 100 passengers from a plane hijacked by the Palestine Liberation Organization (PLO).

Lieutenant-Colonel Yonatan Netanyahu, the leader of the Israeli raid at Entebbe airport which resulted in the rescue of over 100 passengers held captive following the hijacking of an Air France flight. He was killed in the raid – the only Israeli commando to die in the action.

The Sayeret Matkal was formed in 1957 by Avraham Aman, an officer who had formerly been part of the Palmach guerrilla force that pushed the British out of Palestine. Initially a secret organization, its recruits were hand picked. One early recruit was Ehud Barak, who went on to become chief of the general staff, then prime minister. In 1972, it got its first opportunity for a hostage rescue when Palestinian Black September terrorists hijacked an incoming plane at Tel Aviv airport. Sayeret Matkal stormed the plane, freeing the passengers.

The Israeli security forces had to stand helpless when Black September terrorists massacred their athletes at the 1972 Olympics in Munich. Like other security forces around the world, they were forced to up their game. In April 1973, the Sayeret Matkal landed in Lebanon and killed a number of PLO leaders living there. The leader of the assault team was Yonatan Netanyahu, leader of the raid on Entebbe and the brother of another future prime minister, Benjamin Netanyahu.

THE HIJACKING

On 27 June 1976, Air France Flight 139 flying from Tel Aviv to Paris was hijacked soon after it took off from Athens. There were 238 passengers on board, along with 12 crew members. The hijackers were two Palestinians from the Popular Front for the Liberation of Palestine and two Germans, Brigitte Kuhlman and Wilfried Böse, from the militant left-wing 'Revolutionary Cells'. The plane stopped at Benghazi in Libya for refuelling. There a woman who pretended to be pregnant was released. That evening, the plane flew on to Entebbe where more Palestinians awaited them.

The dictator Idi Amin was in power in Uganda at the time. He made no secret of his pro-Palestinian sympathies. Inside the terminal building passengers were separated into Jews and non-Jews. Meanwhile, the hijackers demanded the release of 40 Palestinian prisoners in Israel and others held in West Germany, Switzerland, France and Kenya – otherwise, they threatened, the hostages would be killed.

EXTENDING THE DEADLINE

As the days passed some hostages were released, but the Air France crew refused to leave while the terrorists continued to hold the Jews. Then the Israeli government agreed to negotiate, asking for the deadline of 1 July to be extended to 4 July. Amin supported the extension as he had diplomatic duties out of the country to attend to, and the Palestinians agreed. On 3 July, Sayeret Matkal's rescue plan went into operation. Four Hercules C-130H cargo planes carrying over 100 soldiers flew the 2500 miles (4024 km) from Israel to Uganda, escorted part of the way by Phantom jet fighters. For much of the way they had to fly at under 30 metres (100 ft) to avoid detection by Egyptian, Saudi Arabian and Sudanese radar. They were followed by two Boeing 707 jets. One, an airborne hospital, landed at Nairobi airport in Kenya. The other, carrying General Yekutiel Adam, circled over Entebbe airport as a command and control plane.

There were jubilant scenes following the successful Entebbe raid. Here ecstatic Israelis raise aloft the squadron leader in charge of the rescue planes on their return.

A BLACK MERCEDES-BENZ

The first Hercules landed at Entebbe at 11 a.m.. It was carrying a black Mercedes-Benz, the same model as Idi Amin's official car. Israeli Land Rovers and troops lined up alongside it as if they

In order to get close to the hijacked planes at Entebbe without being challenged, the Sayeret Matkal commandos rode in a black Mercedes-Benz identical to the one used as Idi Amin's official vehicle. Here it is being loaded onto one of the Hercules transport planes prior to the mission.

were an escort. They drove to the terminal building where they were challenged by Palestinian sentries – who were immediately shot. The Sayeret Matkal stormed the building, killing the terrorists.

By then, the other three Hercules had landed. They were carrying APCs which guarded the planes while they were being refuelled. To ensure a clean getaway, the Sayeret Matkal destroyed the 11 Ugandan Air Force MiG fighters parked on the runway.

COMMANDER KILLED

Only one Israeli commando was killed during the raid. The commanding officer of the Sayeret Matkal, Yonatan Netanyahu, was shot dead by a Ugandan sniper from the control

OPERATION ISOTOPE

On 8 May 1972, four terrorists from the Palestine Black September group hijacked a Boeing 707 en route from Vienna. On the ground in Tel Aviv, the hijackers demanded the release of 315 Palestinian terrorists in prison in Israel, otherwise they would blow up the aircraft and everyone on it. However, negotiations failed.

At 16:00 on 9 May, a group of 16 Sayeret Matkal commandos, dressed in white overalls, approached the plane, ostensibly as service crew. Catching the terrorists off guard, they stormed the aircraft.

Within ten minutes, two of the hijackers were dead and their two female accomplices were arrested. They were sentenced to life imprisonment, but were released in a prisoner exchange following the Lebanon War of 1982. Three of the passengers were wounded; one woman later died from her wounds. The commandos who took part in the assault were led by Ehud Barak. One of his men was Benjamin Netanyahu. During the assault, Netanyahu was accidentally shot by another member of the rescue team, but he survived.

tower. Five other commandos were wounded. Forty-five Ugandan soldiers were killed. Of the 105 hostages, three were killed and ten were wounded. They were flown to Nairobi for medical attention, then on to Israel.

Seventy-four-year-old widow Dora Bloch had been released on 2 July, but was taken to Mulago General Hospital in Kampala when a piece of food stuck in her throat. When news of the Israeli raid came through, she was dragged from her bed and murdered.

Although the raid boosted morale in Israel, the terrorist onslaught intensified. On 7 April 1980, five terrorists entered the Misgav Am kibbutz at night. In the nursery, they killed the kibbutz secretary and a boy. Holding the other children hostage, the terrorists demanded the release of 50 Palestinians held in Israeli prisons. When the security forces stormed the building, all the terrorists were killed, along with two kibbutz members and one soldier. Four children and 11 soldiers were wounded. Immediately after the attack, the Sayeret Matkal entered southern Lebanon and wiped out the terrorist nests thought to be responsible.

DISSIDENTS IN THE RANKS

A number of other hostage rescues and raids on terrorist haunts in neighbouring countries have been ascribed to the Sayeret Matkal, but for years it remained in the shadows. Then on 21 December 2003, 13 Sayeret Matkal reservists wrote to Prime Minister Ariel Sharon refusing to serve in the Occupied Territories any longer. The letter said:

> 'We say to you today, we will no longer give our hands to the oppressive reign in the territories and the denial of human rights to millions of Palestinians, and we will no longer serve as a defensive shield for the settlement enterprise.'

The contents of the letter were strongly condemned by Ehud Barak and Benjamin Netanyahu. However, a similar letter had been received from the Israeli air force, and it is thought that they influenced the Israeli government's decision in June 2004 to pull out of Gaza the following year. In an interview with the newspaper *Haaretz* in October 2004, Sharon's chief adviser said:

> 'Domestically … everything was collapsing. The economy was stagnant, and the Geneva Initiative had gained broad support. And then we were hit with the letters of officers and letters of pilots and letters of commandos. These were not weird kids with green pony-tails and a ring in their nose with a strong odour of grass. These were really our finest young people.'

ISRAEL'S SAYERET MATKAL

1957 Sayeret Matkal formed under Avraham Aman

1959 Ehud Barak joins Sayeret Matkal

1967 Benjamin Netanyahu joins Sayeret Matkal

1972 Sayeret Matkal storms hijacked plane at Tel Aviv airport; Yonatan Netanyahu appointed deputy commander

1973 Sayeret Matkal attacks PLO in Lebanon

1975 Yonatan Netanyahu becomes commander of Sayeret Matkal

1976 Hijacked plane taken to Entebbe, where it is stormed by the Sayeret Matkal

2003 Sayeret Matkal dissidents refuse to serve in the Occupied Territories

2005 Israel pulls out of Gaza

'We are proud not only because we have saved the lives of over a hundred innocent people – men, women and children – but because of the significance of our act for the cause of human freedom.'

CHAIM HERZOG, ISRAELI AMBASSADOR TO THE UNITED NATIONS, REGARDING THE RAID ON ENTEBBE, 1976

Germany's GSG-9

Operation Feuerzauber *in Mogadishu*

After the Second World War, the German authorities were reluctant to create élite military units for any purpose. What changed their minds was the hostage taking and subsequent massacre of Israeli athletes at the Munich Olympics in 1972. As a result, the German Federal Police set up GSG-9, on which many counter-terrorist units around the world have modelled themselves.

West German police prepare to intercept terrorists holding hostage nine Israeli athletes in 1972. The mission ended in the deaths of all the hostages as well as some of the terrorists.

On 5 September 1972, Palestinian terrorists infiltrated the athletes' village at the Munich Olympics, killed two Israelis and took nine others hostage. They demanded the release of 200 Palestinians held in Israeli jails and free passage out of West Germany. Although 12,000 men surrounded the building where the hostages were being held, the West German police were neither trained nor equipped to handle the situation.

The Israelis refused to release the prisoners, but the West German government agreed to give the terrorists safe passage out of the country. That night, helicopters flew the kidnappers and their hostages to the Fürstenfeldbruck military airfield where a plane was waiting to take them to Cairo. But when the terrorists appeared on the tarmac, a German sniper opened fire. In the resulting firefight, all nine hostages were killed, along with four of the seven terrorists and one policeman. A helicopter pilot was also critically wounded. The disaster was compounded when, the following month, more Palestinian terrorists hijacked a Lufthansa jet and forced the German authorities to release the three surviving terrorists.

THE FEDERAL BORDER POLICE

In April 1973, six months after the Munich massacre, West Germany set up a dedicated anti-terrorist squad. However, due to German sensitivity, it would not be part of the military, rather it would be manned and controlled by the Federal Border Police. It would be known as *Grenzschutzgruppe 9*, or Border Guard Group 9. Recruits were volunteers from the

'Releasing these eleven terrorists would only have led to new crimes. We weighed the risks as thoroughly as we could.'

WEST GERMAN CHANCELLOR HELMUT SCHMIDT, 1977

In October 1977, four PLO terrorists hijacked a Lufthansa Boeing 737-200 as it flew from Majorca to Frankfurt, West Germany. The aircraft is seen here at Dubai. Eventually, the plane landed at Mogadishu in Somalia, where it was stormed by GSG-9 troops who secured the safe release of all the passengers, and either killed or captured the terrorists.

Federal Border Police, or *Bundesgrenzschutz*. Soldiers who wanted to join had to leave the army and sign up for the *Bundesgrenzschutz* before they were eligible. Initial training for the unit takes 22 weeks. The drop-out rate is high; it can reach 80 percent. The first 13 weeks of training are spent on counter-terrorism and police operations, but the unit also combines military specialities. Some graduates are sent on to the Long Range Reconnaissance Patrol School in Weingarten.

GSG-9 is divided into three primary units, specializing in counter-terrorism, marine counter-terrorism and airborne operations. There are 250 members in all. No expense is spared on equipment – the British SAS adopted the Heckler & Koch MP-5 submachine gun after seeing it in action with GSG-9. GSG-9 members each get through more than 4000 rounds of ammunition during practice every year.

MOGADISHU HIJACKING

In 1977, GSG-9 had its baptism of fire. On 13 October, four terrorists hijacked Lufthansa Flight 181 en route from Majorca to Frankfurt, diverting it to Rome. The terrorists demanded the release of seven members of the Baader-Meinhof gang held in Germany and two Palestinians held in Turkey. For that, and $15 million, they would release the hostages.

GERMANY'S GSG-9

For the next four days, the plane skipped from airport to airport across the Middle East. Finding the runway at Aden blocked, Captain Jürgen Schumann landed the Boeing 737, now short of fuel, on a sand strip nearby. When he returned to the plane after inspecting the landing gear and talking to the authorities, the terrorists shot Captain Schumann in the head, then ordered the co-pilot Jürgen Vietor to fly the plane on to Mogadishu.

A GSG-9 team had already been alerted. Its commander, Ulrich Wegener, loaded his men on a specially outfitted 707, which landed at Mogadishu on 17 October – just hours behind the hijacked plane. By that time, Captain Schumann's body had been flung out on the tarmac and the terrorists were threatening to blow up the plane, having already doused the passengers with duty-free liquor. However, the terrorists were told that the West German government had agreed to their terms and were asked to extend their deadline to the following morning as it would take time for the freed prisoners to reach Mogadishu.

Meanwhile Wegener had surrounded the 737 with snipers. Within an hour of landing, he was running through the assault plan with his 20-man GSG-9 force, along with two SAS observers Wegener had invited to join the rescue. They had brought with them 'flash-bang' stun grenades, recently developed by the regiment. When detonated, these create a deafening bang and a blinding flash, causing disorientation for a couple of seconds – long enough for the rescuers to gain an advantage over the kidnappers.

Around midnight, GSG-9 scouts crawled to within 30 metres (100 ft) of the 737 and, through infrared goggles, identified the location of two of the terrorists. The order for Operation *Feuerzauber* – 'Magic Fire' – to go ahead was given. At 1 a.m., GSG-9 men with blackened faces approached the plane from the rear. Climbing rubber-tipped ladders, they placed magnetic charges on the doors. Then GSG-9 and Somali militiamen started a bonfire in front of the cockpit as a diversion to draw the terrorists towards the front of the plane. At 2:08 a.m., the rear doors were blown and the SAS men threw the flash-bangs in. GSG-9 men

West German chancellor Helmut Schmidt (right) congratulates the commander of the GSG-9 team after ending the Mogadishu hijack. Other members of the unit are also visible in the photograph.

rushed into the plane. One woman terrorist was shot in the head. A second, wounded, took refuge in the toilet as the hostages were being evacuated from the rear doors

Terrorists in the cockpit threw grenades into the cabin but, fortunately, they exploded under the seats, only slightly injuring a flight attendant and one GSG-9 man. The two male hijackers were then dispatched with multiple shots to the head. Within seven minutes the plane was secure, and by 5 a.m. the 86 hostages and their rescuers were on their way back to Germany.

The surviving terrorist spent a year in jail in Somalia. In 1994, she was found living in Norway and extradited to Germany where she was sentenced to a further 12 years in jail, but was released after three years due to ill health.

FURTHER ANTI-TERRORIST MISSIONS

In November 1982, a five-man surveillance team waited for six days at a site in woods outside Frankfurt. Then two top woman terrorists arrived. GSG-9 arrested them and captured their arms cache, which contained weapons, explosives, forged documents, maps and information about US military bases, and maps showing 14 other supply caches. These were placed under surveillance. Five days later, leading Red Army Faction terrorist Christian Klahr turned up at one of the supply stations where he was arrested.

Then, on 27 June 1993, 30 GSG-9 operatives staking out the railway station in Bad Kleinen tried to arrest Birgit Hogefeld and Wolfgang Grams, the two most-wanted members of the Red Army Faction terrorist group. Grams managed to shoot and kill one of the GSG-9 men before turning the gun on himself. There were allegations, since dismissed, that in fact a GSG-9 operative had killed Grams in cold blood as he lay on the tracks. This allegation damaged the unit's reputation. However, later in 1993 their image was restored when they successfully apprehended a terrorist that had hijacked a KLM flight from Tunis to Amsterdam that was diverted to Dusseldorf. A GSG-9 squad subdued the lone hijacker without a shot being fired.

Like most counter-terrorist organizations, the GSG-9 is secretive. It is said that it has conducted over 1500 missions, but has opened fire only five times. Following 9/11, it was responsible for several of the terrorist arrests in Germany. It has also been deployed in Iraq, where they are responsible for protecting German embassy property and personnel in Baghdad. On 7 April 2004, two members were attacked and killed near Fallujah while in a convoy travelling from Amman (Jordan) to Baghdad. The men were travelling in a car at the rear of the convoy, where they received most of the enemy fire after passing the ambush. Subsequently, in a later statement, the attackers apologized for mistaking the German convoy for an American convoy.

THE ORIGINAL SWAT WORLD CHALLENGE

Since 2004, America has been host to the SWAT World Challenge, renamed the Original SWAT World Challenge due to sponsorship by the Original SWAT footwear company. Special weapons and tactics teams from around the world are invited to compete in eight events that include Zodiac attack, vehicle assault, masked entry, high-risk warrant service, sniper challenge, gun challenge and Glock pistol shoot off.

All eight events are conducted over two days. All are performed in full tactical gear and live fire is used. Teams compete head-to-head, and officers are given only one round for each target. Teams are scored on time and hits. Each target missed adds penalties to the team's overall time. Time bonuses can also be earned. In 2005, the GSG-9 won all eight events. The following year they won the competition again, coming first in four of the events.

Poland's GROM

The Grupa Reagowania Operacyjno Manewrowego *in action in Iraq*

Poland's Operational Manoeuvre Reconnaissance Group – or GROM, which also means 'thunderbolt' – is the nation's élite special forces unit. Created in 1990 to combat terrorist threats, the GROM is Poland's equivalent to Delta Force and Britain's SAS, and has fought alongside them in Iraq and Afghanistan. However, it traces its origins back to the *Cichociemi* – 'dark and silent one' – Poland's secret army during the Second World War.

In the late 1980s, Poland faced threats from the Popular Front for the Liberation of Palestine and Hezbollah because they were assisting Jews to emigrate to Israel from the rapidly disintegrating Soviet Union. The Polish response was to create a new special operations unit, initially known as JW2305, with the help of specialists from the United States and the UK. This unit became the GROM.

Answerable directly to the minister of internal affairs, the GROM was the first Polish military unit to co-operate with the US army. It is a highly secretive organization. The first mention of its existence in the press came in 1992, but the Polish government only admitted publicly that the unit existed in 1994, when the GROM joined the US-led Operation Uphold Democracy in Haiti.

The GROM's first commanding officer was Slawomir Petelicki, a career soldier who joined the Polish army in 1946.

'We are especially happy if we can co-operate with and support our American allies. They helped us create this unit.'

GROM COMMANDER BRIGADIER-GENERAL SLAWOMIR PETELICKI
REFERRING TO THE PEACEKEEPING MISSION TO KOSOVO, 1998

He worked in counter-intelligence in Sweden, North Vietnam, China and at the Polish consulate in New York. It is said that during the First Gulf War he led a secret operation behind the lines to rescue CIA agents. When two Polish diplomats involved in 'Operation Bridge' – the international effort to repatriate Soviet Jews to Israel – were killed in Beirut, Lieutenant-Colonel Petelicki was sent to take charge. It was then that he conceived the idea of starting a security force to defend Polish citizens abroad.

PERSONNEL AND TRAINING

Like Delta Force, the GROM is modelled on the SAS. It has some 300 personnel, including women who are used in intelligence gathering. Combat units operate in four-man teams, and men are allowed to select their own weapons. Like the SAS, they favour the Heckler & Koch MP-5 submachine gun for close-quarters fighting. Other favourites include the Browning HP, the Czech CZ-85 pistol, the Glock Model 19, the SIG-Sauer P228 and the 7.62-mm calibre AK. Snipers employ the Heckler & Koch PSG-1 7.62-mm calibre marksman's rifle.

The GROM looks for recruits who are around 30 – family men who are level-headed

Co-operation between the special forces in different countries is an important aspect of helping to counter threats such as global terrorism. Here GROM troops and US Navy SEALs take part in an exercise near Gdansk, Poland, designed to hone boarding skills.

POLAND'S GROM

1990 JW2305 created; expands to form the *Grupa Reagowania Operacyjno Manewrowego*

1994 GROM joins Operation Uphold Democracy

1997 GROM hunts war criminals in the former Yugoslavia

1998 GROM guards peace envoys to Kosovo

1999 GROM transferred from the Ministry of the Interior to the military as Poland joins NATO

2001 GROM joins Operation Enduring Freedom

2003 GROM joins Operation Iraqi Freedom

– and speak at least two foreign languages. Candidates undergo intensive psychological testing. Members serve until they are around 45 years of age, at which time ex-GROM men often become instructors in other units. Training for the GROM takes at least three years and costs an estimated $1 million per person.

GROM members are trained in hostage rescue, close-quarters battle, intelligence gathering, long range reconnaissance and diversionary activities. Since the GROM are responsible for protecting oil-drilling rigs in the Baltic, they are trained in open-sea rescue, diving in adverse conditions and making free-fall parachute jumps into the sea.

All members of a GROM team are fully trained combat assault personnel, while some 75 percent are certified paramedics or male nurses. Doctors are also attached to the unit, along with technicians, analysts and explosive ordinance disposal experts.

OVERSEAS OPERATIONS

In 1994, the GROM made its first appearance on the world stage when 51 men were sent to assist the UN mission on Haiti. Their commander, Colonel Petelicki, was awarded the US Army Commendation Medal and is an honorary member of the 5th and 10th Special Forces Group, the Green Berets. He was dismissed on 19 December 1995, though he returned as commander two years later, serving until he retired in September 1999.

In 1997, the GROM was the first unit in the former Yugoslavia to arrest a suspected war criminal – Slavko Dokmanovic. Known as the 'Butcher of Vukovar', Dokmanovic was apprehended without a single shot being fired, despite the presence of his bodyguards. In 1998, the chief of the Organization for Security and Co-operation in Europe, William G. Walker, asked for GROM soldiers to serve as his own bodyguards on his peacekeeping mission to Kosovo, believing that the Poles would have a greater understanding of the warring Serbians and Croatians.

In January 1999, when Poland joined NATO, the GROM was transformed into a special military formation to comply with alliance standards. They were considered to be the best of the special forces units among the nations newly joining NATO, and they joined the coalition of the willing in Afghanistan during Operation Enduring Freedom.

ACTIVITIES IN IRAQ

During Operation Iraqi Freedom, the Poles sent the GROM to join the US-led invasion force. They were sent out into the western desert of Iraq along with the SAS, Australia's Special Air Service Regiment and US special operations forces to destroy Scud missile batteries threatening Israel. They also helped the SBS, Royal Marines Commandos and US Navy SEALs in the Persian Gulf, to capture and secure the oil platforms there.

Dropped into the sea by helicopter at night, they had to swim in full kit to the legs of the platform, then scale them using ropes and magnetic pads. Then, with MP-5SDs and stun grenades, they stormed the rig. They did not know whether the platforms were manned, whether those who might be on board were armed or whether the platforms were booby trapped. On one platform taken by the GROM, the phone began to ring. The team froze, fearing the telephone might be rigged to detonate explosive charges. After a while it stopped and the Polish officer commanding the assault team joked that it must have been a wrong number – to everyone's great relief.

THE *CICHOCIEMI*

In December 1939, with the fall of Poland, Polish army officer Captain Jan Górski managed to escape to France. There he suggested to his superiors that they set up a special forces unit to aid the guerrilla force left behind. When the Polish forces in exile were forced to withdraw to Britain, a detachment was set up to prepare for covert operations in Poland. Of the 2413 who volunteered, only 605 managed to pass the rigorous training course devised by the Polish General Staff and Britain's Special Operations Executive.

The Cichociemi, *the Polish army in exile in the Second World War, assisted the Warsaw Ghetto Underground Movement, seen in action here.*

forces. Much had changed since they had left. Then they were given false identities and were ready to go into action.

The first party was airdropped into Poland on 16 February 1941. In all, 483 missions carrying men and materials were sent, though 68 planes were lost. Some 316 soldiers were dropped, along with 28 agents. Others were dropped over Albania, Yugoslavia, Greece, Italy and

As well as being taught sharpshooting, intelligence gathering, ambush, handling explosives and mines, and the workings of British, German, Italian, Russian and Polish weapons, they needed detailed courses on life in Poland under occupation and the new regulations imposed by the occupying

France, where it was hoped they could mobilize the half-a-million strong Polish minority. In Poland, many became officers in the Polish Secret Army and the Polish Home Army. They took part in the uprisings in Lvov and Warsaw. However, when the Germans withdrew, the Polish guerrillas – though supported by the West – were crushed by the Soviets.

The GROM was also used to take over oil facilities on land, but after the fall of Umm Qasr, members of GROM were photographed by Reuters alongside the DEVGRU, to the embarrassment of the Polish authorities who wanted their commitment kept secret. The GROM was withdrawn from Umm Qasr and sent to join the Royal Marines Commandos attacking Basra, in the belief that the British were less likely to court publicity.

The GROM stayed on in Iraq after the initial invasion to join Task Force 30, the US-UK special forces outfit whose role was to kill or capture 'high value targets', or HVTs, such as Iraqi mujahideen leaders and former Ba'ath party members and leaders of the regime.

France's GIGN

In action against pirates in Somalia

Following the Munich massacre of 1972 and occupation of the Saudi embassy in Paris in 1973, the French government set up the *Groupement d'Intervention de la Gendarmerie Nationale*, or National Gendarmes Intervention Group. Although it is technically part of the police force and retains its power of arrest, the unit takes its orders from the Ministry of Defence.

A graduate from the Saint-Cyr military academy, Christian Prouteau, shown here in 1980, was involved in setting up the GIGN. He led over 60 operations and freed many hostages during his nine years with the GIGN unit.

The GIGN became operational on 1 March 1974 with, initially, just 15 men under the command of Lieutenant Christian Prouteau. Even this was divided into separate commands covering northern and southern France. In 1976, these were combined when the GIGN shipped out to Djibouti to rescue 30 school children being held on a school bus by the FLCS – the *Front de Libération de la Côte Somalienne*, or the 'Somali Coast Liberation Front'.

In 1979, the GIGN's manpower was increased to two officers and 40 NCOs. They were called in to free diplomats being held in the French embassy in San Salvador, but the kidnappers surrendered before they could go into action. That year they were also on hand to advise the Saudi National Guard prior to their assault on the terrorist-held Grand Mosque in Mecca after it had been taken over by fundamentalists. The following year they were in Corsica, where they arrested an important separatist terrorist.

By 1984, GIGN could field four 12-man strike units with one on call 24 hours a day. By 1988, it had 57 men and a global reach. On 22 April 1988, terrorists demanding the independence of New Caledonia in Melanesia seized a judge and 27 gendarmes, holding them hostage in caves on the island of Ouvea. Four hostages were murdered. On 5 May 1988, 14 GIGN men led a mixed team of parachutists and combat divers into the Gossannah cave to rescue them. Confronted by an old, looted AA-52 machine gun, the GIGN responded with flame throwers. Nineteen terrorists and two soldiers were killed in the action.

HIJACKING IN ALGIERS

On 24 December 1994, four armed men took over Air France Flight 8969 bound for Paris while it was on the ground at Houari Boumedienne airport in Algiers. They discovered an Algerian policeman on board and shot him in the back of the head. When the control tower refused permission for the plane to take off, they dumped his body on the tarmac, warning that more would follow.

Philippe Legorjus, who had been commander of the GIGN from 1985 to 1989, was then head of security at Air France. He called Capitaine Denis Favier, his successor at GIGN. The plane was surrounded by Algerian commandos. A GIGN team, trained on an identical Airbus to Flight 8969, set off for Algiers, but was refused permission to land. Meanwhile, the terrorists killed a Vietnamese diplomat and a young chef from the French embassy, and threatened to kill one more hostage every hour the plane was on the ground. When it was discovered that there were 20 sticks of dynamite on board, it was decided to let the plane leave for Paris. On the way it was diverted to Marseilles on the pretext that it had run short of fuel after running the auxiliary power units all the time it was on the ground.

The GIGN storm an Air France plane at Marseilles in 1994, after it has been hijacked by Algerian terrorists known as the Armed Islamic Group. GIGN operatives can be seen entering the plane via the steps leading into the aircraft as well as taking aim on the ground.

HEADING FOR THE EIFFEL TOWER

In Marseilles, the hijackers demanded that the plane be filled with far more fuel than it would need to reach Paris. Intelligence reports suggested that the terrorists intended to fly it into the Eiffel Tower. But before they could leave Marseilles, the GIGN caught up with them. They approached the plane on a mobile staircase while snipers fired at the terrorists. The co-pilot jumped out of the cockpit window and escaped. GIGN troopers tossed stun grenades in and stormed the aircraft. They shot and killed one terrorist as he ran down the aisle and injured another hijacker.

But the terrorists in the cockpit held out, raking the cabin with AK-47 fire that dented body armour, smashed face shields and literally shot the weapons out of the GIGN men's hands. They flung another stun grenade towards the cockpit, but it landed outside. The hijackers responded by rolling a fragmentation grenade down the aisle. Everyone in the first class cabin – both GIGN men and hostages – suffered injuries to the legs. A second wave of troopers entered the plane, and the gunfire continued until the pilots shouted that all the terrorists were dead. Thirteen hostages and 11 GIGN men were injured, and the plane was so badly damaged that it had to be scrapped.

The GIGN was sent to the Comoros in the Indian Ocean in 1995 to arrest the mercenary Bob Denard who was trying to stage a coup. Then it went to Bosnia to hunt for war criminals. Currently it is seeing service off the coast of Somalia, pursuing pirates from its base in Djibouti.

The GIGN team and rescued hostages arrive at Orly airport in France following the ending of the aircraft hijack in Marseilles on 26 December 1994. The battle was so fierce that the aircraft had to be written off after the event.

ARRIVING IN 30 MINUTES

The GIGN has conducted well over 700 operations, freeing more than 500 hostages. It has lost five men and dozens have been wounded. With 11 officers and 380 men, it now aims to field a team within 30 minutes. It deployed with the commandos of the *Régiment de Parachutistes d'Infanterie de Marine* for long range anti-terrorist missions.

Each team consists of a command cell comprising four assault units and a logistical element manned by former assault troops. Each operations unit has one officer and 15 men. Two of these groups specialize in waterborne operations; the other two in HALO/HAHO insertion. And two groups are on 24-hour alert. The GIGN also has its own intelligence component – *Section de Renseignement* – to assess situations which might need GIGN intervention.

To avoid the use of violence if at all possible, the GIGN maintains a four-man negotiations team, staffed by operatives who have served more than six years with the unit.

OPERATION THALATHINE

On 4 April 2008, the 850-tonne luxury yacht *Le Ponant*, en route from the Seychelles to the Mediterranean, was seized by Somali pirates and the 30-man crew held hostage. The yacht was moored near the port of Eyl in the Puntland regions of northern Somalia while the pirates held negotiations with the owners.

A ransom of some $2 million was paid, and the crew were brought ashore safely. Then the GIGN moved in on attack helicopters. As the pirates attempted to flee the scene, a sniper hit the engine of the getaway car, putting it out of action. Three GIGN men then arrested six pirates who were taken back to France to stand trial.

The governor of the region said that three bodies had been recovered after the operation and eight people had been wounded, though President Nicolas Sarkozy's office denied that anyone was killed in the operation. Chief of Staff of the French army, General Jean-Louis Georgelin, said that troops had also recovered 'interesting bags' and 'some of the ransom that was probably paid'.

Also, unlike other counter-terrorist forces, GIGN marksmen are taught to disable suspects rather than to kill them, if they can.

NINETY PERCENT FAILURE

Recruits come from the regular *gendarmerie,* with the majority coming from riot control teams. Those selected must then complete commando-style obstacle courses, escape and evasion drills, marksmanship courses and other tests. Only 10 percent pass. A further two months of physical and marksmanship training follow. In the third month, the recruit is issued his personal weapons and given instruction in long-range shooting.

Official insignia of the GIGN (Groupe d'Intervention de la Gendarmerie Nationale), which is the elite counter-terrorism and hostage rescue unit of the French gendarmerie.

After six months, the recruit is assigned to a GIGN team where he is trained in advanced techniques of suspect apprehension, riot suppression, VIP protection and other specialist duties. Only then does the trooper get his GIGN badge. But the training does not end there. All troopers are encouraged to learn HALO and HAHO parachuting, high-speed vehicle operation, skiing and mountain climbing. They also spend at least two hours each day in firearms training, with the average trooper firing between 100 and 300 rounds a day. It is reckoned to take three years for a gendarme to become a fully fledged GIGN operative.

'The president expresses his deep gratitude to the French armed forces and all the state services which enabled a rapid and peaceful solution to this hostage-taking.'

FRENCH PRESIDENT NICOLAS SARKOZY SPEAKING ON
THE RELEASE OF HOSTAGES ON THE YACHT LE PONANT, 11 APRIL 2008.

Glossary

Achaemenian Of the founding dynasty of ancient Persia, named for their eponymous ancestor Achaemenes.

Amazon A female warrior from the ancient world, possibly mythical.

Aquitaine Province of southwest France that was gained by England after the marriage of Eleanor of Aquitaine to Henry II in 1152.

Assegai A slender spear or lance of hard wood, often tipped with iron.

Astrakhan Region of southern Russia.

Azab Ottoman service corps.

Baker Street Irregulars Britain's Special Operations Executive during the Second World War.

Bardice A long poleaxe.

Battle of the Bulge German counter-attack in the Ardennes during the winter of 1944.

BEF British Expeditionary Force.

Berchtesgaden Hitler's Bavarian retreat.

Boeotian An inhabitant of the Boeotia region of ancient Greece.

Caique A small sailing ship.

Carlist Supporter of Don Carlos, the second son of Charles IV of Spain and his heirs.

Cebeci Ottoman logistical corps.

Chasseur A French unit equipped and trained for rapid deployment.

Chasseurs à pied Chasseurs on foot.

Chindits British irregular forces in Burma during the Second World War.

Chiricahua One of the nomadic Apache tribes of Native-Americans living in the southwestern United States and northern Mexico.

Chunin Middle man in a ninja clan.

Claymore A two-handed Scottish broadsword.

Covenanter A member of the covenant to defend the Scottish Presbyterian church during the 17th century.

Cuirass A breast plate and, usually, a back plate joined to make one piece of light armour.

Cuirassier A mounted soldier wearing a cuirass or upper-body armour.

Dardanelles The narrow strait between the Gallipoli Peninsula and Asia Minor, in northwestern Turkey.

DEVGRU United States Navy Special Warfare Development Group.

Devsirme The Ottoman system of enforced recruiting.

Dirk A Scottish dagger.

Éclaireurs Scouts.

Elamite Of, or belonging, to the kingdom of Elam in ancient Iran.

Esprit de corps The sense of pride, fellowship and loyalty among the members of a group.

Freiwilligen Volunteer.

Führer Leader; specifically Adolf Hitler.

Fusilier Originally a soldier armed with a fusil: a light musket or firelock; in the British army, for certain regiments of the line distinguished by wearing a fur busby.

Gempei War The struggle between the Taira and Minamoto clans between 1180 and 1185 that resulted in the establishment of the Kamakura shogunate (1192-1333).

Genin Ninja foot soldier.

GIGN French anti-terrorist force.

Grenadier Soldiers armed with grenades or grenade launchers.

Grenadiers-à-cheval Mounted grenadiers.

GROM Poland's Operational Manoeuvre Reconnaissance Group.

GSG-9 Germany's anti-terrorist force.

Gurkha A Nepalese soldier serving in the British army.

HAHO High altitude, high opening (of a parachute).

Hajj The pilgrimage to Mecca that every Muslim who can afford it should make once in their lifetime.

HALO High altitude, low opening (of a parachute).

Harquebus An early portable gun that rested on a forked post, or was suspended by a hook from a tripod.

Heniochoi A Greek charioteer.

Hetairoi Macedonian 'companion'.

Homoioi A Spartan citizen.

Hoplite A heavily armed infantryman in ancient Greece.

Hypaspist Shield-bearing infantry guard.

Impi A Zulu soldier.

Jacobite A supporter of James II and the Stuart dynasty after he was deposed.

Janissary A Turkish imperial guard.

Jonin Head of a ninja clan.

Kaiser The emperor of Germany.

Knobkerrie A short, thick stick with a knobbed head used as a missile or a weapon by South African peoples.

Kopis A short, slashing sword.

Koppojutsu Japanese martial-arts technique of breaking bones.

Kraal An African village that is surrounded by a fence.

Kristallnacht 9 November 1938, when Jews and Jewish property, in particular synagogues, were attacked throughout Germany; also known as the 'night of broken glass'.

Kukri Long curved knife used by the Gurkhas.

Lacedaemon Ancient Sparta.

Lacedaemonian A Spartan.

Lewes bomb An explosive and incendiary bomb designed by Jock Lewes of the SAS to blow up planes.

Luftwaffe The German air force.

Lurp A member of a Long Range Reconnaissance Unit.

Mahdi The 'divinely guided one' who will bring justice, quality and the true religion before the end of the world.

Mahdi army Shi-ite paramilitary force in Iraq.

Mameluke Enslaved Turks who fought for Egypt.

Maquis The French resistance movement that fought against the German occupation during the Second World War.

Marine Originally, a soldier that served on board a navy ship.

Median Of, or belonging to, the Medes, an ancient Iranian people.

Mfecane Shaka's 'crushing' of rival clans in Natal.

Middle Guard Soldiers who served in Napoleon's *Grande Armée* in the campaigns of 1805 and 1809.

Mons Star The campaign medal give to members of the British Expeditionary Force sent to defend Belgium and France in 1914.

Mtetwa The native people of northern Zululand, later absorbed into the Zulu empire.

NCO Non-commissioned officer.

Ninja Japanese guerrilla and 5th columnist.

Nom de guerre Pseudonym used in war.

NVA North Vietnamese Army.

Old Contemptibles Members of the British Expeditionary Force sent to defend Belgium and France in 1914.

Old Guard Members of Napoleon's *Grande Armée* who joined before 1805.

Old Noll Oliver Cromwell.

Ottoman A member of the Turkish people who conquered lands in the 13th century.

Panzerkorps Tank unit.

Paraibatai A Greek charioteer's companion.

Peloponnese The large southern peninsula of Greece.

Perioeci Free non-citizens in ancient Sparta.

Peshmerga Kurdish forces in Iraq allied to the US-led coalition.

Poniard A small dagger with a slim blade that is triangular and square in cross section.

Praetor A magistrate in ancient Rome.

Prikazy A Russian regiment.

Prodromoi Macedonian scout.

Qing The Manchu dynasty that ruled China from 1644 to 1911.

Red Army The Russian army; also the communist army that took Mao Tse-tung to power in China in 1949.

Reichsführer A Nazi state leader.

Ryu A Japanese school.

Sapper An army engineer.

SAS Britain's Special Air Service.

Sasanian Of the dynasty of Ardashir I in Persia (224-651).

SBS Britain's Special Boat Service.

Scholae palatine A palace guard.

Schutzstaffel The SS, the dedicated Nazi élite, recognized by their black uniforms.

Scotch-Irish Ulstermen.

SEAL A soldier who deploys by Sea, Air and Land.

Sepoy An Indian soldier serving the British Army.

Sesterce An ancient Roman coin or monetary unit equal to a quarter of a denarius.

Shuko A spiked band that is worn around the hand.

Shuriken Steel blades.

Sicherheitsdienst The SD, the Nazi's security force.

Spartiate Spartans by blood.

Spetsnaz Russian special forces unit.

Statholder Viceroy or lieutenant governor of a Dutch province.

Stiletto A short dagger with a thick blade.

Streltsy Russian militiamen.

Sturmabteilung The SA, the Nazi 'Assault Battalion'.

Sultan The sovereign ruler of a Muslim country, particularly Ottoman Turkey.

SWAT Special weapons and tactics.

Swazi The native people of Swaziland and parts of the eastern Transvaal.

Syssitia The quarters of a Spartan army unit.

T'ang Dynasty that ruled China 618–907.

Targe A light shield strapped to the body for protection.

Tetsubishi Small spiked weapons that were scattered on the ground.

Totenkopf The 'death's head', or skull-and-cross-bones, insignia of the SS.

Triailleurs Skirmishers.

Verfügungstruppen Or VT, Nazi 'Order Troops'.

Victoria Cross Britain's highest award for valour introduced by Queen Victoria in 1856 and first awarded during the Crimean War.

Viet Minh The nationalist independence movement that fought the Japanese and the French in Indochina between 1941 and 1954; the forerunner of the Viet Cong.

Vizier A high official in Muslim countries, especially in Ottoman Turkey.

Waffen SS The 'Weapons SS': the combat units of Hitler's dedicated Nazi élite.

Wehrmacht The German army.

Xiphos A short double-edged sword.

Xyston A long wooden spear.

Zouave A French North African soldier and those that imitate them.

Zulu The Bantu people of Zululand and Natal.

Index

Further reading

Adleman, Robert H. and Walton, George H. *The Devil's Brigade* (US Naval Institute Press, 2004).

Ankony, Robert C. *Lurps* (Hamilton Books, 2006).

Astor, Gerald. *The Jungle War* (Wiley, 2004).

Bahmanyar, Mir. *Shadow Warriors* (Osprey Publishing, 2006).

Beaumont, Roger A. *Military Elites* (Robert Hale & Company, 1976).

Beaven, Colin. *Operation Jedburgh: D-Day and America's First Shadow War* (Viking, 2006).

Bennett, Richard M. *Elite Forces* (Virgin, 2003).

Blok, Josphine H. *The Early Amazons* (Brill, 1995).

Blond, Georges. *La Grande Armée* (Arms and Armor, 1997).

Buckingham, William F. *Paras* (Tempus, 2005).

Campion, Garry. *The Good Fight* (Palgrave MacMillan, 2009).

Cartledge, Paul. *Alexander the Great* (Overlook Press, 2004).

Carter, Forrest. *Watch for Me in the Mountain* (Delta, 1990).

Casler, John O. *Four Years in the Stonewall Brigade* (University of South Carolina Press, 2005).

Cawthorne, Nigel. *The Mammoth Book of Inside Special Forces* (Blake, 2008).

Cawthorne, Nigel. *Alexander the Great* (Haus, 2004).

Chinnery, Philip D. *Air Commando* (St. Martin's Press, 1997).

Cohen, Aaron and Century, Douglas. *Brotherhood of Warriors* (Ecco, 2008).

Colins, John M. *Green Berets, SEALs and Spetsnaz* (Pergamon-Brassey, 1987).

Connolly, Peter. *Greece and Rome at War* (Greenhill Books, 2006).

Cross, J.P. and Buddiman Gurung. *Gurkhas at War* (US Naval Institute Press, 2007).

Delve, Ken. *RAF Fighter Command 1936-1968* (Pen and Sword, 2008).

Eshel, David. *Elite Fighting Units* (Arco Publishing, 1984).

Falconer, Jonathan. *Life as a Battle of Britain Pilot* (Sutton, 2007).

Featherstone, Donald. *Bowmen of England* (Pen & Sword, 2003).

Geronimo (ed S.S. Barrett). *Geronimo, His Own Story* (Ballantine Books, 1971).

Goldsworthy, Terry. V*alhalla's Warriors* (Dog Ear, 2007).

Goodwin, Jason. *Lords of the Horizons* (Picador, 2003).

Grote, George. *A History of Greece* (Routledge, 2001).

Haney, Eric. *Inside Delta Force* (Delta, 2005).

Hatsumi, Masaaki. *The Way of the Ninja* (Kodansha, 2004).

Hayes, Stephen K. *The Ninja and their Secret Fighting Art* (Tuttle, 1981).

Heath, Ian. *The Taiping Rebellion 1851-66* (Osprey Publishing, 1994).

Hennessy, Maurice N. *The Wild Geese* (Devin-Adair, 1973).

Hook, Patrick. *The Stonewall Brigade in the Civil War* (Zenith Press, 2009).

Hughes, Dana T. *The Old Breed* (Outskirts Press, 2008).

Jordan, David. *The US Navy SEALs* (New Line Books, 2006).

Kennedy Shaw, W.B. *Long Range Desert Group* (Greenhill, 2000).

Koskimaki, George. *D-Day with the Screaming Eagles* (Presidio Press, 2006).

Lang, Walter N., Eliot, Peter, and Maguire, Keith. *The World's Elite Forces* (Salamander, 1987).

Liptak, Eugene. *Office of Strategic Services 1942-45* (Osprey Publishing, 2009).

Lonsdale, David. *Alexander the Great, Killer of Men* (Carroll & Graf, 2004).

Mackenzie, William. *The Secret History of SOE* (Little Brown 2002).

Mann, Jay. *The Green Berets: Action in Iraq* (iUniverse, Inc., 2007).

Micheletti, Eric. *Le GIGN: Trente Ans d'Actions* (Histoire and Collections, 2004).

Moremann, Tim. *Chindits 1942-45* (Osprey Publishing, 2009).

Morris, Donald R. *The Washing of Spears* (Pimlico, 1994).

Neillands, Robin. *The Old Contemptibles* (John Murray, 2005).

Nicholson, Helen. *The Knights Hospitaller* (Boydell & Brewer, 2006).

Nicolle, David. *The Janissaries* (Osprey Publishing, 1995).

O'Connell, Robert L. *Soul of the Sword* (Simon & Schuster, 2002).

Parker, John. *Royal Marines Commandos* (Headline, 2007).

Parker, John. *SBS* (Headline, 2004).

Parris, Bill. *The Making of a Legionnaire* (Cassell, 2005).

Quarrie, Bruce. *The World's Elite Forces* (Octopus, 1985).

Read, Piers Paul. *The Templars* (Weidenfeld & Nicolson, 1999).

Ryan, Mike. *Secret Operations of the SAS* (Zenith Press, 2003).

Sadler, John. *Culloden* (Tempus, 2006).

Scholzen, Reinhard. *GSG-9* (Motorbuch Verlag, 2007).

Sekunda, Nicholas. *The Spartan Army* (Osprey Publishing, 1998).

Sledge, E.B. *With the Old Breed* (Presidio Press, 2007).

Smith, Robing, and Younghusband, Bill. *American Civil War Zouaves* (Osprey Publishing, 1996).

Sutherland, Jonathan. *Elite Troops of WWII* (Airlife, 2003).

Tyerman, Christopher. *God's War* (Allen Lane, 2006).

Westwood, Dr David. *The Waffen SS 1933-1945* (MLRS Books, 2004).

Picture credits

ZENITH PRESS

Visit **zenithpress.com**

This edition published in 2009 by Zenith Press, an imprint of MBI Publishing Company, 400 First Avenue North, Suite 300, Minneapolis, MN USA

First published in 2009

ISBN: 978-0-7603-3752-3

Printed and bound in China

1 3 5 7 9 10 8 6 4 2

Designed and edited by BCS Publishing Limited, Oxford.